DEVELOPMENT CENTRE STUDIES

# NEW FORMS OF INTERNATIONAL INVESTMENT

## IN DEVELOPING COUNTRIES

BY

CHARLES OMAN

DEVELOPMENT CENTRE
OF THE ORGANISATION FOR ECONOMIC CO-OPERATION AND DEVELOPMENT

Pursuant to article 1 of the Convention signed in Paris on 14th December, 1960, and which came into force on 30th September, 1961, the Organisation for Economic Co-operation and Development (OECD) shall promote policies designed:

- to achieve the highest sustainable economic growth and employment and a rising standard of living in Member countries, while maintaining financial stability, and thus to contribute to the development of the world economy;
- to contribute to sound economic expansion in Member as well as non-member countries in the process of economic development; and
- to contribute to the expansion of world trade on a multilateral, non-discriminatory basis in accordance with international obligations.

The Signatories of the Convention on the OECD are Austria, Belgium, Canada, Denmark, France, the Federal Republic of Germany, Greece, Iceland, Ireland, Italy, Luxembourg, the Netherlands, Norway, Portugal, Spain, Sweden, Switzerland, Turkey, the United Kingdom and the United States. The following countries acceded subsequently to this Convention (the dates are those on which the instruments of accession were deposited): Japan (28th April, 1964), Finland (28th January, 1969), Australia (7th June, 1971) and New Zealand (29th May, 1973).

The Socialist Federal Republic of Yugoslavia takes part in certain work of the OECD (agreement of 28th October, 1961).

*The Development Centre of the Organisation for Economic Co-operation and Development was established by decision of the OECD Council on 23rd October, 1962.*

*The purpose of the Centre is to bring together the knowledge and experience available in Member countries of both economic development and the formulation and execution of general policies of economic aid; to adapt such knowledge and experience to the actual needs of countries or regions in the process of development and to put the results at the disposal of the countries by appropriate means.*

*The Centre has a special and autonomous position within the OECD which enables it to enjoy scientific independence in the execution of its task. Nevertheless, the Centre can draw upon the experience and knowledge available in the OECD in the development field.*

Publié en français sous le titre :

LES NOUVELLES FORMES
D'INVESTISSEMENT INTERNATIONAL
DANS LES PAYS EN DÉVELOPPEMENT

The present study is a product of the first phase of the Development Centre's research project on new forms of investment in developing countries. This project was initiated in 1980 as part of the Centre's research programme on Interdependence and Development. The first phase of the project has involved the collaboration of researchers and institutions in ten developing countries and five OECD Member countries.

# TABLE OF CONTENTS

## Chapter 5
## CONSEQUENCES OF THE NEW FORMS

## Appendix
## SOME AGGREGATE MEASURES OF NEW FORMS OF INVESTMENT

# ACKNOWLEDGEMENTS

The Development Centre wishes to thank all of the researchers and institutes who collaborated in Phase I of this research project. They are, from Algeria: Mr. Kemal Abdallah-Khodja (ex-Minister of Planning); Brazil: Messrs. E.A. Guimaraes, P.S. Malan, and J. Tavares de Araujo Jr. (Research Institute for Economic and Social Planning – IPEA/INPES); India: Mr. Ashok Desai (National Council of Applied Economic Research); Malaysia: Professors Tan Siew Ee and Kulasingam (Universiti Sains Malaysia); Mexico: Mr. Edgardo Lifschitz (Centre on Transnational Economy); Peru: Messrs. Carlos Parodi Zevallos and Fernando Gonzalez Vigil (Development Studies and Promotion Centre – DESCO); Philippines: Ms. Lilia Bautissta (Governor, Board of Investments; Vice-Chairman and Acting Executive Director, Technology Transfer Board; and Asst. Secretary, Ministry of Trade and Industry); Republic of Korea: Mr. Bohn-Young Koo (Korea Development Institute); Singapore: Mr. Pang Eng Fong (Director, Economic Research Centre); Tunisia: Professor Abdelfettah Ghorbel (University of Sfax). The project was also joined in 1981 by researchers from a number of industrialised countries. They are, from the Federal Republic of Germany: Mr. Christian Pollak (Institut für Wirtschaftsforschung – IFO); France: Professors Claude Berthomieu and Anne Hanaut (Univerity of Nice); Japan: Professor Terutomo Ozawa (Colorado State University); United Kingdom: Professor John H. Dunning and Mr. John A. Cantwell (University of Reading); United States: Professor Lawrence Franko (The Fletcher School of Law and Diplomacy); OECD Secretariat: Mr. Graham Vickery (DSTI).

The Centre also gratefully acknowledges the financial support given to this project by the Government of Switzerland.

The author further wishes to extend his personal gratitude to all those who provided comment and criticism on early drafts of this book. A special note of thanks is due to Professor Terutomo Ozawa and Mr. Henry Ergas for their very useful suggestions. Any errors and shortcomings which remain are the sole responsibility of the author.

# PREFACE

Foreign direct investment constitutes, with official development assistance and private bank lending, a major external source of investment resources for many developing countries. It also constitutes an activity of crucial importance for a sizeable and growing number of firms based in the industrialised countries. As such, it lies at the heart of economic relations between the developing and industrialised countries.

A crucial distinction between official development assistance and bank lending on the one hand, and direct investment on the other, is that whereas the host country retains ownership of the investment project in the case of the former, in the latter the foreign investor normally retains ownership and control. This charcteristic of foreign direct investment has led, particularly since the mid-1960s, to some controversy over the extent to which such investment fully corresponds to the needs of the host country. It has also led some developing countries to seek to increase local ownership and control by a variety of means. These have included nationalisation of foreign investment; promotion of local equity participation in joint ventures with foreign firms and limitations on levels of foreign ownership; performance requirements and other regulations on the activities of foreign investors; and the use of turnkey, licensing, management and other such contractual arrangements as an alternative to the "package" of assets normally provided by foreign direct investors.

Both the importance of and the controversy associated with foreign investment in developing countries led the Development Centre in late 1979 to hold a meeting of international experts on the subject. Among the topics most actively debated at that meeting was the argument, put forward by some participants and questioned by others, that in the North-South context foreign direct investment was becoming obsolete and being replaced by new forms of investment. The term "new forms of investment", defined and discussed by Mr. Oman in Chapter 1 of the present study, was used in this meeting precisely to refer to the contractual and joint-venture arrangements alluded to above. This debate, and the Centre's earlier research into the role of multinational enterprises, technology transfer and international sub-contracting in developing countries all pointed to the importance and timeliness of undertaking a study of the new forms of international investment in developing countries.

The objective of this study is not to come up with a list of policy proposals as such. Rather, in keeping with the Centre's mandate to focus on and contribute to an improvement of relations between industrialised and developing countries, its aim is to clarify actual trends in the use of new forms of investment, the causes of those trends, and some of their possible implications. This approach reflects a conviction that by contributing to conceptual clarification and shedding factual light on what is actually taking place, as well as on the strengths and weaknesses of alternative views and their underlying assumptions, research can make an important contribution to greater understanding and improved relations between industrialised and developing countries. Insofar as this objective is attained, policy implications may become apparent to decision makers concerned with international investment, in both host and home countries, according to how they define their specific interests and policy objectives.

The present study is based on Phase I of the Centre's research on new forms of investment in developing countries. It draws to a considerable extent on research carried out in 1980-1982 on the basis of collaborative agreements with researchers and their institutes in ten developing "host" countries: Algeria, Brazil, India, Korea, Malaysia, Mexico, Peru, Philippines, Singapore and Tunisia. Preliminary work was also undertaken by collaborating researchers in five OECD "home" countries: France, Germany, Great Britain, Japan and the United States. Some of these studies will be made available in a "Development Centres Papers" collection, entitled *"New Forms of International Investment in Developing Countries: The National Perspective".*

Phase II of the Centre's research is now getting underway. It will analyse the use of new forms of international investment by firms in specific industries, by generating data in – and looking at the implications for – firms' home economies. The latter will include both a number of OECD countries whose firms are active in developing countries, and a few developing countries whose firms are becoming increasingly active in other developing countries via new forms of investment. Many of the ideas put forward in the present study will serve as hypotheses to be tested and further developed with the firm- and industry-specific data to be generated in this research.

Just Faaland
President of the OECD
Development Centre
January 1984.

*Chapter 1*

# INTRODUCTION

## I. BACKGROUND AND OVERVIEW

International investment in less developed economies is not a new phenomenon. Nor is such investment in forms other than direct (i.e. equity) investment particularly new.

If one looks back to the 19th century, for example, one finds that the Industrial Revolution was accompanied not only by a massive worldwide expansion of trade but also by significant increases in the flow of investment capital from the more industrialised countries to many less developed regions of the world. While some disagreement has emerged in recent years as to the share of direct investments in the total flow of investment capital to the less developed economies prior to World War I[1], it is clear that the latter half of the 19th century and the early years of the 20th witnessed substantial amounts of non-equity foreign investment in these economies – often in the form of bonds issued by developing-country governments and floated in the financial markets of London, Paris and New York. Such was the importance of portfolio investments during this period, in fact, that shortly after the turn of the century some economists were arguing, apparently mistakenly, that financial capital had replaced industrial capital as the dominant form in the world economy[2].

Be that as it may, the World War I years saw a general contraction of international investment flows. Despite a brief resurgence during the 1920s, at a time when the United States was clearly replacing Great Britain as the dominant economy in both industrial and financial terms, the Depression and War years of 1930-1945 brought stagnation of direct investment and the virtual collapse of portfolio investment in developing countries.

The postwar period thus stands out in the history of international investment on at least two counts. First, the *volume* of international investment in developing countries has grown very rapidly, surpassing by far that which took place prior to World War I. Second, contrary to the pre-World War I period, the *form* of this investment has been predominantly direct private investment. The rapid growth of multinational, often U.S.-based, firms through the establishment of wholly or majority-owned subsidiaries in developing as well as developed countries during the 1950s and 1960s has undoubtedly been the clearest manifestation of these trends.

The 1970s witnessed a continued rapid expansion of international investment in developing countries. What is less certain is the significance of the growing diversity of forms which such investment has taken since the late 1960s/early 1970s. On the one hand there can be little doubt, as we shall discuss in Chapter 2, that the amount of

11

foreign direct investment (FDI) in developing countries has continued to grow. But it is equally clear that over the last decade or so not only has the flow of financial capital grown more rapidly than that of FDI, but also a variety of *new forms* of international investment has come to play an increasingly important role in the North-South context.

The term "new forms of investment" used in this study may be defined, generically, as international investments in which foreign investors do not hold a controlling interest via equity participation, that is, as investments in which foreign-held equity does not constitute majority ownership. More specifically, new forms of investment refer to:

*a)* joint international business ventures in which foreign-held equity does not exceed 50 per cent;

*b)* various international contractual arrangements which involve at least an element of investment from the foreign firm's viewpoint[3] but which may involve no equity participation by that firm whatsoever, as is frequently the case with licensing agreements, management, service and production-sharing contracts, and occasionally with sub-contracting and turnkey operations.

The new forms of investment may be thought of as constituting a grey area between the "classic" international activities of firms, namely wholly/ majority-owned foreign direct investment and exports. The new forms are rather heterogeneous, and can perhaps be defined most simply by distinguishing them from what they are not. They are not investments in majority- or wholly foreign-owned subsidiaries – which we refer to as the traditional form of foreign direct investment – nor are they bank lending or other purely financial operations, although these may be used to finance new forms of investment. In Section II of this chapter we present a taxonomy of new forms of investment, and in Section III we attempt to further clarify the concept of new forms of investment, particularly our use of the terms "new" and "investment".

In Chapter 2 we present three working hypotheses regarding overall trends in the use of new forms of investment and traditional FDI in the North-South context. One is that traditional FDI is becoming obsolete and is being replaced or superseded by new forms of investment; we argue that FDI data do not sustain this "obsolescence-of-FDI" hypothesis. A second hypothesis is that during the 1980s FDI may gain renewed importance in relation to international borrowing and "indebted industrialisation" in a number of developing countries, including many of the heavy borrowers of the 1970s. A third hypothesis is that there is emerging a new division of risks and responsibilities among the three principal sets of actors involved in international investment in developing countries – host-country élites, multinational firms and international lending organisations – such that the new forms of investment will continue to gain importance, if not actually supersede traditional FDI, in the North-South context over the coming years.

Chapter 3 summarises trends in the use of new forms of investment on a sectoral basis. It is in the extractive industries of petroleum and metals mining that one finds the strongest empirical support for both the first and third hypotheses. Evidence from the manufacturing industries is less clearcut, both on the extent to which the new forms may be superseding traditional FDI, and the extent to which a new division of risks and responsibilities among the three major actors is superseding the traditional FDI "package" supplied and owned by multinational firms. Although it is clear that globally the new forms have gained increasing importance in manufacturing industries over the last ten to fifteen years, what stands out is the wide variation among host countries both as regards the importance of certain new forms relative to others, and as regards the importance of the new forms as a group relative both to traditional FDI and to gross industrial capital formation.

Chapter 4 discusses a number of reasons why firms using new forms of investment in developing countries may do so. It distinguishes between factors which are essentially endogenous to developing countries and several which are largely exogenous. Among the former, host-government regulations which favour reduced- or non-equity forms of foreign investment are of course crucial. But structural changes in developing countries which are creating new opportunities for, and/or reducing the costs of, doing business via the new forms of investment are also important. Factors largely exogenous to host countries include the relative stagnation of growth in the industrialised countries as a group; a diminishing of the "technological gap" separating the U.S. and other industrialised countries; the appearance in the late 1960s early 1970s of structural tendencies toward balance-of-payments disequilibria in countries whose firms reveal different propensities to insist on majority ownership of foreign investments[4]; the instability of international currency exchange rates; the marked increase and instability of interest rates; and a globalisation of oligopolistic inter-firm competition in numerous key industries.

These macro-economic factors appear to have been accompanied during the 1970s by an important micro-economic phenomenon: a tendency on the part of many investors to shorten their investment time-planning horizons, and a growing appreciation by some of them of the leverage-increasing and risk-reducing or risk-shedding advantages offered by the new forms of international investment. This behaviour may have received additional impetus from possibilities created by the new forms, at least under some circumstances, to separate ownership and control internationally.

Chapter 5 explores several possible implications of the new forms of investment. One hypothesis considered, and questioned, is that as the new forms become institutionalised, in the sense that familiarity with their use and potential spreads worldwide, numerous OECD-based small- and medium-size firms will use them as a vehicle to internationalise their activities – with potentially important consequences for home and host countries alike. Another hypothesis discussed is that, by combining the strengths and assets of local élites and the international business and financial communities, the new forms of investment may lead to the capitalisation of important branches of economic activity which hitherto have remained largely un- or under-developed, notably the so-called traditional sectors which lie at the heart of underdevelopment in many host countries. Put simply, the idea here is that in the coming decades the institutionalisation of new forms of international investment in developing countries could conceivably do for investment and accumulation in the international sphere what the advent of the joint stock corporation in today's industrialised countries did for investment and accumulation in the national context about a century ago.

This chapter also devotes considerable attention to a number of more immediate possible implications or interpretations of the new forms of investment. Discussion focusses on their potential advantages and disadvantages, relative to traditional FDI, for economic development in the host country, and for specific groups within the latter.

It is not the aim of this study to come up with a set of policy recommendations as such. Rather, in keeping with the Development Centre's mandate to focus on and contribute to an improvement of relations between industrialised and developing countries, our aim is to shed light on these relations – in this specific case, on the use of new forms of investment – with the purpose of clarifying what is taking place, why, and some of the possible implications[5]. Our approach reflects the belief that one of the most important ways in which research can contribute to resolving controversy and, thus, to the advancement of relations between industrialised and developing countries, is by focussing on and attempting to demystify opposing interpretations and pre-conceived ideas. To the extent we succeed in this aim, policy implications may become apparent to decision makers according to how they define their specific interests and objectives.

## II.  A TAXONOMY OF NEW FORMS

Included in the following taxonomy are types of international business operations which may, in any given case, fulfil the definition of "new forms of investment" cited in the preceeding section. But a word of caution: not every known case of each type of operation listed below necessarily conforms to that relatively strict definition. To cite one of the more obvious and important examples, turnkey contracts usually represent important investments for host countries, but from the foreign contractors' viewpoint, many turnkey contracts *per se* are a form of sales, not of investment. Nevertheless, because some turnkey operations represent investments for supplying firms as well as for host countries – and given the importance of these operations as investments for some host countries – we include turnkey contracts in our taxonomy of new forms of investment in developing countries.

We proceed, in Section III of this chapter, to discuss criteria which may be used to distinguish between business operations that conform to the stricter definition of new forms of investment cited earlier, i.e., operations involving at least some elements of investment for the supplying firm as well as for the host country, and those which conform only to a broader definition: investment as seen from the host-country's standpoint, but not necessarily from that of the supplying firm. There we explore the relevance of the stricter definition of new forms of investment, and attempt to clarify the concept of "investment" which underlies that definition. We also comment on the significance of the adjective "new", since many of the phenomena included in our taxonomy have obviously been in existence for some time.

### Joint Ventures

A joint venture normally implies the sharing of assets, risks and profits, and participation in the ownership (i.e. equity) of a particular enterprise or investment project by more than one firm or economic "group". The latter may include private corporations, public corporations or even states. The distribution of equity shares in a joint venture may be determined according to each partner's financial contribution, or it may be based on other forms of capital contribution, such as technology, management, access to world markets, etc.

International joint ventures in developing countries which meet our definition of new forms of investment are those in which the host developing-country partner holds at least 50 per cent of the equity. We would not include as new forms of investment those joint ventures which are majority foreign owned. Nor, at least conceptually, would we include joint ventures where a wide dispersion of local ownership means that the foreign partner's equity, although less than 50 per cent, represents a controlling interest on the basis of equity shares alone; in practice, though, our lack of refined data renders this distinction irrelevant.

The so-called fade-out agreement, sometimes referred to from the host country's perspective as a "phase-in" agreement, generally involves an initial equity participation by the foreign investor of more than 50 per cent, often 100 per cent. But it is agreed contractually that ownership will subsequently be transferred to one or more local parties, in either the private or public sector, often gradually or in several stages. Once the fade-out (or phase-in) process has been completed, the foreign investor may retain minority participation, or no equity whatsoever. Even in the latter case, however, the foreign investor may retain a direct interest in, or even control over, certain aspects of the business, such as in international marketing and/or via licensing, management or other contractual arrangements cited below.

14

## Licensing Agreements

Licensing Agreements are contracts in which a foreign licensor provides the local licensee with access to one or a set of technologies or know-how, in return for value. The latter may take a variety of forms: an initial lump-sum fee, a percentage of sales, royalties, shares of equity (and hence profits), or goods bought at a discount, as in a counter-purchase or buy-back arrangement. Agreements may also provide for access to any technological improvements or adaptations the licensee may make.

The licensee, on the other hand, gains access to either "know-how", that is, secret unpatented technology, trademarks, copyrights or patents, or a combination of these, for a specified or un-specified duration. And, as is the case with many of the new forms of investment, licensing agreements may call for the training of local personnel by the licensor, or, in the case of technical-assistance agreements, by the supplier of technical assistance.

Although the term "technology sale" is often used to describe licensing agreements, the term "sale" is generally inexact, since strictly speaking, a sale implies the transfer of property rights from the seller to the buyer. Rather, under licensing agreements, the licensee is usually given carefully defined rights of access to and use of proprietary knowledge possessed – and retained – by the licensor. This is reflected in the fact that payments to the licensor frequently take the form of a percentage of sales or, occasionally, of profits. Even where the payment or "price" paid by the licensee is a lump sum, it may be argued that what the licensor is selling is in fact not the technology *per se*, but his rights to future income from his contribution of technological capital to the licensee's operation.

## Franchising

Franchising may be regarded as a particular type of licensing or technical-assistance agreement. The franchisor usually provides the locally owned franchisee with a "package" including not only trademarks and know-how but also local exclusivity and management assistance, in return for a down payment fee, royalties, and compliance with certain corporate regulations.

## Management Contracts

Management Contracts stipulate that the foreign company manage a project or enterprise in the developing country. They may also call for training of local personnel and handing-over management authority to locals after a certain period, although in some cases, notably in Middle Eastern petroleum-exporting countries, the host-country government will use independent consultants/experts to monitor the activities of the managing company instead. Under management contracts, the local firm/group may benefit from such intangibles as the managing firm's international reputation, worldwide procurement capabilities, knowledge of international product and financial markets, and access to funds.

One difference between a licensing agreement and a management contract is that whereas the former often relies on an already functioning enterprise in the host country, in the latter the managing company often builds up the local operation from scratch. And, in contrast to "product-in-hand" operations, cited below, the managing firm is not usually the direct supplier of plant and equipment.

## Turnkey Contracts

Under a turnkey contract, the contractor is responsible for setting up a complete production unit – factory, energy plant, etc. – or infrastructure project in the host country. The specific responsibilities of the contractor may vary from project to project, but frequently cover feasibility studies, provision of technology and know-how, basic design and engineering, supply of complete plant and equipment and/or construction of civic works. The term "turnkey" derives from the fact that the contractor's responsibility is normally fulfilled only when the plant or project is fully operational. In some cases these contracts call for operation and/or maintenance by the contractor as well.

Turnkey contractors are often engineering firms whose assets – and profits – are rooted in their ability to bring together what have come to be called temporary systems, that is, in their capacity to mobilise large groups of technicians, engineers, managers, construction workers, as well as the equipment, technology and the like, required for projects which are one or few of a kind. Turnkey contracts do not necessarily involve a single contractor carrying out all the requisite activities alone; principal contractors often sub-contract portions of the job, and the technologies supplied generally include some which are licensed or embodied in machinery and equipment supplied by other firms.

The first turnkey contracts were reportedly developed in the United States by capital-goods producers as a means for increasing sales during the Great Depression; the first international turnkey agreements appeared in the East-West context during the 1960s, and were being used in a limited number of developing countries by the end of that decade. More recently, the recycling of petro-dollars through multi-million and even billion-dollar contracts calling for entire industrial complexes to be set up by foreign firms, notably in some of the major petroleum-exporting countries, has drawn considerable attention to turnkey operations.

### Product-in-Hand

Product-in-Hand contracts are turnkey operations in which the contractor's responsibilities are fulfilled only when the turnkey installation is completely operational with local personnel. That is, they include provisions whereby the contractor assumes legal responsibility for preparing local management and workers to run the installation.

### Production-Sharing Contract

First developed in Indonesia in the early 1960s and now used extensively in the petroleum industry and sometimes in mining as well, production-sharing agreements call for the foreign company to undertake exploration in specified areas and, if petroleum (or a minerals lode) is found, to undertake production in conjunction with the host country's state-owned company. This is done for a specified period of time in return for a pre-determined share of the physical output, once the foreign firm has recovered its costs. The pre-determined production "split" varies considerably among countries, from a 15 per cent host-government share, as in Chile, to an 85 per cent host-government share, as in Egypt; differential tax rates on foreign companies' share of output may effectively narrow the nominal difference among host countries, however.

The term "production sharing" is also sometimes used to describe rather different phenomena. For example, certain types of joint ventures or management contracts in manufacturing or mining, where the foreign partner assumes no exploration risk but is either remunerated with – as a form of dividend – or can purchase a given proportion of output, are also sometimes referred to as production-sharing arrangements. Such is the case, for example, of a number of Japanese manufacturing ventures in China, and some mining operations in Indonesia[6]. Intra-industry international sub-contracting arrangements have also occasionally been referred to as "production sharing"[7]. Our use of the term will generally refer to the definition cited in the preceding paragraph.

**Risk Service Contracts**

Risk Service Contracts used primarily in the petroleum industry, are similar to production-sharing contracts in many ways, with the crucial distinction that the foreign company's share of output is paid in cash rather than physical production. The company, however, may be permitted to buy back an amount of crude at international prices from established production. Unlike the pure non-risk service contract, where the foreign contractor is paid a pre-determined fee for services rendered, say in exploration or production, the risk-service contract typically places the burden of risk on the foreign contractor, who must provide the investment capital for exploration and production. If no oil is found, the contract ceases to exist, as in the case of production-sharing agreements. If oil is found, the contractor develops the find, which may then be operated either by the local government – normally its state oil company – or by the contractor. Capital is reimbursed, with interest and a risk fee, out of production revenues.

**International Subcontracting**

International Subcontracting normally involves a "principal" contractor based in an industrialised country – often a multinational firm or trading company, occasionally an importer or wholesaler – that places orders with a sub-contractor in a developing country to produce components or assemble finished products with the inputs it provides. The final product is normally sold by the principal, sometimes in its home market, sometimes in third-country markets.

The growing importance of international sub-contracting is closely related to tariff regulations in some industrialised countries, notably U.S. tariff regulations 806.30 and 807.00, and to the rapid proliferation in recent years of free export-processing zones in developing countries[8].

Strictly speaking, we would include as a new form of investment only those international sub-contracting arrangements in which ownership of the subcontractor is at least 50 per cent local. That is, according to the stricter definition of new forms cited earlier, international subcontracting between majority foreign-owned subsidiaries in developing countries and foreign principals (be they parent firms of the sub-contractors or not) is an intra- or inter-firm relationship associated with "traditional" FDI, not a new form of investment.

As a concluding note to this taxonomy of new forms of investment, it should be pointed out that any given international investment project or enterprise in a developing country may simultaneously involve two or more of the new forms. To cite only a few common examples, management contracts are often used in conjunction with joint ventures and turnkey operations, and the latter are more often than not accompanied by licensing agreements. International joint ventures are often also accompanied by international marketing agreements.

## III. ON THE DEFINITION OF "NEW FORMS OF INVESTMENT"

In subsequent chapters we explore the evidence on trends in the use of new forms of investment and traditional FDI in the North-South context. But first a few more words on our definition of the term "new forms of investment". The attentive reader may well ask, for example, whether all the new forms of investment are really so new. The answer of course is no. Joint international business ventures and various types of international subcontracting, to cite only two examples, have existed for many years. But to the extent that a significant quantitative increase in the use of the new forms of investment as a group has led to a qualitative change in their global importance in recent years, we feel justified in referring to them as "new" forms of investment. One of the objectives of this study is precisely to provide insight into the growing importance – new importance – of these phenomena, in relation to "traditional" FDI, in the North-South context.

It can also be asked – and it is an important question indeed – whether certain new forms of investment can properly be called forms of *investment*. At least from the point of view of the supplying firm, are not some of them really forms of *sale?* Would it not be more accurate to describe a licensing agreement, for example, as a form of sale of technology by the licensor to the licensee, rather than as a form of investment by the licensor? Or, to cite another example, would it not make more sense to describe a turnkey contract (which may indeed represent a major investment from the host-country's point of view) not as an international investment but, from the supplying firm's point of view, as a sale of plant and equipment?

These questions, in our view, call for a reasonably rigorous definition of the concept of "investment", as distinct from other forms of economic activity, notably "sale". (Exports, of course, are an international form of sale.) True, one frequently finds the expressions "new forms of involvement" or "new forms of industrial co-operation" used to describe many of the phenomena we are calling new forms of investment. But the terms "involvement" and "co-operation" avoid the issue, they do not resolve it. They are all-encompassing terms which are not necessarily incorrect, but do not clarify the nature of the relationships among participants in a specific international business operation. As we shall explain below, the nature of those relationships – sources of conflict or tension on the one hand, convergence or commonality of interests on the other – is likely to vary considerably according to whether the supplying firm approaches the operation as a sale, or as an investment. Hence the relevance of the stricter definition of new forms of investment cited in Section I.

As a first step towards clarifying the distinction between an investment and a sale, it could be argued that a pure sale is a "spot" transaction involving no risk for the seller. Investment – which refers to the use, creation or acquisition of capital – can be defined as the acquisition of assets expected to yield revenue in future periods. Current investment decisions reflect investors' expectations of future, hence uncertain, events. Investment therefore entails risk. The extent to which an investment in physical assets yields the expected flow of income or quasi-rents will depend on the evolution of demand, the pace of technical progress and the changing nature of competition. The return on a financial investment will be sensitive to change in the price level, interest rates and the attractiveness of alternative financial investments.

Since investment entails risk, it could be argued that any transaction involving some risk for a firm supplying resources involves at least an element of investment by that firm. For example, although a firm contracted to build a turnkey plant may be selling the plant as such, insofar as the firm incurs costs prior to payment and thereby incurs some risk, the operation might be said to involve an element of investment by that firm, during the period prior to payment, even assuming the price of the finished plant has been pre-negotiated. Conceivably, the firm could even sell its investment, i.e., its contractual right to future income, to a third party – such as an export-credit agency or other financial organisation – who thereby "invests" in the plant purchaser's ability and willingness to pay.

This reasoning suggests that virtually all international business operations other than "spot" market transactions involve an element of international investment. It could thus be cited to justify use of the term "investment" in accordance with the broader definition of "new forms of investment" cited earlier. In focussing on the risk associated with investment, this reasoning also brings attention to an aspect of international investment which is particularly relevant for our analysis of the new forms: the distribution of risk among parties involved in the investment process.

But the reasoning requires refinement. The distribution of risk was often thought in the past to coincide with the distribution of ownership and control. In a joint stock corporation, for example, the bulk of income risk was thought to be borne by the holders of equity, who were also thought to exercise control; those providing debt capital were seen as reasonably secure from unexpected variations in income, but did not have voting rights. Subsequent research has pointed out that ownership rights – particularly when fragmented – do not necessarily confer control. Formal ownership, actual control over operations, and powers of allocation of income can be quite distinct, and the relationship among them depends more on the economic factors shaping the bargaining relations among parties than on the legal nature of their association[9]. There is no straightforward correspondance between the distribution of risk and that of control; it depends on economic circumstances which vary from investment to investment.

Three conclusions may nevertheless be inferred from this reasoning as we have developed it so far. First, since investment implies acquisition of rights to future income, transactions which procure such rights may be regarded as forms of investment. Second, insofar as risk is inherent in investment, the distribution among parties involved in an investment of the costs to which risk and uncertainty give rise may vary from one form of investment to another. And third, the distribution of effective control need not coincide with the distribution of risks.

Returning to our example of the firm contracted to build a turnkey plant, although the builder (or party which finances construction) incurs the risk of non-payment by the purchaser of the plant, it is the purchaser alone for whom the plant as such represents an investment, upon termination of the contract, according to our stricter definition. While the builder (or lender) may be said to invest "in the host country" during the period prior to payment, the builder can only be described as selling the plant to the host country insofar as it is the host country which fully assumes the risks associated with the decision to invest in the plant once the plant is paid for. Only insofar as payment for the plant depends not simply on the purchaser's ability to pay, but on the productivity or revenue-generating capacity of the plant itself, once it is in operation – as would normally be the case in a joint venture, for example – could it be said that the builder (or lender) is also investing in the plant as such.

This last observation suggests a way to shed additional light on the distinction between investment and sales operations. The reasoning focusses on the stricter definition of "investment" cited earlier, and has the advantage of avoiding the potentially confusing distinction between "investment in the host country" and "investment in the plant as such". It is that whereas an investment is normally undertaken by the investor with the intention of increasing the value of the resource (capital) he controls, that is, with the intention of using the resource he supplies to create and appropriate new value ("value-added"), a sale is normally carried out to realise (monetise) value already created. Whether or not a given international business operation involves at least an element of investment from the standpoint of a firm supplying a given resource thus depends not so much on the presence or absence of risk *per se,* or on any intrinsic characteristic of the good or service supplied, but simply on whether or not the supplying firm seeks to use the resource to gain access to, and control at least part of, the new value to be created in the host country with that resource. In other words, it depends on whether the firm uses the resource it supplies as an asset, to participate in the return on the activity in which the resource will be employed in the host country[10]. We illustrate this reasoning, and develop it further, in the appendix to this section.

The distinction between a new form of investment (strict definition) and a *sale,* then, derives from whether the foreign firm gains some degree of access to and control

19

over the value created by the investment project in the host country[11]. The distinction between a new form of investment and *traditional FDI,* on the other hand, is that whereas the former implies whole or majority local ownership of the investment project – though not necessarily of all the invested resources[12] – the latter implies whole or majority foreign ownership of the investment project.

These differences in turn imply that the type of relationship between foreign firms and host countries generally characteristic of new forms of investment (conflicts and convergences of interest) may be significantly different from those characteristic of arm's-length sales, on the one hand, and of traditional FDI, on the other. To illustrate this point, it is useful to briefly compare the logic of the relationship typical of licensing agreements with that typical of turnkey contracts. According to the conceptual distinction we have established between "investment" and "sale", our research results indicate that from the licensor's point of view, the bulk of licensing agreements correspond to the logic of an investment operation, but that the bulk of turnkey contracts correspond to the logic of an export rather than an investment operation for a supplying firm.

Let us look first at turnkey contracts. While many host countries have increased pressure on foreign firms to reduce their equity participation in traditional FDI projects, a number of developing countries have begun to provide incentives and to press firms supplying industrial complexes under turnkey contracts to *take* (minority) equity positions in the investment projects[13]. The logic is not difficult to understand: in the case of an investment operation, both parties have an interest in maximising the difference between the costs of setting up and running the investment project – the costs of producing the project's output – on the one hand and the value of that output on the other. Possible conflicts arise primarily over how that difference is shared between the two parties, as we shall show in the case of licensing agreements. But in a sales operation, the foreign supplier's interest lies in maximising the difference between the value of resources it commits to the project – the cost to the firm of setting up the plant in the case of a turnkey contract – and the price it is paid. The host country's interest is just the opposite[14]. It is understandable therefore that some host countries try to induce supplying firms to approach turnkey operations not as arm's-length sales but as investment operations. Hence the pressure on firms, often including lucrative incentives in the form of long-run oil-supply contracts, to take equity in the investment project.

For international technology licensing agreements, the logic of the potential conflict can be just the reverse. Developing countries often seem to regard technology as an intangible commodity which they can purchase through a licensing agreement and which is then at their disposal to use as any owner uses a good he has bought. Licensors, on the other hand, generally look on the technology they provide as a resource (asset) which they still own. They may cede some degree of access to independent parties in return for sharing part of the value created through their exploitation of the technology. In other words, licensors generally see a licensing agreement as a vehicle through which technology they possess can be used to generate or participate in investment income.

This conflict of interest between licensors and host countries often takes two, partially contradictory, forms. Because the technologies (including patents, brand names, etc.) involved in international licensing often offer possibilities for generating monopoly or oligopolistic rents in the host country, the local licensee and foreign licensor tend to share a common interest in maximising such rents. But the host government may seek to minimise or eliminate such rents at least in so far as it seeks to defend the interests of local purchasers of the licensee's product (as seems to be the case particularly when the product is an important input to local industry)[15]. Here the government is in a position of opposition to the alliance of interests between foreign licensors and local licensees. At the same time, however, the interests of licensees are opposed to those of licensors on their respective shares of those same rents. In these negotiations the host government often sides with the local licensee, not only for political reasons but also for reasons of balance of payments, i.e., to try to minimise the foreign-exchange cost to the local economy of the licensing agreements. We shall return in more detail to these issues in discussing implications of the new forms of investment for the host country, in Chapter 5.

To sum up, the concept of investment used in our term "new forms of investment" is important, and should be clearly distinguished from the concept of sale or export. It sheds important light on the nature of relationships among participants involved in these international business operations. The terms "co-operation" and "involvement" are less than fully satisfactory for our purposes precisely because they fail to bring out this distinction.

As we point out in the appendix to this section, it is not always easy to distinguish empirically those international business operations which involve at least an element of investment, for the supplying firm as well as the host country, from those that do not[16]. Nor are matters simplified by the fact that what few aggregate statistics exist on international value transfers resulting from new forms of investment tend to be found not in statistics on investment stocks or flows, but in trade and current-accounts data[17]. But in both conceptual and practical terms, and given our interest in analysing the role of the new forms of investment in the current evolution of international business strategies and in the dynamics of North-South investment relations, it may be hypothesised that at least under some circumstances each of the new forms included in our taxonomy contains aspects of investment which could not be adequately understood if they were analysed either as arm's-length export operations or as traditional FDI. One of the objectives of our empirical research, whose results are summarised in subsequent chapters, has been precisely to test the validity and examine the implications of this hypothesis.

# ON THE CONCEPT OF "INVESTMENT"

A simple model may serve to illustrate the distinction between sales and investment. Suppose, for example, that a firm owns a piece of machinery which it can either invest (i.e., use as capital) in a foreign investment project, or sell to the same foreign country for $100. (For our purposes it does not matter whether the sales price reflects highly price-competitive conditions of supply and demand for this type of machinery, or whether it includes some degree of monopoly rents; our point is simply to assume that the machine has a sales value of $100.) If the firm sells the machine, the firm's profit (or loss) is derived from the difference between what it cost the firm to produce (or otherwise obtain) the machine and the sale price of $100. If the firm invests the machine, its profit (or loss) is derived from the difference between the value of the machine ($100) and the value created in the production process in which the machine is employed. In the case of the sale, $100 of machinery is transformed into $100 of money; in the case of the investment, a value of $100 is transformed into, say, $110, over the life of the investment project – corresponding to a "value added" of $10, from which the firm's profit is derived[18].

Another ostensibly important difference, and a relatively easy way to establish the difference empirically, is that whereas in the case of a sale the transformation of value occurs instantaneously (the seller's profit or loss being realised at the time of sale), an investment inherently involves a *time dimension,* since the production process takes time and the investor's profit or loss is derived from the value created during the life of the investment process. In other words, while there is not necessarily a lasting relationship between a seller and a buyer, the relationship in the case of an investment between a supplying firm and the host-country inherently involves a time dimension – with potentially important implications for the nature of that international relationship.

In trying to judge empirically whether a given business operation is in fact a sale or an investment, one must however treat this time-dimension argument with considerable caution. Appearances may be deceiving for any of several reasons. For example, although the time dimension of a "spot" sales agreement cannot be compared to that of an investment project, payments in multiple installments may take on a time dimension. Also, and more importantly for our purposes, continuous supply agreements may imply a lasting relationship between buyers and sellers.

Perhaps even more confusing for the empirical observer is the fact that the time dimension of an investment project may be collapsed when the investor discounts expected future earnings and "capitalises out", that is, when he sells his rights to a future income flow from the investment project. Take the case of a technology licensing agreement. The licensor may discount his share of expected future earnings from the investment project or firm to which his technology is licensed, and sell them. Rather than receiving an income flow – say, 5 per cent on sales – for an indefinite period, the licensor may be paid in the form of (larger) lump-sum fees, royalties or a "price" paid by the licensee over a fixed period. The point is however, that what is being sold, in this example, is not the technology *per se* but the licensor's rights to future income from his contribution of technological capital to the investment project or enterprise. The amount of fees, or price, paid by the licensee depends at least in part on the value which the investment project or firm in which the technology is employed may itself be expected to generate. It does not depend simply on the value already embodied in the technology, or on the marginal cost of producing the technology, prior to the investment project's operational start-up, as price theory suggests would be the case in a strict arm's-length sale of technology under competitive market conditions. (Of course if the licensor has discriminating monopolistic power over the technology in question, the determining factor becomes the licensee's overall ability-to-pay, which may not even reflect the specific investment project's expected revenue-generating capacity. In other words, under conditions of perfect monopoly in segregated markets, the distinction between sale and investment becomes irrelevant; what counts is the host-country partner's ability to pay.)

In short, the time dimension and form in which supplying firms are remunerated for their contribution to a given business operation are not necesssrily a good indicator of whether the operation represents a sales or investment from the supplying firm's standpoint. With this major caveat, it is nevertheless interesting to note that under international licensing agreements, payments to technology licensors are frequently based on, among other things, the sales volume of the firm or project using the licensed technology. In contrast, this is rarely the case in turnkey arrangements. Payment is rarely based on the plant's output or on the income flow (sales or profits) to be derived therefrom. These contrasting tendencies suggest that whereas licensing agreements often represent a type of investment and not simply a sales operation from the licensors' standpoint, turnkey contracts often represent a sales but not an investment operation from the contractors' standpoint.

Returning to our simple $100-machine model, then, it should also be noted that when the machine is sold, legal ownership of the machine is invariably transferred from the firm to the purchaser, whereas under a traditional form of investment the firm retains ownership of the machine in order to ensure its control over the value created by the production process in which the machine is employed. However, from the firm's standpoint, what fundamentally distinguishes an investment from a sale is not the transfer or non-transfer of ownership rights over the invested resources (i.e., the machine) *per se*, but whether the firm's profit is or is not derived at least in part from the output of (value created by) the investment project. If the profits of the firm which supplies the machine are derived at least in part from the value created in the production process in which the machine is employed, it may be argued that the operation is not simply a sale but involves at least an element of investment from the standpoint of the firm, *even if the firm uses means other than legal ownership of the resources invested (i.e. the machine in this case) to ensure its control over at least part of the value produced by the investment project.* This is the distinguishing characteristic of new forms of investment.

# NOTES AND REFERENCES

1. Nurkse, Dunning and many others have emphasised the importance of financial capital in total international investment flows to the less developed regions of the world prior to World War I. Svedberg argues that direct investment accounted for a larger share of the stock of private foreign investment in the Third World (and globally) than is generally understood, and therefore that the argument that the share of direct investment greatly increased after World War II may be based on at least partially false premises. Cf. R. Nurkse, "The problem of international investment today in the light of nineteenth century experience", *Economic Journal,* September 1954. J. H. Dunning, *Studies in International Investment,* London, 1970; and P. Svedberg, "The Portfolio – Direct Composition of Private Foreign Investment in 1914", *Economic Journal,* December, 1978.

2. Cf. Rudolf Hilferding, *Finance Capital (Das Finanzkapital),* first published in Vienna, 1910.

3. In Section III of this chapter, and its appendix, we explain what we mean by "an element of investment from the foreign firm's viewpoint."

4. It was during this period that major balance-of-payments surpluses led the Japanese government to begin to encourage outward investment; and deficits led the U.S. government to restrict, if briefly and somewhat ineffectively, capital outflows.

5. We focus in this text primarily on implications for host countries and relations between these and foreign investors; phase II of this research project, now getting underway, will focus more extensively on implications for home countries.

6. Terutomo Ozawa kindly brought this use of the term "production sharing" to my attention.

7. Cf. Article on "Production Sharing" by Peter Drucker in the *Wall Street Journal,* March 15, 1977.

8. Cf. D. Germidis (ed.) *International Sub-contracting: A New Form of Investment,* OECD Development Centre, 1981; and A. Basile and D. Germidis, *Policies to Attract Export-Oriented Investment: The Role of Free Export-Processing Zones,* OECD Development Centre, forthcoming.

9. Cf. A. Berle and G. Means, *The Modern Corporation and Private Property,* New York, MacMillan, 1932.

10. One prominent student of FDI and multinational enterprise has urged us to describe what we are calling new forms of investment as forms of *internationalisation of production* instead. While we have no quarrel with the concept in its own right, our use of the term "investment" is intended to focus on the role of a firm's assets (tangible or intangible), not only as inputs to production abroad but also as means for the firm to control at least part of the value added in the production process located abroad. That is, a firm may create an asset within its home economy and then internationalise the asset, and hence its sources of profit on the asset, via new forms as well as traditional FDI. Under such circumstances, the new forms are, in our view, quite appropriately described as forms of *international investment.*

11. Thus, for example, in its publication *International Licensing* (1977), Business International Corp. concludes that "although from an ownership and legal standpoint, an unaffiliated licensee is certainly an independent party and not 'part of the corporate family', nevertheless, from a managerial viewpoint, in some sense a licensee is 'part of the family'. The underlying, often unspoken, but critical bond between a licensor and a licensee is that they are collaborating on a business venture in which, in effect, they are sharing profits. The sharing may be spelled out in black-and-white terms (e.g., 5 per cent of sales), yet still in key ways a licensing agreement is more involved for both sides than a straight arm's-length sale..." (p. 120).

12. The need for this distinction between "the investment project" and "invested resources" becomes apparent when unembodied technology or other intangible assets are among the resources supplied by the foreign firm. For example, a licensor who holds no equity in the investment in the host country will nevertheless normally retain legal ownership of the technology which he supplies to – the technological resource he invests in – the project. As pointed out in our discussion of licensing agreements in Section II, a licensee normally does not acquire ownership of technology through such agreements, but certain rights of access to technology owned by the licensor (in return for which the licensor acquires part of the value created in conjunction with its technology in the host country).

13. Such has been the case, for example, of Saudi Arabia, which requires firms setting up petrochemical plants to take a 25 per cent equity position. Such was also reportedly the case of Mexico in its recent negotiations with Nippon Steel to set up a steel plant under a turnkey contract. In both cases commitments by the host country to provide long-term crude petroleum supplies have apparently been a major inducement to otherwise relatively reluctant firms to take equity positions – reluctance presumably due in part to the existence of overcapacity in these basic industries (especially steel).

14. For a useful exposition of some of the implications of conflicting interests in the case of turnkey contracts, see in particular K. Abdallah-Khodja, "Algeria's Experience with New International Investment Relations", in C. Oman, ed., *New Forms of International Investment in Developing Countries: The National Perspective*, Development Centre Papers, OECD Development Centre, Paris, forthcoming.

15. See for example C. Pollak, "Non-equity forms of German Industrial Co-operation", in *ibid.*

16. The Development Centre has just begun a follow-up study which is expected to include, among other things, a much more systematic and in-depth analysis of firm-level data, which should provide useful additional empirical evidence on the extent to which specific operations are approached as investments by firms, under what conditions, etc.

17. See the Appendix by Graham Vickery.

18. This simple model considers only one factor of production (the machine), assumes that the gross value of output is $110, and that the machine has no scrap value at the end of the life of the investment project. Our model could of course be amplified by assuming, for example, that the gross value of output is $150 and that other production costs (e.g. labour) amount to $40, giving the same profit of $10.

*Chapter 2*

# NEW FORMS VS. TRADITIONAL FDI
## AGGREGATE TRENDS AND ALTERNATIVE HYPOTHESES

In the late 1970s a number of economists were arguing that, in the North-South context, traditional FDI was becoming obsolete and was being replaced or superseded by new forms of investment[1]. This argument, which we shall refer to as "the obsolescence-of-FDI hypothesis", raises a number of important questions. Is it true that the traditional form of FDI has become obsolete, or is it becoming so? Are the new forms of investment replacing or superseding FDI? To what extent are the new forms of investment a substitute for, and to what extent do they complement traditional FDI?

This chapter and the following one address the general question of what is happening in the North-South context as regards trends in the use of new forms of investment and traditional FDI. In this chapter we focus on aggregate trends and review a number of broad working hypotheses. In Section I we review existing data on FDI and financial flows in order to test the obsolescence-of-FDI hypothesis; in Sections II and III we discuss alternative hypotheses which can be deduced from these data. In Chapter 3 we review the empirical evidence on trends in the use of new forms and FDI at a more disaggregate level, i.e., on a sectoral basis. Subsequent chapters explore some of the reasons why firms may use new forms of investment (Chapter 4), and examine some of their implications (Chapter 5).

## I. IS FDI OBSOLESCENT?

Statistics cited by proponents of the obsolescence-of-FDI hypothesis are usually of two types:

1.  those which reveal trends in the flows and stocks of FDI *per se;*
2.  those which show FDI trends in relation to other types of capital flows to developing countries, notably private bank loans.

The arguments which focus on FDI trends *per se* can in turn be broken down into three points. First, and most importantly, data on average annual flows of FDI from the group of DAC countries[2] to developing countries are cited to show that while the flow increased in real terms during the 1960s, it tended to stagnate and even decline in real terms during the 1970s. Secondly, data on the share of locally reinvested earnings in FDI showing it to be higher on average in developed countries than in developing countries are cited to point up stagnation of FDI in developing countries. Third, and closely related to the preceding point, estimates showing the developing countries' share of the worldwide stock of FDI to have decreased over the last decade, relative to the share of the industrialised countries, are sometimes cited.

Perhaps even more important for purposes of this study are the arguments referred to under category[2] above, which compare FDI trends with those of other financial flows to developing countries. Here the proponents of the obsolescence-of-FDI hypothesis generally cite data showing the spectacular growth of international bank lending to developing countries during the 1970s. While such loans were still of only limited volume as late as 1970, by mid-decade they surpassed FDI in yearly volume, and more than doubled it by the end of the decade. This is felt to be unmistakable evidence of the relative obsolescence of FDI in the North-South context.

To assess the validity and usefulness of the obsolescence-of-FDI hypothesis, we should begin by taking a careful look at year-by-year statistics on the flow of FDI from the DAC countries to the developing countries[3]. If we are to shed light on the significance of the new forms of investment, to see for example whether they are actually replacing or simply complementing the traditional form of FDI, at least two points merit careful consideration. The first concerns the data base itself. Since statistics on international investment *flows* are derived from data on financial movements (as reflected in the capital-account figures collected for national balance-of-payments purposes) and those on investment *stocks* are derived largely from corporate-survey estimates of the book value of assets controlled by foreign residents (including reinvested profits), neither set of data is even supposed to measure transfers of real resources from developed to developing countries. In other words, in as much as the obsolescence hypothesis holds that the new forms are replacing the traditional form of FDI as the principal international investment vehicle of North-South flows of "real" resources (as distinct from financial flows on the one hand and ownership of assets on the other), these data are unfortunately inappropriate for our purposes[4]. To this problem must be added the virtual absence of comparable aggregate data on the new forms of investment, not to mention the serious difficulties with cross-country aggregation of data on direct investment. We feel, therefore, that one cannot reliably either accept or reject the obsolescence-of-FDI hypothesis on the basis of available investment statistics.

But insufficient as these statistics may be for our purposes, they are the best we have. So, with the reservations just expressed, we proceed to the second point: how best to interpret the data if we ignore the reliability problem. Do we draw the same conclusions, after taking a careful look at the numbers, as do the proponents of the obsolescence hypothesis? The answer is no. Let us consider their arguments one by one.

The data in Table I show that in current dollars the average annual growth rate of FDI during the decade 1960-1970 was 7.6 per cent and from 1970-1980 it was 9.9 per cent. Because of the significant increase in the rate of inflation during the latter decade, however, the respective growth rates are approximately 4.3 per cent and –0.5 per cent when reduced to constant (1977) dollars. At first glance, these figures appear to support the obsolescence-of-FDI hypothesis. And even if one includes the estimate for 1981[5], one finds an average annual growth rate of FDI flows over the period 1970-1981 of 3.7 per cent, that is, somewhat lower than the rate during the 1960s, although less markedly so than if one looks only at the 1970s.

However, a closer look at the yearly figures reveals that the growth trends one perceives depend largely on the specific years chosen as inflection points within the twenty-one-year period for which data are available. For example, if one compares growth trends for the periods 1960-68, 1968-71 and 1971-81, one obtains average annual growth rates of FDI flows, measured in constant dollars, of 4.2 per cent, –2.8 per cent, and 6.0 per cent, respectively. One could therefore just as easily argue that although the North-South flow of FDI slowed down in the 1968-71 period, since 1971 it has grown even more rapidly than during the 1960s.

27

Table 1. PRIVATE FOREIGN DIRECT INVESTMENT AND BILATERAL PORTFOLIO
INVESTMENT FLOWS FROM DAC COUNTRIES TO DEVELOPING COUNTRIES

(US $ billion)

| Year | Private Foreign Direct Investment | | Bilateral Portfolio Investment Current $ | Year | Private Foreign Direct Investment | | Bilateral Portfolio Investment Current $ |
|------|-----------|-------------|--------|------|-----------|-------------|--------|
| | Current $ | Constant $[1] | | | Current $ | Constant $[1] | |
| 1960 | 1.77 | (4.69) | 0.63 | 1971 | 3.31 | (5.95) | 0.70 |
| 1961 | 1.84 | (4.74) | 0.61 | 1972 | 4.23 | (6.96) | 1.99 |
| 1962 | 1.49 | (3.78) | 0.15 | 1973 | 4.72 | (6.75) | 3.27 |
| 1963 | 1.60 | (3.95) | 0.33 | 1974 | 1.10 | (1.40) | 3.81 |
| 1964 | 1.57 | (3.77) | 0.85 | 1975 | 10.49 | (11.84) | 9.29 |
| 1965 | 2.46 | (5.72) | 0.69 | 1976 | 7.68 | (8.35) | 10.21 |
| 1966 | 2.17 | (4.90) | 0.48 | 1977 | 9.47 | (9.47) | 10.74 |
| 1967 | 2.10 | (4.66) | 0.74 | 1978 | 11.26 | (9.65) | 21.05 |
| 1968 | 3.03 | (6.50) | 0.91 | 1979 | 12.74 | (10.10) | 23.45 |
| 1969 | 2.78 | (5.70) | 1.19 | 1980 | 9.47 | (6.81) | 17.70 |
| 1970 | 3.69 | (7.11) | 0.70 | 1981[2] | 14.64 | (10.66) | 24.71 |

1. Calculated in 1977 dollars using the GNP deflator.
2. Preliminary estimates.
Source: OECD DAC Secretariat.

It should also be emphasized that the aggregate statistics on FDI flows may be strongly influenced – and, for our purposes, distorted – by a few very large investments or disinvestments reported in a particular year. This was most notably the case of U.S. FDI in the petroleum industry in 1974 and 1975, and to a lesser degree again in 1980[6]. In seeking to identify the underlying longer-run trends in North-South FDI, we have therefore constructed Graphics 1-3 excluding data on FDI in petroleum for the years 1973-76, as shown by the dotted line. Graphic 1 shows yearly FDI flows in current dollars, Graphic 2 in constant dollars, and Graphic 3 a three-year moving average. These data, which refer after all not to levels of accumulated investment but to yearly investment flows, do not appear to support the obsolescence hypothesis. They clearly show that the annual flow of FDI has continued, on average, to increase during the 1970s and, moreover, that the rate of increase has remained roughly comparable, in real terms, to that characteristic of the 1960s.

So what about the data showing that a significantly higher proportion of FDI consists of profits reinvested locally in developed countries than in developing countries? Here again, at first glance the evidence would seem to support the obsolescence hypothesis. For example, data on the share of re-invested earnings in total FDI by U.S. firms during the 1970s indicate this share to have been about a third in developing countries, compared to well over half in the industrialised countries. But a serious flaw in the argument that these data indicate an obsolescence of FDI in developing countries stems from its failure to consider differential rates of return on investment. A counter argument might be that higher rates of profit in developing countries mean that lower rates of re-investment of profits in those countries are required to sustain a given rate of growth of investment. Although it is difficult to reliably estimate developing-/industrialised-country profit-rate differentials – among other reasons because of possible differential trends in the use of transfer pricing – there is in fact considerable evidence that profit rates on FDI do tend, on average, to be higher in developing countries. Data on average rates of return on FDI by U.S. firms from 1975 to 1980, for example, show that the average rate of return in developed countries over the six-year period was about 14 per cent, compared to an average of over 26 per cent in developing countries[7]. Thus, in our view, the fact that a higher percentage of profits on FDI tend to be reinvested locally in the industrialised countries than in the developing countries lends little support to the obsolescence hypothesis.

And thirdly, what about the argument that the developing countries' share of total FDI stock worldwide is diminishing? The problem with this argument, once again, is that one is faced with what for our purposes are considerable distortions in the data caused by the relatively high incidence of nationalisations of FDI, notably in the petroleum and mining industries, in a number of developing countries in the early 1970s. These nationalisations make it difficult to identify underlying trends, as does the fact that no reliable estimate of the global stock of FDI in developing countries has been undertaken since 1967. Nevertheless, DAC estimates show that whereas 30 per cent of global FDI stock was in developing countries in 1970, by 1976 the share had risen again to 36 per cent[8].

In sum, we do not find much support for the obsolescence-of-FDI hypothesis in the data on FDI trends *per se*. In fact, if we choose to ignore the serious problem of data reliability, we would be inclined to argue that these data contradict the hypothesis.

But before jumping to conclusions, let us take a closer look at what appears to be the most important argument put forward by proponents of the obsolescence hypothesis. It runs as follows: whereas FDI was the dominant form of North-South investment during the 1950s and 1960s, since the early 1970s private bank lending has grown much more rapidly than FDI, surpassing it in volume of yearly flows by the middle of the decade and doubling it by the end of the decade. Furthermore, while the foreign investor provides a "package" of assets under FDI, the new forms of investment are characterised by at least some degree of "unbundling" of these assets, with host countries borrowing financial capital when necessary to finance the acquisition of other assets. Proponents of the obsolescence-of-FDI hypothesis consequently deduce that the rapid growth of international non-concessional lending indicates a rapid growth of new forms of investment in developing countries. And the much more rapid growth of such lending suggests to them that traditional FDI is being replaced or superseded by the new forms of investment. In other words, they infer from the rapid growth of bank lending that FDI is becoming *relatively* obsolete in the North-South context.

As shown in Table 1 and Graphic 4, the data do indeed show a spectacular growth of bilateral "portfolio" investment – most of which consists of private bank loans – since the early 1970s. Though not shown in the data, the well known size of loans associated with such lending techniques as "project finance" might also be cited to buttress the obsolescence hypothesis. But for the reasoning referred to in the preceding paragraph to hold water, one has to assume that a significant proportion of these bank loans to developing countries is being used to finance, directly or indirectly, new forms of investment. In our view this assumption is not well founded.

Unfortunately, there are to our knowledge no data on how developing countries have used their international borrowings over the last decade which would permit even a rough estimate of what share of developing countries' borrowings are being used to finance new forms of investment. However, to clarify the picture somewhat, we can distinguish between three broad categories of uses, the first two of which are not new forms of investment. In the first category, we can include loans used to finance both current expenditures of all types, and those used to increase the borrower's foreign exchange reserves[9]. A very large element in this category would of course be balance-of-payments financing to cover current-account deficits due to rising import bills for petroleum, intermediate goods consumed by local industry, food, military hardware, etc.[10]. Also included in this category would be international loans made, directly or indirectly, to local firms which use the funds, converted into local currency, to cover current operating costs. Although it is impossible to ascertain the global importance of the latter phenomenon, it reportedly took on surprising proportions in at least one major borrowing country, Mexico, during a period in the late 1970s when certain large local groups (Alfa is a known example) were unable to borrow further on

**Graphic 1 YEARLY FLOWS OF FOREIGN DIRECT INVESTMENT FROM DAC COUNTRIES TO DEVELOPING COUNTRIES :**
Current Dollars (US billion)

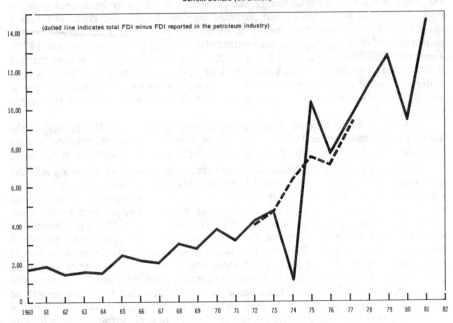

(dotted line indicates total FDI minus FDI reported in the petroleum industry)

**Graphic 2 YEARLY FLOW OF FOREIGN DIRECT INVESTMENT FROM DAC COUNTRIES TO DEVELOPING COUNTRIES :**
Constant (1977) Dollars (US billion)

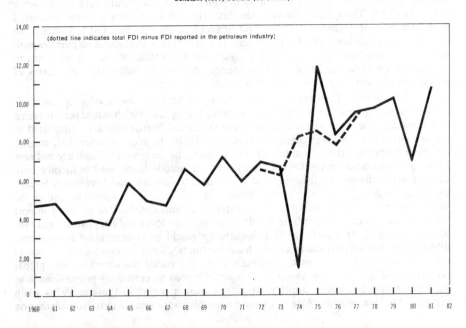

(dotted line indicates total FDI minus FDI reported in the petroleum industry)

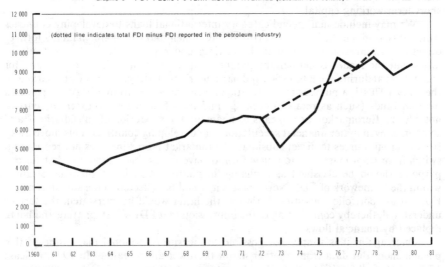

Graphic 3   FDI FLOWS : 3-YEAR MOVING AVERAGE (constant 1977 dollars)

(dotted line indicates total FDI minus FDI reported in the petroleum industry)

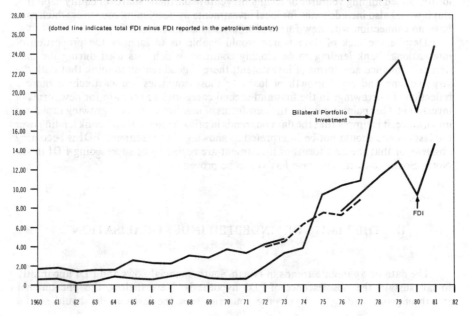

Graphic 4   YEARLY FLOWS OF PRIVATE FOREIGN DIRECT INVESTMENT AND BILATERAL PORTFOLIO INVESTMENT FROM DAC COUNTRIES TO DEVELOPING COUNTRIES : Current Dollars (US billion)

(dotted line indicates total FDI minus FDI reported in the petroleum industry)

Bilateral Portfolio Investment

FDI

31

local capital markets but were able to turn to international financial markets for short-term working capital.

We may include in a second category international loans to developing countries which appear in the statistics as "portfolio" investment but which are, in fact, a form of direct foreign investment. These are borrowings undertaken by foreign-owned subsidiaries, but the lender is neither the parent company nor an affiliate. It appears, for example, that during the late 1960s and particularly with the growth of Euromarkets in the early 1970s[11], a number of multinational firms switched from a heavy reliance on internal funds (such as retained earnings and intra-firm loans) to external sources, notably the Euromarket, as a means of financing the expansion of subsidiaries – and sometimes even major financial speculation – in developing countries. This move away from internal sources to direct subsidiary-Euromarket borrowing does not represent a switch from traditional FDI to a new form of investment, but simply to what for our purposes should be classified as a change in multinational firms' financial strategy within the framework of FDI. Nevertheless it would be reflected in the statistics not as FDI but as "portfolio" investment; that is, the latter would be overstated, the former understated, thereby contributing to the impression that FDI was stagnating and being replaced by financial flows.

Once again, it is simply not possible to measure the global magnitude of this phenomenon. But data from another major borrower are revealing. In 1979, at least 17 per cent of all foreign loans to Brazil went to local subsidiaries of foreign companies; the volume of these loans (some $8.6 billion) was equivalent to half the volume of FDI registered in Brazil that year. Even more impressive are the data from a 1974 study of 115 large foreign-owned firms, which show that the net inflow of foreign loans to these companies was 4.2 times the net volume of investment and reinvestment made by the companies that year[12].

A third and last category would include those international bank loans to developing countries used to finance all types of investment activities undertaken by wholly or majority-locally owned (private or public) enterprises. This category would of course include loans used to finance new forms of investment, such as turnkey plants, locally owned mining ventures or local joint venture partners' shares of equity capital[13]. But it would also include loans for local investments by developing countries which may have no connection with new forms of international investment.

Despite the lack of data which would enable us to identify the proportion of international bank lending to developing countries which was used during the past decade to finance new forms of investment, there is good reason to think that both the large volume and rapid growth of loans to those countries are as much or more a reflection of borrowings in the first and second categories as they are for new forms of investment. Our point is not that the new forms of investment are not growing rapidly in importance; it is simply that the data on trends in private international bank lending over the last decade should not be interpreted as showing that traditional FDI is becoming obsolete, or that the new forms of investment are replacing or superseding FDI in the North-South context. The case has yet to be proved.


II.  THE LIMITS OF "INDEBTED INDUSTRIALISATION"


The data on aggregate trends in North-South financial flows and FDI apparently do not sustain the obsolescence-of-FDI hypothesis. Nevertheless, the phenomenal growth of bank lending to developing countries over the last decade should not be dismissed as irrelevant to our analysis. That is, if the data summarised in Table 1 do not sustain the obsolescence hypothesis, neither do they conclusively show that the new forms are not superseding North-South FDI flows. There are in fact a number of alternative hypotheses which can be derived from the data on FDI and financial flows.

To begin with, bank lending over the last decade has been concentrated in many of the more industrialised developing countries. Many of them are now faced with heavy debt-servicing obligations (a problem exacerbated by the rise in real interest rates in recent years), and for some the only alternative to severe austerity policies in the 1980s – which might even be politically untenable – are strategies of industrial growth which would sustain both increasing manufactured exports, vital for debt servicing, and domestic accumulation and consumption levels. Consequently, many of the heavy borrowers are likely to show not only an ever-greater interest in expanding their exports of manufactured products (a trend clearly visible during the 1970s) but also to show renewed interest in import-substituting industrial growth[14].

Rather than reverting to the "classic" import-substitution policies of the 1950s and 1960s, which tended to inhibit manufactured exports and in general to create structural balance-of-payments imbalances, however, the import-substituting policies of the 1980s are likely to seek increasing ratios of value of output (and exports) to value of imports in industry. Given the importance of capital goods and technology in total imports by the industrial sector, import substitution in these countries during the 1980s will be concentrated not on final products as was the case of "classic" import substitution, but on capital inputs. It therefore stands to reason that considerable attention will be given to minimising the foreign-exchange costs of investment resources coming from abroad (i.e., capital goods, technology, etc.) whether they are acquired through foreign investment or arm's-length purchases.

One interpretation of whether or not the new forms of investment are likely to supersede FDI in such a scenario, is that many developing countries which in the 1970s turned to strategies of debt-financed growth and greater use of new forms of investment will in the 1980s tend to revert to a greater reliance on traditional FDI because it has again become the more cost-effective means of obtaining investment resources from abroad. There are at least two versions of this interpretation.

In the first, "cost effectiveness" is defined in terms of foreign-exchange inflows and outflows in a relatively narrow sense. The reasoning might be summarised as follows: whereas loans require the borrowing country to make interest and principle payments determined at the time of the loan decision and which do not fluctuate in accordance with changes in the state of the borrower's economy (absent default), the advantage of FDI is that the foreign exchange outflow from the host economy is more likely to fluctuate in accordance with local conditions. During periods of vigorous local expansion, profits are likely to be buoyant and repatriation of earnings on FDI may increase relative to periods when conditions in the host economy deteriorate and profits decline. In other words, the foreign-exchange cost of FDI to the host country may be thought to be more sensitive to changes in individual countries' ability to pay, so to speak, whereas terms on international loans tend to fluctuate (sometimes abruptly) more as a function of conditions in international capital markets and too little as a function of local economic conditions.

A second version of this interpretation considers "cost effectiveness" in a much broader context. It calls attention to the power of multinational firms, particularly the monopolistic or oligopolistic advantages of foreign direct investors (cf. Chapter 4) and the foreign-exchange costs which these may entail for the host economy. The advantages held by foreign direct investors may be thought to result, for example, in monopolistic rents on FDI, in foreign investors' greater use of imported technology, equipment, expatriate personnel, and in transfer pricing, all of which tend to raise the foreign-exchange cost of foreign investment resources to – and may also be considered incompatible with the development needs of – the host country. Moreover, this version would also suggest that while foreign direct investors often tend to re-invest their earnings locally during periods of economic buoyancy in the host country, economic downturns may actually witness increased repatriation of funds. The responsiveness of FDI to local economic conditions may therefore have precisely the opposite effect on flows of foreign exchange from that envisioned in the first version (and as such may actually tend to accentuate the business cycle in the host economy as well). The phenomenal growth of bank lending, relative to FDI, in the 1970s may thus be seen as resulting both from resistance on the part of developing countries to increased FDI and a lack of dynamism (or even a tendency to withdraw) on the part of foreign direct investors during a period of relatively slow growth; the latter tendency, at least, may be reversed if growth picks up in the 1980s.

In contrast to the predictions of increased and/or renewed developing-country reliance on traditional FDI in the 1980s, one author has predicted a rise in "Third World indebted industrialisation" based on "indirect" foreign investment. Citing the experiences of Algeria, Brazil, Mexico and South Korea, he portrays an alliance of "nationalist state-capitalist regimes" and "internationalist finance-capitalists of the Euromarkets" in which multinational banks are a major source of finance capital and the local states provide "the muscle and brains to force-march the countries involved into the industrialised world"[15]. He sees the international lending institutions, notably the large banks, displacing multinational firms as the predominant source of foreign capital to developing countries.

In our view this is an oversimplification, not only because of a rather loose use of such terms as "state-capitalist" and "finance-capitalist" but, more significantly, because of what our research suggests is a mistaken appreciation both of the role of multinational firms – which continues to be important in developing countries, whether through FDI or new forms of investment – and of the relationship between these firms and the international financial organisations. We look more closely at this relationship in Section III of this chapter.

The author does, however, make the interesting observation that, because of the crucial role played by developing countries' exports of manufactured goods to the industrialised countries in sustaining their debt-servicing payments, on which the banks depend for profits, the banks may play an active role in resisting protectionist pressures in the industrialised countries. One might infer from this "interdependence" of multinational banks and major borrowing countries that, as their mutual interests converge to reinforce the process of "indebted industrialisation", so will traditional FDI by multinational firms be increasingly replaced by new forms of investment financed by multinational banks in the North-South context.

Such reasoning may turn out to be correct, but it should be treated with caution. By way of counter-argument it is worth noting, for example, that a decade of experience with "indebted industrialisation" may have left a number of borrowing countries (the so-called nationalist state-capitalist regimes) with an impression that, in seeking to circumvent the oligopolistic powers of multinational firms embodied in FDI, they may have jumped from the frying pan into the fire. In the early to mid-1970s, when real interest rates were low and the abundance of OPEC funds created a "borrower's market" in which banks competed aggressively in lending to developing countries, many of these countries may have concluded that it was both easier and cheaper to pursue a strategy of debt-financed growth involving greater use of new forms of investment, than to negotiate with the multinational firms over the terms of FDI. It may in fact have been easier, because for a time bankers were acting in haste to keep up with the wave of lending to developing countries. And it may have looked cheaper not only because of the low (or negative) real interest rates prevalent at the time, but also because it was thought that monopoly rents appropriated by the foreign investor under FDI could be eliminated and/or appropriated by local groups under the new forms of investment.

But by the late 1970s a number of factors may have changed many borrowing countries' perceptions of the advantages of such heavy reliance on foreign debt to finance domestic capital formation. One was undoubtedly the large unexpected increase in real interest rates. Another may have been the perception by some borrowing countries that in trying to avoid or dilute the oligopolistic powers of multinational firms exerted through FDI, they were increasingly confronted with what turned out to be quasi-monopolistic powers of the international banking community and the IMF. Crucial here is the international banking community's adherence to a relatively homogeneous set of lending practices (notably credit ratings which determine terms on "sovereign" loans) at any given time, as well as the pivotal role of the IMF, whose terms of conditionality may effectively if not intentionally limit a borrowing country's scope for taking more effective advantage of competition among potential lenders in seeking a loan and/or more favourable terms.

Furthermore, whereas FDI by even the most powerful multinational firm may offer some leverage to the host country because of the "captive" nature of the investment once it is made, a developing country is likely to perceive that the risks involved in defaulting on its foreign debt are substantially greater than those involved in nationalising the local subsidiary of a foreign firm. In other words, the relatively non-differentiated natural financial capital – which both permits and requires its relatively high degree of international integration, as can be seen in the vast worldwide network of inter-bank linkages, the use of syndicated loans, common credit-risk assessment and the relatively homogeneous set of lending practices – may render it less vulnerable to pressures from host countries (and, for foreign investors, to "political risk" as well) than even relatively concentrated industrial capital, because of the latter's tendency to be more highly differentiated.

Lastly, some countries which turned to debt-financed growth and an extensive use of new forms of investment during the late 1960s and 1970s may have found that multinational firms continue to enjoy oligopolistic advantages as suppliers of equipment, technology, management, etc. From the firm's standpoint the new forms of investment may be just as advantageous as traditional FDI, if not more so, in part because the firm's resources are no longer "captive", and payoff may depend less on the long-term commercial profitability of the investment project. One can only wonder, for example, whether post-1978 changes in Algeria's growth strategy and foreign investment policy do not in part reflect such perceptions.

Whether the "cost effectiveness" of foreign capital in contributing to domestic capital formation is assessed by host governments in the narrower or broader sense, one could reasonably infer that, contrary to the "indebted industrialization" model cited above, many developing countries will look to FDI as an important source of investment resources in the 1980s. The second version of this interpretation (which considers "cost effectiveness" more broadly) would also suggest, however, that in seeking to maximise foreign investment's contribution to domestic capital formation at the lowest possible foreign-exchange cost, many host governments may more actively pursue investment policies that rely on incentives, performance requirements, and screening and approval procedures which are both increasingly sophisticated and more streamlined. To the extent that investors' home governments begin to react to these policies, the result may be greater tensions[16] and/or a growing role for inter-governmental investment agreements[17] in the North-South context. However, the point here is that according to this line of reasoning, whether or not FDI can be said to have been superseded by debt-financed industrialisation and new forms of investment in developing countries during the 1970s, FDI will again tend to dominate North-South investment trends in the 1980s.

## III. A NEW INTERNATIONAL DIVISION OF RISKS AND
## RESPONSIBILITIES?

There is, however, another interpretation which has as its point of departure the same phenomenal growth of North-South financial flows over the past decade, but which reaches another conclusion. It differs from the "indebted industrialisation" model primarily in the role it attributes to multinational firms, and hence in its view of the nature of relations between the major firms and banks and the nature of their relations with host countries. It contends that a new division of risks and responsibilities among the *three* major actors involved in North-South investment is gradually emerging so that, in the long run, the new forms of investment may indeed tend to replace traditional FDI.

The three sets of major actors are:

1.  international firms, based especially but not exclusively in industrialised countries and including, but not limited to, the major multinationals;
2.  international lenders, including especially private multinational banks, international financial organisations (notably the World Bank, IMF and Regional Development Banks), and national public development finance institutions (especially the industrialised countries' export-credit agencies);
3.  host-country élites, including the state, public enterprise, and the private business and financial communities in developing countries.

The hypothesis may be summarised as follows. If many developing countries (notably the more industrialised, which also include many of the heaviest borrowers) can be expected to try to minimise the foreign-exchange cost of foreign investment resources while maximising the contribution of those resources to domestic capital accumulation, the tendency for host countries to seek to "unbundle" the traditional FDI "package" of financial capital, embodied and disembodied technology, management and, where relevant, access to world markets, may be reinforced over the coming years. It may be reinforced because local firms and/or host governments wish to incur the foreign-exchange costs of only those specific resources required, rather than the whole package. Thus, countries like Brazil or Korea, which have a relative abundance of local entrepreneurial and managerial talent, may seek to minimise the foreign-exchange cost of gaining access to high technology (say, computer-production technology) by negotiating joint ventures or licensing agreements with foreign technology suppliers. In return the suppliers get access to an important, growing market. Similarly, a country may use new forms of investment to gain or facilitate access to world export markets for its primary and/or manufactured products.

But – and here is the key point of this interpretation – the multinational firms which have traditionally dominated international investment in developing countries, and relied heavily on FDI to do so, may also increasingly find it more profitable for reasons of cost- and/or risk-reduction (which we discuss in Chapter 4), to rely more heavily on non-financial, non- or reduced-equity forms of investment in developing countries. A good number of firms, including many of the "majors" as well as the so-called new- or late-comers, may increasingly concentrate on such strategic areas as technological innovation (i.e., the upstream side of final output) and/or control over world markets (the downstream side of production), as well as certain key aspects of management. These could become their primary base of control and profits in a world economy characterised by the increasing internationalisation of production, coupled with considerable uncertainty in world product and financial markets. In other words, multinational firms may increasingly play important roles as intermediaries on both the input (technology and management) and output (world market) sides of the production process in developing countries, while shifting a greater share of the risk associated with the investment process on to international lenders and, perhaps even more so, on to the host countries.

The multinational banks and international financial organisations may increasingly play the leading role in channeling financial capital to developing countries in need of liquidity, particularly those with the industrial or primary-products export potential needed to service their debt. Because of the homogeneous nature of financial capital and the risks associated with fluctuating currency and interest rates, financial institutions may be found to have a strong "comparative advantage"[18] internationally and may therefore increasingly assume – or be delegated – control over the financial dimension of the international investment process[19]. Within the international financial community, the division of risks and responsibilities may also vary from project to project and period to period, with private multinational banks playing a clearly predominant role in some cases, and public national or multilateral financial agencies playing an increasingly important role – via co-financing, for example – in others.

Thirdly, host countries may increasingly retain (or be delegated) legal ownership of the investment projects and assume (or be delegated) increasing managerial responsibilities. Some of them, notably a number of the capital-surplus petroleum exporters, may provide financial capital as well. Along with these increasing responsibilities for host countries may go important risks, a topic discussed further in Chapter 5.

In short, we may be witnessing the emergence of a new pattern of international investment strategies affecting all three major sets of actors. According to this hypothesis, the new forms of investment may indeed tend to displace traditional FDI as the predominant form in the North-South context.

# NOTES AND REFERENCES

1. See, for example, P. Judet and R. Chaponniere, "Problèmes liés à la coopération industrielle entre le Nord et le Sud", Université des Sciences Sociales, Grenoble, septembre 1978 (mimeo), paper presented at a meeting on "Foreign Investment and its Impact on Development", held at the Development Centre in November, 1978.

2. "DAC" refers to the Development Assistance Committee of OECD. DAC Member countries are: Australia, Austria, Belgium, Canada, Denmark, Finland, France, Germany, Italy, Japan, Netherlands, New Zealand, Norway, Sweden, Switzerland, the United Kingdom and the United States.

3. These statistics are presented in Table 1 at the end of this chapter.

4. These data suffer from, among other things, inconsistencies in their treatment of reinvested earnings and investment in kind (such as equipment, patents, etc.) which are generally not included, even though their inclusion is required for conformity to the working definitions of foreign direct investment as used in the IMF/OECD Common Reporting System, so that the recorded data present a limited, and distorted, picture of direct investment flows even in a financial sense. Furthermore, to meet analytical requirements for measuring direct foreign investment as a real (as well as financial) phenomenon affecting total investment, employment, output, etc., broader coverage to cover all assets under foreign corporate control, such as local company issues and local and third-country borrowing, should be included. For a systematic discussion of these problems, see the OECD document entitled *The Availability in Member Countries of Statistics on Foreign Direct Investment* (IME(79)15, July, 1979), especially pp. 3-10. See also the World Bank Staff Working Paper No. 348, *Private Direct Foreign Investment in Developing Countries*, prepared by K. Billerbeck and Y. Yasugi (1979), especially Annex I.

5. Although the figure for 1981 is a preliminary estimate, for our purposes it is not significantly less reliable than figures for earlier years.

6. The amount of direct investment shown for 1974 reflects a drastic drop because of the U.S. Authorities' 1978 decision to classify nationalisations during the 1972-74 period in the petroleum sector as "disinvestment" in 1974 by their nationalised firms (thus net U.S. investment was estimated at minus $2.17 billion in 1974, as compared with the positive figures of $895 million in 1973 and $7.24 billion in 1975).

7. *Survey of Current Business*, several years.

8. OECD DAC Secretariat, *Investing in Developing countries*, Fifth Revised Edition.

9. Since the figures we present in Table 1 refer to net rather than gross portfolio investment, we do not mention borrowing to service previous debt. Such loans do account for an increasingly important share of gross loans to developing countries, of course, and would be included in this category if we were using gross figures.

10. Non-oil-exporting developing countries covered some 85 per cent of their import bill with exports in 1973, but only 67 per cent in 1975. It is well known that developing countries with access to financial markets made up much of the difference by borrowing from the banks.

11. The late 1960s/early 1970s was a period of relatively low real interest rates in international financial markets. It also witnessed the U.S. government's restrictions on capital outflows, including FDI. The period closely coincided with the acceleration of private bank lending to developing countries.

12. Cited in E.A. Guimaraes, P.S. Malan and J. Tavares, "The New Forms of Investment in Brazil", 1982 (mimeo).

13. Loans to local joint venture partners which the latter use to pay up their share of equity capital are reportedly a common practice by Japanese minority joint venture partners (Cf. Y. Tsurumi, *The Japanese Are Coming*, Cambridge, Mass., 1977).

14. Cf. A. Fishlow, "Debt, Growth and Hemispheric Relations: Latin American Prospects in the 1980s", University of California, Berkeley, 1979 (mimeo).

15. J. Frieden, "Third World indebted industrialization: international finance and state capitalism in Mexico, Brazil, Algeria and South Korea, *Industrial Organization,* Summer 1981.

16. Cf. C. Fred Bergsten, "Coming Investment Wars?" in *Foreign Affairs,* October 1974.

17. Cf. Alexandra Gourdain Mitsotaki, "Les Accords Intergouvernementaux Relatifs aux Investissements", July 1982 (mimeo).

18. The greater vulnerability of industrial capital than financial capital to "political risk" in developing countries, alluded to towards the end of Section II, would be included in this notion of "comparative advantage".

19. Though it lies beyond the scope of our analysis, the potential power of the international financial community to influence trends in industrial structure worldwide is worth noting. See for example, R. Cohen, "Structural Change in International Banking and Its Implications for the U.S. Economy," in *Special Study on Economic Change,* Vol. 9, Joint Economic Committee of the U.S. Congress, December 1980; and R. Cohen, "The Transnationalization of Finance: Bank Lending to Multinational Firms in the Early 1970s" (mimeo).

*Chapter 3*

# SECTORAL TRENDS IN THE USE OF NEW FORMS

As we have seen, the principal statistical arguments for "obsolescence of FDI" are based on inconclusive aggregate data, though there seem to be logical reasons for a new pattern of division of risks and responsibilities among the three major actors. Since no sweeping generalisations can be made as to whether or not the new forms are tending to supersede traditional FDI, we shall try to shed further light on investment patterns in the North-South context by exploring trends in the use of new and traditional forms on a more disaggregated basis.

## I.  EXTRACTIVE INDUSTRIES

If there is one sector where it seems safe to conclude that new forms of investment are replacing traditional FDI, it is in the petroleum and metals-mining industries. It is also in these extractive industries that one finds the strongest evidence of the emerging trilateral division of risks and responsibilities.

### A.  Petroleum[1]

Traditional FDI clearly predominated in the petroleum industry from the time of the first international investments in developing countries (reportedly in 1901, in Iran) until the late 1950s. These petroleum investments were usually based on agreements between host countries and foreign investors known as "concessions", under which the firms were traditionally given exclusive rights of exploration and production, and sometimes even surface rights, within a specified area for extended periods of time. The firms held exclusive property rights over all output. Profit-sharing agreements, which provided the host country with significantly increased revenues, were introduced in 1948 by Venezuela and in 1950 by Saudi Arabia[2]. But the first new form of investment, as we have defined the term, was the joint venture between Iran's state petroleum company (NIOC) and Italy's state company (AGIP) in 1957[3]. A second joint venture was set up by NIOC in 1958 with a wholly owned subsidiary of Standard Oil of Indiana (AMOCO).

Indonesia pioneered the *production-sharing contract*. The first such agreement was reportedly set up in 1960 with a Japanese consortium (Kobayashi) for a liquified gas project. The first production-sharing contract in petroleum was signed in 1966, with an "independent" company (IIAPCO), and Conoco appears to have been the first "major" to sign such an agreement, in 1967. By 1968, more than a dozen had been signed by Indonesia. In Latin America, the first such contract was the Peru-Occidental Petroleum Co. agreement of 1971[4]. Since 1973, Malaysia has been using production-sharing

40

arrangements, and since 1974, India for offshore production; these contracts are also found in the Philippines and Chile. In Africa, countries using production-sharing contracts include Angola, Egypt, Libya, Nigeria and Sudan.

One of the earlier *service contracts* was undoubtedly that signed by Mobil with Venezuela in 1962, but it was of limited scope and importance. The modern service contract was reportedly pioneered by France's ERAP (Elf-Aquitaine) with Iran in 1966 and with Iraq in 1968. Such contracts are commonly used in conjunction with *joint ventures,* in which the host country's state petroleum company holds at least majority equity and the multinational company is paid a fee and ensured access to supplies of oil at either market or discount prices. This type of arrangement is expected to predominate during the 1980s in such major producing countries as Saudi Arabia, Kuwait and Qatar.

In Algeria, the classical concessional arrangement was replaced in 1965 by the Franco-Algerian agreement of "Cooperative Association", whose distinctive feature was the predominance of inter-governmental negotiations. With the nationalisation of the industry in 1971, however, this agreement was superseded by a formula known as "association of enterprises", in which Algeria's state petroleum company (SONA-TRACH) negotiates directly with foreign firms. Although SONATRACH contributes to the cost of production, for our purposes the formula used in Algeria since 1971 may be described as being of the production-sharing type.

Most recently introduced, and perhaps of least global importance to date, are the so-called *risk contracts,* as initiated by Brazil with BP in 1976. Brazil has signed similar contracts with such companies as Shell, Elf/AGIP, Exxon, Hispanoil and several "independents". Guatemala has also sought to develop her petroleum industry through similar agreements (though they are called production-sharing contracts) since 1975, but with apparently limited success.

The trend towards "obsolescence" of traditional FDI in North-South petroleum investment may, in a sense, be traced to the first major assertions of nationalist aspirations in developing countries: the nationalisation of foreign oil companies and the creation of state petroleum companies in Mexico (PEMEX) in 1938, and in Iran (NIOC) in 1951[5]. But the shift to new forms of investment really began in the 1950s, and by the late 1970s it was virtually complete[6]. Whether they involve contractual arrangements with no foreign equity participation, or joint ventures in which substantial amounts of FDI from both state- and privately owned "major" and "independent" petroleum companies are involved (but in which the host country retains majority ownership[7]), the new forms of investment have almost completely replaced the traditional concession-based form of wholly foreign-owned FDI in petroleum extraction in the developing countries.

The production-sharing formula seems more prevalent in petroleum producing countries that do not have large financial surpluses (many are major borrowers), whereas service contracts – with joint ventures in many cases – seem more common in major capital-surplus countries. The Peruvian experience illustrates this point: from the time of expropriation of the major foreign petroleum investment in 1968 until 1971, Peru used service contracts and was quite satisfied with the results; but as the country's foreign debt rose considerably the switch was made to production-sharing arrangements[8].

As regards the hypothesis that there may be emerging a new division of risks and responsibilities among the multinational firms, financial organisations and host countries, the evidence from the petroleum industry is not as clearcut. This is probably largely due, however, to two factors which do not in themselves contradict the hypothesis. The first is that the three-way relationship, in which the banks assume the financial dimension of the international investment process, is most likely to apply to countries in need of liquidity, i.e., foreign exchange, whereas several of the major petroleum producers have been large net lenders of financial capital (although this may be changing). The second factor is the high degree of liquidity characteristic of many petroleum companies, particularly since 1973-1974 as a result both of the spectacular price increases and compensation received for some of the nationalisations of their investments[9]. Both in petroleum-producing countries which are net borrowers and in those which are major lenders, however, one finds ample evidence that the firms are increasingly concentrating on supplying technology, certain key managerial functions, and international marketing, with the host countries assuming ownership and some managerial aspects, as predicted by the "new division of risks and responsibilities" hypothesis[10].

More specifically, there is good reason to believe that, in the long run, the basic strength of the major multinational petroleum companies as well as the competitive weapon of the "independents" will remain the technical and managerial services they supply in return for assured access to crude supplies[11]. It is less clear to what extent the developing countries will continue to rely on the petroleum corporations for access to international crude markets as well. On the one hand several major producing countries continue to rely on these firms for their international marketing operations. Thus, for example, at end-1980 Saudi Arabia continued to rely on Aramco to market most of her production. But many producing countries' national oil companies (e.g., Kuwait's KNPC) are moving aggressively into downstream activities, including marketing. These moves are often facilitated – and here the petroleum industry may prove exceptional – by the burgeoning financial strength of the producing countries, particularly the capital-surplus countries, as well as the growing role of importing countries' state companies as purchasers[12]. Perhaps even more important, many producing countries, including Saudi Arabia, are increasingly by-passing private oil companies, and in some cases importers' national oil companies as well, and are handling large crude transactions on a government-to-government basis. This trend may be reinforced when downward pressures on petroleum prices mount, and/or if political considerations prevail over short-term market forces in the allocation of oil supplies.

Investment patterns in petroleum-producing developing countries which have also been important borrowers tend to reinforce the "three way division of risks and responsibilities" hypothesis. In these countries, the financial dimension of international investment in the petroleum industry is increasingly handled by international financial organisations – despite the high liquidity characteristic of many of the petroleum corporations. The high level of international borrowing by Mexico's PEMEX and Brazil's PETROBRAS to finance their exploration, production and refining investments during the 1970s is common knowledge. This was also the case, if on a less spectacular scale, of the state oil companies in Peru, Indonesia, Nigeria and Algeria, for example[13].

Our discussion would not be complete without some mention of the growing investment role played by both multilateral public financial institutions, such as the World Bank and its International Finance Corporation, and the governments of a number of industrialised oil-importing countries. For example, in 1977 the Board of Directors of the World Bank approved the expansion of its lending program in this sector to $1.5 billion per year by 1984, with 40 per cent of the loans for exploration and other pre-production activities and 60 per cent to be invested in production facilities[14]. At the national level, Japan, for example, has been particularly active in financing petroleum-related investments in return for long-run supply agreements[15].

Therefore, despite the fact that several major petroleum-producing countries are net lenders to the international financial organisations and despite the high degree of liquidity characteristic of the petroleum industry as a whole during the past decade, the evidence generally appears to corroborate the hypothesis that a new division of risks and responsibilities among the major actors is emerging, as posited in Chapter 2. A possible discrepancy in this hypothesis may be the potential for government-to-government marketing agreements, which could gradually supplant the multinational petroleum companies' control over international crude markets. Such a long-term trend, however, remains to be seen.

## B. Mining

North-South investment trends in non-fuel minerals extraction (referred to hereafter as the mining industry) are remarkably similar to those just described in the petroleum industry, though with a few years' time lag. In mining, as in petroleum, the predominant form of investment through the 1950s was FDI based on traditional concessional agreements[16]. The shift towards new forms of investment which took place in the petroleum industry in the late 1950s appeared clearly in the mining industry in the late 1960s. Joint ventures, production-sharing arrangements, and service and management contracts had largely replaced FDI in mining by the late 1970s, just as they had in petroleum.

The similarity between the two sectors is not surprising. A common factor has undoubtedly been the importance given by almost all developing countries to the concept of permanent sovereignty over natural resources. This concept has of course been stressed internationally by numerous U.N. General Assembly Resolutions, most notably those of 1962 and 1974[17]. And at the national level, the assertion of permanent sovereignty was expressed, particularly during the early 1970s, in the greatly expanded ownership of mining operations by state or private national enterprises[18].

A second factor that may help to explain the similarity of trends in petroleum and mining is the growing involvement of multinational petroleum companies in worldwide mining investment. Though their importance is difficult to weigh, it should not be underestimated. Quite independently from the host countries' wish to emulate the oil-producing countries' success in increasing revenues from their extractive industries, the petroleum companies' familiarity with the use of, and with the benefits derivable from, the new forms of investment in such activities may have encouraged these companies to take an active role in setting up joint ventures, production-sharing arrangements and service and managerial contracts in the mining industry as well[19].

Although these fundamental similarities exist, one should not overlook some potentially significant differences between North-South investment trends in the petroleum and mining industries. The three-way division of risks and responsibilities appears more clearcut in the mining industry than in any other industry or sector, including petroleum. Then, too, risk- and especially production-sharing contracts are employed more intensively in petroleum than in mining[20], whereas other contractual arrangements, notably turnkey contracts, appear more frequently in the mining industry, particularly where infrastructure and minerals-processing complexes are involved.

To an important extent, all these differences are probably due to the major difference in worldwide price/production-cost trends in mining compared to petroleum: whereas in petroleum world market prices rose much more rapidly than average production costs during the post-1973 period, in mining rapidly rising average investment costs[21] were accompanied by fluctuating, and on average depressed, world market prices during the same period. One result is that relatively few new mining projects have come to fruition in recent years. Another result is that following a period of increasingly stringent host-country regulations in the late 1960s and early 1970s (which largely paralleled trends in the petroleum industry), a number of mineral-producing developing countries have more recently switched from limiting foreign direct investment to promoting it. In the early 1970s, few investment incentives appeared in the foreign investment laws of some major mining countries, but such advantages as, for example, accelerated depreciation allowances are increasingly being offered today, albeit frequently in conjunction with specific performance requirements. Lastly, the previously clear trend towards increasing government ownership of mining ventures in developing countries is now less evident.

Given the relatively limited number of major mining investments undertaken in recent years, and given our interest in identifying current patterns in the use of new forms versus traditional FDI in North-South mining investment as a whole, it might be useful to cite a few concrete examples. One important minerals producer where the shift to liberalised treatment of foreign mining investment occurred relatively early is Chile. Soon after the 1973 coup d'état, the country withdrew from the Andean Pact and, in 1977, issued a foreign investment act with comprehensive guarantees of government non-interference, foreign-exchange privileges, etc. While the representativeness of Chile's experience for other host countries is unclear because of the radical nature of the country's global policy reorientation, which had little to do with international trends in mining investment *per se,* it is nevertheless interesting to note the reluctance shown by foreign mining corporations to reassume ownership of the mining operations which had been nationalised under previous governments[22].

Perhaps more representative of general trends in mining investment agreements during the latter 1970s is the contract signed in 1977 between Indonesia and RTZ, which gave the foreign investor a majority equity position in a base metal project; the agreement did, however, call for a majority of shares to be offered to the Indonesian state or private nationals over a ten-year period after production began. Two major copper projects were also negotiated by Papua New Guinea, in 1974 and 1976, in which foreign corporations took 80 per cent equity positions and the host country no more than 20 per cent[23]. These examples, as well as a number of recent contract negotiations providing relatively more favourable terms to foreign investors[24] illustrate the point that the "obsolescence" of traditional FDI is less clearcut in mining than in petroleum production.

The experience of Peru with foreign investment in copper is particularly interesting[25]. In 1969 the government signed an agreement providing for majority ownership by the the U.S.-owned Southern Peru Copper Corporation in the development of the large Cuajone mine. At the time Peru was in the midst of renegotiating its foreign debt, and the terms of the Cuajone contract reflected the Government's need to inspire the confidence and backing of the international financial community. In 1971, a new General Mining Law was promulgated which included provisions for state control of refining and international marketing[26]. Though this legislation was explicitly designed to bring about state ownership of refining and marketing, and not of mining *per se,* the government was unable to induce foreign mining corporations to invest in the development of other mines or to set up joint ventures with the local state enterprise to do so. The reason, apparently, was that the multinational mining corporations felt that control over downstream activities was vital to make their investment in mining production worthwhile, despite the relatively high price of copper on the world market at that time.

Following the 1971 law, two of the largest foreign mining companies in Peru – Cerro de Pasco and Marcona (the latter producing iron ore) – accelerated the process of diversification of their assets and curtailed their mining re-investments. The latter in turn led to the nationalisation of Cerro de Pasco Corporation in December, 1973, and of Marcona in 1975. Negotiations focussed not on whether the nationalisations should take place but on the value of assets for compensation. Thus, faced with the mining companies' reluctance to invest and contrary to its original intention, the Peruvian Government turned to two British construction and engineering firms to develop the mining and refinery complex at Cerro Verde under turnkey contracts. External finance for the project came in the form of loan capital, principally from the Euromarket.

The Peruvian mining experience of the 1970s serves to illustrate several important points regarding the role of new forms of investment in the development of mining activities. One is the growing importance of turnkey contracts. Engineering and construction firms now sometimes contract directly with host countries rather than work as subcontractors to mining corporations, as was frequently the case under traditional FDI cum concession agreements. Of course, this is not always the result of the host country's inability to induce FDI. Algeria, for example, has chosen to develop her mining industry through turnkey arrangements just as she has done in manufacturing (see Section II of this chapter). Turnkey arrangements are also found in many mining projects that require significant investments in associated infrastructure.

In fact, the major mining companies have shown considerable reluctance in recent years to undertake major equity investments in developing countries. Though we shall explore more fully in Chapter 4 the reasons which may induce firms to use new forms of investment in developing countries, the Peruvian experience suggests that one must treat with considerable caution the frequently advanced argument that mining firms' reluctance to invest in developing countries is the result of host-country restrictions on FDI. An alternative possibility is that the role of mineral rents (i.e., rents derived from mineral extraction *per se*) in multinational mining companies' global profit strategies may be of limited, or decreasing, importance relative to profits and rents derivable from such downstream activities as processing and especially marketing. In Chapter 5 we cite some evidence which seems to support this interpretation[27].

In other words, whereas the strong and relatively price-inelastic demand for oil worldwide and the considerable degree of control by some of the major petroleum companies over retail outlets, especially in their home-country markets, have allowed the oil companies to pass along to consumers post-1973 increases in rents derived by crude-oil producing countries (and increased downstream profits as well), in the mining industry different market structure and demand conditions mean that mineral rents may compete more directly with downstream profits. In mining just as in petroleum, the producing countries' growing assertiveness for national ownership of production may have induced multinational firms which once looked to rents from extraction *per se* as an important source of profit, to turn increasingly to supplying technology and management and/or to controlling international output markets as their primary sources of control and profits. But whereas, in the petroleum industry, producing countries and multinational companies may have found it possible to join forces in passing along increased rents and downstream profits in the form of higher prices to the final consumer, in the mining industry this may be less feasible because increases in mineral rents would threaten downstream profit margins. It is even possible that, in contrast to the petroleum companies, multinational mining firms may increasingly have an interest in keeping a lid on mineral rents *per se* insofar as these rents compete with profits in downstream activities in this sector[28]. As mining corporations' profits are increasingly "delinked" from minerals rents, it is also logical that they would have substantially less interest in taking equity positions than in serving as intermediairies in setting up major mining investments in developing countries.

A third and closely related point highlighted by the Peruvian experience, then, is the changing division of risks and responsibilities over the past decade among multinational firms, international financial organisations and host countries. As posited in Chapter 2, international financial markets and national export-credit institutions of some industrialised countries are playing a growing role in financing mining projects. Multinational mining corporations are increasingly focussing on supplying technology, management and marketing, and often serve as intermediairies in setting up the financial "package" as well. Host countries are assuming ownership and many of the financial risks.

Curiously enough, according to one author, while the developing countries' apparent share of worldwide investment in mining has decreased in relation to that of the developed-country minerals producers (notably Australia, Canada, South Africa and the U.S.), their role as minerals suppliers has been maintained or even increased[29]. He resolves the paradox by pointing to the growing role of host-country equity and above all the large-scale substitution of loan for equity capital in the international financing of exploration and mining projects in developing countries. Whereas some 80 to 90 per cent of investment funds in developing countries' mining projects came in the form of equity capital up till about 1960, during the 1970s the proportion was only about a third[30].

Two reasons are cited by this author to explain the marked increase in debt to equity, and implicitly the growing use of new forms of investment. First, interest and principle payments on debt are less subject to taxation than are profits and dividends on equity. Second, and probably more importantly, equity investments are considerably more vulnerable to nationalisation and other political risk than are loans, particularly when the latter take the form of syndicated loans involving numerous banks, often from several different countries[31].

Other possible reasons might also be cited. One is the skyrocketing in recent years of physical-capital costs in mining which appear to have accelerated even more rapidly than worldwide inflation rates[32]. Another important reason might be the need for creating new assets (i.e., profitable lending opportunities) on the part of many multinational banks, particularly since the 1973-74 oil price increases. And thirdly, the acute and persistent need for foreign exchange on the part of a number of minerals-producing developing countries (not to mention the political advantages which a host government may derive from a major mining project) may induce borrowing by these countries to develop mineral lodes even when world-market minerals prices are relatively unfavourable. Though conditions may be such that major mining companies are discouraged from investing, in other words, host countries sometimes even subsidise local production costs in order to obtain the foreign-exchange income generated by minerals exports[33].

Whatever the reasons, there seems to be a general consensus among students of the mining industry that, regardless of equity structures, the multinational mining corporations are tending to transform their role from that of equity investors to one of mobilisers of international loan capital (from public and private sources), innovators and suppliers of production and processing technology and management, and above all providers of access to world-market outlets for many developing-country minerals producers. Thus, for example, Brazil's state-owned CVRD – one of the world's largest exporters of minerals – reportedly enters joint ventures with foreign mining corporations "mainly to facilitate access to the external market; also for external financing"[34]. Another very interesting illustration is Japan's "loan and import" strategy, which provided some 50 per cent of her copper-ore and 30 per cent of her iron-ore imports in 1978, for example. Under this strategy, Japanese importers (notably trading companies) arrange concessionary long-term loans to host-countries' extractive companies in exchange for assured – and, they hope, favourable – long-term supply contracts[35].

In sum, the evidence on North-South investment patterns in mining suggests that over the last ten to fifteen years the new forms of investment have superseded traditional FDI to a considerable extent. It also suggests however that the trend towards "obsolescence" of traditional FDI is not as marked in mining as in petroleum. Wholly/majority-foreign-owned mining subsidiaries have continued to emerge in some developing countries, particularly since the latter 1970s. That the new forms have not rendered traditional FDI as obsolete as appears to be the case in the petroleum industry might seem paradoxical, since according to the industrialised countries' official statistics, the flow of FDI to developing countries has been much greater in petroleum than in mining during this same period. The paradox is not difficult to resolve, however. First, the statistics generally record petroleum companies' expenditures – e.g., for petroleum exploration – undertaken in conjunction with a production-sharing or risk contract as FDI even though the companies hold no equity in the investment project. To this technical explanation should be added the fact that whereas total investment (host-country plus foreign) in mining has been relatively stagnant over the last decade, the volume of total investment in petroleum exploration and production has grown spectacularly, surpassing that of mining many times over. Finally, however, it should be noted that the extent to which initially majority FDI equity positions in mining projects continue as such over the life of the project remains to be seen; fade-out agreements or renegotiations may often lead to majority host-country ownership.

Be that as it may, the evidence is more clearcut in the mining industry than in any other that there is indeed emerging a three-way division of risks and responsibilities. (See Section II, Chapter 5, for a fuller discussion of some of the possible implications of this emerging division of risks and responsibilities.) Because of the light it sheds on the nature of relationships between multinational mining corporations and financial organisations, as well as between these and host countries, it is appropriate to conclude this discussion of new forms of investment in mining by citing the widely held view that, "the requirements of finance are so critical that the attitudes of lenders, be they international agencies, banks or export credit insurers, are likely to be of critical importance and may well seriously limit the freedom of manoeuvre of the host countries and mining enterprises as they reach for new models of mining agreements for the remainder of this century."[36].

## II.  MANUFACTURING

The fragmentary evidence we have on new forms of investment in developing countries' manufacturing industries reveals no clear worldwide trends. Compared to the extractive industries, it suggests that the traditional form of FDI is by no means becoming obsolete or being systematically superseded by the new forms. There is some evidence consistent with the hypothesis on the emergence of a three-way division of risks and responsibilities, in the sense that banks and other financial organisations are playing a growing role in the provision of financial capital to manufacturing investments in developing countries. But it is by no means clear that this implies the obsolescence of FDI since, as pointed out in Chapter 2, foreign-owned subsidiaries rather than host countries may often be the direct borrowers. That is, the growth of international bank lending to manufacturing industries in some developing countries may reflect changes in multinational firms' financial strategies rather than the obsolescence of FDI.

Two distinctions are useful to describe patterns apparent in the use of new forms in the manufacturing sector. One is between investment projects or firms whose output is destined primarily for the export market, and those whose output is primarily oriented towards the national or regional market of the host country. The other distinction is between industries characterised by relatively stable, mature or "low" technology, and industries with sophisticated, rapidly changing or "high" product or process technologies. Ceteris paribus, the new forms of investment appear to have gained somewhat more importance in firms or industries whose output is destined primarily for the host-country's domestic market, particularly when relatively mature technologies are involved, than in either export-oriented or "high" technology industries.

47

Apparent exceptions to this general pattern may of course be found. For example, international subcontracting is obviously characterised by a high degree of production for export. Another exception might be the involvement by numerous Japanese manufacturing firms in minority-owned joint ventures, notably in Asia, of the export-platform type. But in this case it should be noted that while they are export-oriented, these firms use relatively "low" technology[37]. And even in the case of sub-contracting, a careful distinction between operations where local subcontractors are not majority foreign-owned (i.e., those which strictly qualify as a new form) and those which are subsidiaries of foreign firms (which do not so qualify) suggests that the general pattern may still hold. Scattered evidence suggests that, overall, the role of locally owned subcontractors has grown less rapidly than that of foreign-owned subcontractors producing for their parent or affiliated companies, and that the role of majority-locally owned subcontractors has grown much less rapidly in "high" than in "low" technology industries. Both these "exceptions", in other words, may in fact at least partially confirm the general pattern cited above.

More serious is the fact that one can reliably predict neither the extent to which a new form is likely to be used rather than traditional FDI, nor the specific new form most likely to be used, simply by identifying the market orientation and level of technological sophistication of the industry of a particular investment. Within a given industry, one may find traditional FDI to predominate in one host country, joint ventures to be the rule in others and, say, turnkey contracts in still others. In the manufacturing sector even more than in the extractive industries, in other words, industry-specific factors tend to be outweighed by others, particularly those which are host-country specific.

It therefore makes more sense to compare trends in the use of new forms of investment in manufacturing on a country-by-country rather than industry-by-industry basis. Space limitations prevent us from even summarising here the relevant findings from each of the host countries covered by this study[38]. Instead, we shall highlight those from four countries – Algeria, Brazil, South Korea and Singapore – which illustrate well the diversity and complexity of patterns of new forms and traditional FDI in manufacturing. Investment patterns in these countries should not be considered representative of those in all developing countries – clearly they are not since, with the exception of Algeria, these countries are all "NICs" – nor even of those in other countries covered by this study. Nevertheless, these four countries offer the advantage of being quite diverse in terms of their size, location, degree of export-orientation of their manufacturing sectors and, perhaps most importantly, their state policy towards foreign investment and their overall development strategy. These four countries also cover a wide spectrum in terms of the degree to which new forms are used in manufacturing, the specific new forms which are most important, and the extent to which the new forms complement or replace traditional FDI in this sector. We return to a summary of global trends in sub-section B.

## A. Country Analysis

*Algeria*[39]: In any country-by-country comparison of the degree to which the new forms have replaced traditional FDI, Algeria clearly lies at one end of the spectrum. During the period 1966-1971 almost all foreign firms were nationalised (starting with mining concerns in 1966 and culminating with hydrocarbons in 1971) and national State monopolies were set up in most sectors of the economy. Though Algerian legislation has never formally prohibited FDI, both local and foreign private direct investment have generally been discouraged. Capital formation in Algeria, which grew at an average rate of over 30 per cent per year from 1967 to 1978, has thus been based almost entirely on the new forms of investment.

48

Besides hydrocarbons, the sector which has absorbed the bulk of Algerian investment since the late 1960s, is manufacturing. In this sector contractual relations between Algeria's state enterprises and foreign firms involving no equity investment or provision of financial capital by the foreign firms have completely dominated. Some 97 per cent of the total value of contracts in the manufacturing sector from 1962 through mid-1976 (the last date for which we have data) was accounted for by six industries or industry groups: steel (25 per cent); metallic, mechanical and electrical construction (21 per cent); construction materials (17 per cent); chemicals (15 per cent); food (10 per cent) and textiles (9 per cent). All of these industries were, and are, oriented towards the domestic market, with virtually no emphasis having been given to export manufacturing in Algeria throughout the 1960s and 1970s.

In the early years of Algeria's industrialisation process, notably during the three-year plan of 1967-1969, considerable emphasis was given to "unbundling" the supply of investment resources from abroad. Separate contracts for the delivery and setting up of plant and equipment were the general rule during this period. During the first four-year plan, of 1970-1973, however, turnkey contracts gained increasing importance, and the first "product-in-hand" contract was signed. With the second four-year plan (1974-1977) turnkey and product-in-hand contracts became the general rule, not only in terms of the amount of investment but also in terms of the number of contracts.

As to the type of foreign firms involved in these contractual arrangements, engineering firms dominated in virtually all industries, generally working alone in such industries as steel, chemicals and construction materials, and sub- or co-contracting with licensors of technology and manufacturing firms in other industries, notably motor vehicles (classified under "metallic, mechanical and electrical construction"). But even in the latter case, rarely did the licensors or manufacturers play the leading role. In other words, the new forms of investment in Algeria have been generally characterised by a reversal of roles, compared to traditional FDI, in the sense that even where major manufacturers have been involved they have usually supplied technology, maintenance services, initial management of production, etc., to the engineering firms, whereas under traditional FDI manufacturers usually play the leading role with engineering firms supplying support services of various types.

The new forms of investment in Algeria therefore have involved many "outsiders", as distinct from the "major" multinational firms which tend to dominate traditional FDI in most developing countries. There has also been a considerable degree of diversification of home countries of the firms involved, especially after 1970, with firms from several European countries, the U.S. and, since 1974, Japan. France is still by far the most important single home country however.

These trends do not mean that many small- or medium-size firms have been among the "outsiders" to do business in Algeria. In fact, the process has been dominated by relatively large firms. Given the comparatively large number of small- to medium-size French firms involved through FDI in Algeria at the time of her independence, one could even infer that the use of new forms of investment in Algeria has been characterised by a tendency towards greater concentration among foreign, as well as local, capital operating in Algeria, with the average size of the foreign firms involved having increased considerably. (Possible implications of such a tendency will be discussed in Chapter 5.)

The relative diversification of home countries does however bring to light another important issue: the role of financial flows, and particularly of export credits, in the new forms of investment in Algeria's manufacturing industries. In our discussion of new forms of investment in the petroleum industry, we noted both that most of the international capital markets' loans to Algeria were for the exploration and production of hydrocarbons, and that Algeria's possibilities of negotiating the terms of these loans were relatively limited. In the manufacturing sector, export credits – usually guaranteed by the government of the lending country, i.e., the contracting firm's home country – have been a major source of financial capital. These credits reportedly offered greater possibilities for Algeria to negotiate the terms, suggesting that what competition existed among foreign firms to do business in Algeria may have exerted itself as much or more at the level of the conditions of availability of credit as at the level of the terms of the contract itself.

In any case, Algeria's experience with new forms of investment in manufacturing, notably with turnkey and product-in-hand contracts, provides an important illustration of the three-way division of risks and responsibilities. While on the one hand multinational firms (including, in this case, engineering firms) have played a leading role in supplying both embodied and disembodied technology, and in some cases management – access to world export markets being largely irrelevant to the development of Algeria's manufacturing sector during the 1960s and 1970s – financial organisations, including public institutions in the home countries of the supplying firms, have played an important role in providing financial capital, notably export credits. The host country has retained full ownership, assumed responsibility for certain crucial aspects of management – notably, deciding which industries should receive the investment – as well as a major share of the economic and financial risks of the investment process.

The volume and the industrial distribution of capital formation in Algeria's manufacturing sector have thus reflected not so much the expected rate of financial return on individual investments – as is normally the case with FDI – as they have the host country's global industrialisation strategy. They have, of course, been subject to the limitations imposed by perceptions of the country's "ability to pay", which in turn have depended largely on surpluses generated in the hydrocarbons sector. In other words, the trilateral division of risks and responsibilities which has emerged in conjunction with the new forms of investment in Algeria has also been characterised by the possibility of divorcing a given investment project's expected surplus-generating capacity and the decision to invest – a divorce made possible by the availability of surpluses in other sectors (notably hydrocarbons) and realised through the trilateral division of risks and responsibilities.

Algeria's experience with the new forms of investment in manufacturing could thus be summarised, in the words of Abdallah-Khodja, as involving a double mutation of traditional FDI. First, international *contractual* relations have completely replaced the traditional form of direct investment. Second, *commercial* relations between supplying firms and the host country have largely replaced the investment relations embodied in FDI.

This latter characteristic of the new forms of investment in Algeria's manufacturing sector implies that the turnkey and product-in- hand contracts on which so much of that investment has depended are more accurately described as export, not investment, operations from the point of view of the supplying firms. It goes a long way towards explaining some of the problems experienced by Algeria with the new forms of investment in her manufacturing sector, as discussed by Abdallah-Khodja. The country's new policies on foreign investment, implemented as of mid-1982 and which appear to place less emphasis on turnkey and product-in-hand operations relative to FDI, may reflect a desire to reintroduce the logic of foreign investment in a context of continued heavy reliance on the new forms.

*Brazil*[40]: In marked contrast to Algeria, the traditional form of FDI has continued to play a central role in the process of capital formation in Brazilian manufacturing. Measured in constant (1980) dollars, the total stock of FDI in Brazil (which already amounted to over US$4 billion in 1966) grew at average annual rates of about 4.7 per cent from 1966 to 1970, and over 15 per cent from 1970 to 1979. The manufacturing sector accounted for approximately 75 per cent of FDI stock in Brazil at end-1980.

Industries with the largest shares of FDI registered in manufacturing at end-1980 were: chemicals (13.9 per cent of all FDI), transport equipment (13.4 per cent), machinery (9.8 per cent), electrical and communications equipment (8 per cent) and metallurgy (7.9 per cent). Foreign-owned firms accounted for about 25 per cent of sales and 18 per cent of assets in 1975 (the only year for which figures are available), but when the country's highly capital-intensive state enterprises are excluded, foreign firms' shares of sales and assets represent about 30 per cent in the Brazilian economy as a whole. Their shares surpass 50 per cent in several manufacturing industries, notably electrical and communications equipment, transport equipment, chemicals, rubber, pharmaceuticals, perfumery and tobacco. Clearly one cannot speak of any obsolescence of traditional FDI in Brazil's manufacturing sector.

Two new forms of investment nonetheless appear to be of some importance in this sector: technology contracts and joint ventures. Looking first at the use of technology contracts during the 1960s, the data show a concentration of contracts in the country's major growth industries, which were also major recipients of FDI. Transport equipment alone accounted for 40 per cent of all contracts – of which some 1,516 were reportedly signed during the decade – the largest number being in the motor vehicle and parts industries. Metallurgy (especially steel) accounted for 11 per cent, communications and electrical equipment for 9.2 per cent, chemicals for 7.6 per cent and pharmaceuticals for 5.2 per cent.

By country of licensors, 41 per cent of all contracts were signed with U.S. firms, but these contracts accounted for slightly less than 30 per cent of total technology payments. Western European firms, on the other hand, accounted for 62.7 per cent of total technology payments (West Germany alone for over 33 per cent) and 50 per cent of the number of contracts signed (Germany 18 per cent). Japan accounted for less than 4 per cent of both payments and number of contracts during that decade.

Approximately two-thirds of the technology contracts in the 1960s were signed by local firms, about a third by foreign subsidiaries in Brazil. Foreign subsidiaries nevertheless accounted for fully three-quarters of the amount of payments made in conjunction with these contracts, the average payment per subsidiary-parent contract being nine times the average of those signed by locally owned Brazilian firms. These and other data clearly suggest that on the whole technology contracts were used to a significant extent during the 1960s as a means to facilitate profit remittances on FDI by foreign direct investors, and should probably not be regarded as having been of major importance as a new form of investment in their own right.

For the 1970s, a lack of data on payments and a change in the data base on the number of contracts make comparisons of trends problematic. It appears that, due in part to increasing Brazilian state regulation of international technology agreements, the share of contracts accounted for by subsidiaries of foreign firms decreased during the 1970s and that the extent to which technology agreements were used as a new form of investment in their own right rather than simply as a legal mechanism to facilitate the transfer of funds within multinational firms, may have increased somewhat. But there is little reason to believe that FDI was actually being superseded by technology agreements; on the contrary, the role of such contracts appears to have remained largely complementary to FDI in Brazil's manufacturing sector during this period.

According to Guimaraes, et al., the new form of investment in Brazil is the minority-foreign-owned joint venture. An early example was USIMINAS, a state steel enterprise established in the late 1950s, in which Japan's Nippon Steel today holds

19 per cent of equity. It was not until the early 1970s that the first major joint ventures involving minority foreign participation were established. The pioneering ventures, so to speak, were in the petrochemical industry and were largely the result of government policy designed to enable local private capital to participate more significantly in an industry where technological sophistication and capital requirements were felt to be important barriers to entry. The explicit aim of the policy was to support local capital and forestall an exclusive dependence on foreign capital, while simultaneously avoiding excessive state intervention in the economy. The result was a strategy of "three-legged" joint ventures involving equity participation by Brazil's state petrochemical enterprise (PETROQUISA), private local and foreign firms. Of the 15 joint ventures set up in the Northeastern petrochemical complex, in no case do the foreign partners hold a majority equity position, and of the $46 million of voting capital held by foreign groups about 35 per cent is derived directly from these groups' technological contributions to the projects, particularly in the form of process know-how and the provision of engineering services. Among the foreign groups participating in these joint ventures, Japanese petrochemical producers are the most heavily involved.

The experiment with joint ventures in the petrochemical industry in the early 1970s came to be seen as a pattern to be followed in other sectors. Thus, Brazil's Second National Development Plan emphasized that financial and fiscal assistance was to be provided to Brazilian firms for joint venture projects, and that along with petrochemicals and basic raw materials, the capital goods industry was to be given priority. One result was the creation of three subsidiaries of the country's National Economic Development Bank which offered credit on very favourable terms and participated as minority shareholders in firms set up in these sectors. As of 1980, there existed some 68 joint ventures with state enterprise participation in the manufacturing sector as a whole, about 40 of which had local private firms participating as well.

A somewhat different policy was followed as of the late 1970s for the computer and telecommunications equipment industries. The policy designed to promote the emergence of a micro- and mini-computer industry limited entry into the Brazilian market to local firms and joint ventures with minority foreign ownership. But, contrary to the petrochemical and capital goods industries, the state was not expected to hold equity. As it turned out, five enterprises have been selected by the state to manufacture micro- and mini-computers, three of them fully owned by local private capital, only one involving 3 per cent foreign equity participation and one involving majority state ownership. The foreign suppliers of technology are British, German, French and Japanese firms, with none of the "major" computer firms present either as investors or suppliers of technology. A debate is reportedly in progress on the presence of two large producers (IBM and Burroughs) in the medium-sized computer market, given their unwillingness to accept the state's policy guidelines and to enter into joint ventures with local capital in the micro- and mini-computer industry.

Brazilian state policy on the telecommunications equipment industry has been similar, but the major multinational producers have shown greater willingness to follow policy guidelines. ITT, Ericsson and NEC, which had been producing standard equipment in Brazil for many years, entered as minority shareholders into joint ventures with local private firms for the production of new government telecommunications equipment.

Unfortunately, the only economy-wide statistics on international joint ventures without state equity participation are from data on the 200 largest non-financial companies in Brazil. Of these firms only 21 appear to involve substantial sharing of ownership between local and foreign firms, and of these six are majority state-owned and six are majority foreign-owned. That leaves only nine majority Brazilian owned joint ventures without state equity participation among Brazil's 200 largest companies.

Among the 21 joint ventures, five are in the mining industry (mostly majority state owned) and 16 are in manufacturing: four in metallurgy, three in electrical and communications equipment, three in chemicals, two in transport equipment, two in non-metallic minerals products, one in food products and one in cellulose.

In sum, there is little evidence that the new forms of investment are in any way replacing or superseding the traditional form of investment in Brazilian manufacturing as a whole. FDI clearly continues to play a predominant role, although international joint ventures with minority foreign equity participation have gained some importance, particularly in a number of growth industries. With the exception of technology contracts – whose use was already widespread in the 1960s but whose role as a new form of investment independent of FDI appears somewhat limited even in the 1970s – it seems that other new forms of investment are of little global significance in Brazilian manufacturing.

There is some evidence of an increasing division of roles between foreign firms and international financial organisations in the provision of financial capital to the investment process. A comparison of financing schemes in the early 1970s for the steel and petrochemical industries brings out an interesting point. Major investments were made in both, involving the active participation and ownership of Brazilian state enterprises with foreign producers holding minority equity positions. In the case of steel, international credits amounting to over $600 million, or about 48 per cent of total investment funds, were contracted independently of decisions as to the kind and sources of equipment to be used. In the petrochemical industry, on the other hand, foreign credits amounted to less than 24 per cent of total investment funds (48 per cent were provided by Brazil's state Development Bank) and, most importantly, these credits resulted from prior decisions concerning the type of equipment required and the suppliers of basic engineering. In addition to this lower degree of reliance on international credits in the petrochemicals industry, a major difference was "an unnecessary rise in expenditures on imported equipment and foreign engineering services" in the steel industry: 75 per cent of equipment expenditures were on imports in the case of steel, compared to about 50 per cent for petrochemicals[41]. There is thus an interesting parallel between the somewhat more favourable balance-of-payments implications for Brazil of suppliers' credits compared to international loans, and Algeria's experience in negotiating somewhat more favorable terms on suppliers' credits than on loans from the international capital market during this same period.

In contrast to the Algerian experience, however, the major growth of international lending to Brazil since the early 1970s has not accompanied any obsolescence of FDI. On the contrary: signs of an increasing division of roles between multinational firms and suppliers of financial capital in Brazilian manufacturing investment over the last ten to fifteen years undoubtedly reflect in part a shift by some direct foreign investors towards financing the growth of their wholly or majority-owned subsidiaries in Brazil by means of direct subsidiary borrowing from international capital markets, as mentioned in Chapter 2. It has thus been predicted that, "paradoxically enough, Brazil will probably move toward more selectivity and control of foreign investment, precisely because it needs to expand foreign participation in the economy, but as a net foreign-exchange earner..."[42] Whether the result will be greater emphasis on the use of new forms of investment, continued emphasis on FDI but subject to more stringent performance requirements and greater use of equity as opposed to debt financing, or some combination of the two remains to be seen.

*South Korea*[43]: Korea's reputation as a relatively open economy which welcomes foreign investment might lead one to expect the traditional form of FDI to predominate in this country as it does in Brazil. That such is not the case is illustrated by Harvard Business School's finding that among 66 host countries with investment by U.S. multinational firms in joint ventures and wholly owned subsidiaries in 1975, Korea had the lowest proportion of wholly owned subsidiaries – less than 30 per cent, as compared for example with Japan's 33 per cent. .

In fact, one could argue that FDI is itself a new form of investment in Korea. Whereas the first turnkey plants were set up in the 1950s, the first FDI was not made until 1962, the same year the first licensing agreements were signed. Since 1962, furthermore, more than half of all foreign equity investment in Korea has been in less than majority foreign-owned enterprises (the very first FDI was a fifty-fifty joint venture involving a U.S. firm in the nylon industry). At end-1980, over three-quarters of all firms in Korea with some foreign equity were less than majority foreign owned, and almost two-thirds of the value of FDI in Korea was in such firms.

Korea's government policy on FDI may be roughly divided into three phases. In 1960, the first legal basis was drawn up whose aim was to induce foreign investment. No regulations were imposed on foreign ownership and extensive incentives were provided; but these early attempts to attract FDI met with relatively little success, reportedly due to investors' concern over the country's unproven political stability and uncertain economic outlook. Relations with Japan were normalised in 1965, further support measures were introduced in 1967 and 1969, and in 1970 the first free export zone was created[44]. It was not until the late 1960s and particularly the early 1970s that the inflow of FDI began to accelerate, notably Japanese investments in export-oriented manufacturing firms.

A major policy change occurred in 1973, when high government priority was given to joint ventures. The detailed "Guideline for Foreign Direct Investment" adopted that year established criteria on project eligibility, foreign ownership and minimum investment size. This Guideline, which was the backbone of Korea's investment policy until the late 1970s, set 50 per cent foreign ownership as the maximum in principle, although there were a number of grounds for exception.

The third policy phase began in September 1980, with substantially liberalised guidelines established on minimum amounts of investment and areas of investment, and majority- and wholly foreign-owned investments allowed in many more cases. The aim of the new guidelines is reportedly to promote the technological development of more sophisticated industries and to enhance the efficiency of previously protected firms by promoting greater competition in Korean industry.

Foreign equity investment first began to expand rapidly in the latter half of the 1960s. The stock of FDI grew at the remarkable average rate of 46.5 per cent per year (in current U.S. dollars) from 1967 to 1974. From 1974 to 1980 growth continued at an average annual rate of about 11.8 per cent. By end-1980, about 84 per cent of firms with foreign equity (minority- and majority-foreign-owned firms combined), and some 75 per cent of total FDI stock, were in Korea's manufacturing sector.

Four industries or industry-groups have received the bulk of FDI in this sector. Japanese investments in relatively labour-intensive export-oriented industries, notably textiles and electronics, were particularly important during the latter 1960s and early 1970s. Since about 1974, when Korean labour costs began to rise more rapidly, Japanese investment has not grown as rapidly as that by U.S. and European firms, which tend to invest in technically more sophisticated production for Korea's domestic market, notably in the chemical and machine industries.

At end-1980, about 22 per cent of total FDI stock was in chemicals, 16 per cent in metals and machinery, 13 per cent in electrical and electronics industries, and 12 per cent in textiles[45]. Japanese investment accounted that year for 57 per cent of total FDI stock and was involved in 76 per cent of all firms with foreign equity; the respective figures for U.S. investment are 22 per cent and 16 per cent, and those for European investment are 12 per cent and 5 per cent[46].

The contribution of FDI to gross capital formation in Korean manufacturing is not easy to estimate. On one hand, official FDI statistics show FDI to have accounted for barely over 5 per cent of gross capital formation in manufacturing for the 1962-1980 period as a whole. The proportion apparently rose to as high as some 14 per cent for the three-year period of 1972-74 (reaching a maximum of 15.7 per cent in 1973) and steadily tapered off since then, dropping to about 2 per cent in 1978-1980 (the last three-year period for which we have data). But the proportion varies considerably from one industry to another and, more important, the official FDI figures apparently do not include long-term loans even when they are made by the parent company. Official data on total foreign capital inflows which exclude loans with maturities of less than three years and inter-bank loans, but include other long-term loans, show that about 94 per cent of the total flow has come in the form of loan capital (56 per cent "commercial" and 38 per cent "public" loans) and only 6 per cent as FDI. It is also widely known that both local and foreign firms in Korea tend to be characterised by relatively high ratios of debt to equity. It is thus quite conceivable that the role of FDI in gross capital formation in Korean manufacturing is seriously underestimated by the FDI figures cited above. But, to the extent they can be relied upon, these figures suggest that FDI has on the whole played a quantitatively less important role in the development of Korean manufacturing than in the case of, say, Brazil.

So what about the role of the new forms of investment in Korea's manufacturing sector? If Korea appears to have been relatively far from Brazil (and perhaps unexpectedly close to Algeria) during the 1960s and 1970s in our inter-country comparison of the role of traditional FDI in manufacturing, and if both Korea and Algeria have very recently made important changes in their policies towards foreign investment in the direction of greater liberalisation, what can be said about these countries' degree of reliance on new forms of investment for growth of their manufacturing industries? Here the apparent similarities between Algeria and Korea end, and the differences are crucial. Whereas in Algeria capital formation in manufacturing was almost totally dependent on the new forms during the 1960s and 1970s, in Korea private domestic investment appears to have played a central role; and in comparison with Brazil, the role of state enterprise has been more limited in Korea. Also, whereas in Algeria the two new forms of major importance were turnkey and product-in-hand contracts, in Korea, as in Brazil, by far the most important new forms of investment have been joint ventures and technology licensing agreements.

True, as mentioned previously the first new form to appear in post-colonial Korea was the turnkey contract. During the early stages of industrialisation a fair number of such contracts were used by the State to develop such capital-intensive industries as petrochemicals, chemical fertilizers, cement and synthetic fibres. Partial turnkey contracts have also been used, in which foreign firms provide engineering and key components required for plant construction. In many cases contractors have been engineering firms designated by foreign technology licensors, which were themselves often sought out by the Korean partner. Because of their large capital requirements, many of the turnkey plants were originally contracted by government-owned corporations, but most of the corporations have since been sold to the private sector. And, with the development of the local engineering and machine industries (reinforced by their participation in overseas development projects, for example in the Middle East), by about the mid-1970s turnkey projects had lost their significance in Korean manufacturing.

Management contracts do not appear to have ever been of any significance in this sector, even in the early stages of industrialisation.

As to the role of international subcontracting, the only data available are on bonded processing industries, which show exports from these industries to have declined in importance from 24 per cent of Korean exports in 1974 to 9 per cent in 1980. A serious problem with the data on bonded processing industries is that they do not allow us to distinguish between processing firms which are majority locally owned (and which qualify as a new form of investment for our purposes) and those which are majority foreign-owned (traditional FDI). In any case, the data on export shares cited above and others[47] suggest that international subcontracting has been of decreasing, and in recent years limited, importance in Korean manufacturing.

Turning to joint ventures – one of the two principal new forms in Korean manufacturing today – it is worth recalling that at end-1980 over three-quarters of all firms with some FDI were minority-foreign-owned or fifty-fifty joint ventures, and that these firms accounted for almost two-thirds of all FDI in the country. Time-series data reveal no significant shifts during the 1960s, when the value of FDI was relatively small, but they suggest a gradual increase in the role of minority-foreign and fifty-fifty joint ventures since the early 1970s. Thus, for example, whereas in the latter 1960s about 63 per cent of all firms with foreign equity were not majority foreign owned, the figure had risen to about 73 per cent by the 1978-1980 period. Data on the share of total FDI stock registered in firms which are not majority-foreign owned show a decrease from over 60 per cent in the latter 1960s to barely under 50 per cent in 1973, followed by a steady if gradual increase, to 63 per cent in 1980. And finally, data showing ownership structure by foreign investors' home countries indicate an increasing share of minority-owned joint ventures by firms from all countries: whereas 37 per cent of Japanese firms were minority joint ventures in 1972, the figure had risen to 46 per cent in 1980; corresponding figures for U.S. firms are 28 per cent and 34 per cent; and for European firms they are 30 per cent and 39 per cent.

The relatively high proportion of minority-foreign and fifty-fifty joint ventures viewed for the 1962-1980 period as a whole is probably more important for highlighting the relative importance of new forms of investment – in this case joint ventures – in Korea's manufacturing sector, than is the comparatively slight increase which appears to have occurred in this proportion since the early 1970s. These trends are nevertheless significant not only because they suggest a tendency for the globally important role of new forms to have been somewhat reinforced during the 1970s, but also because they point to a positive correlation between the increasing role of new forms and the shift from a concentration of foreign manufacturing investment in the labour-intensive export-oriented industries towards more investment in domestic-market-oriented investments since around 1973. Such a correlation would of course be consistent with our hypothesis that the new forms are more likely to be used, *ceteris paribus,* in investments oriented towards the domestic market than in those oriented towards the export market. It might also imply – given the somewhat greater technical sophistication of the domestic-market-oriented investments – that the market orientation of a given investment tends to weigh more heavily, at least up to a point, than the degree of technical sophistication in determining whether foreign investors are likely to accept minority equity positions. The correlation could also be evidence that the market orientation of an investment tends to be more important than the nationality of the foreign investor in determiing whether the investor is likely to accept a minority equity position. This last inference might be drawn from the fact that although U.S. and European firms generally display a lower propensity than do Japanese firms to take minority ownership positions, the continued increase in importance of minority joint ventures coincided with a more rapid growth of U.S. and European investments since the mid-1970s[48].

Turning now to the second principal new form of investment in Korean manufacturing, the growth pattern of international licensing has been remarkably similar to that of FDI. Just as the first FDI was made in 1962, so was the first licensing agreement signed that year (with a Taiwanese firm in the food processing industry). And just as FDI grew rather slowly in the early 1960s, accelerating in the late 1960s and 1970s, so did licensing agreements. The number of agreements signed from 1962 through 1965 averaged only about four per year, then grew steadily from 1966 (18 contracts) through 1970 (92 contracts), representing an average growth of almost

50 per cent per year in the late 1960s. The number of agreements signed in 1971 fell to 47, but then steadily grew to 296 in 1978, representing an average annual growth rate of about 30 per cent during the period. And finally, just as the growth of FDI tapered off in 1979 and 1980, so the number of licensing agreements signed in these two years declined slightly, to 288 and 222 respectively.

Some 92 per cent of all licensing agreements have been in the manufacturing sector. Metals and machine industries account for 41 per cent of the agreements, electrical and electronics for 21 per cent, and chemicals and petroleum refining for 20 per cent. In terms of the home country of licensors, Japan accounts for 59 per cent of the agreements, the U.S. for 23 per cent, Germany for 4.5 per cent, the U.K. for 3.4 per cent, France 2.1 per cent and other countries 8.6 per cent.

Approximately 25 per cent of all licensing agreements and 40 per cent or more of royalty payments are made by Korean subsidiaries of foreign firms. These figures show that average payments per contract tend to be greater when the agreement involves a parent-subsidiary relationship than when it involves independent local firms. They are consistent with, though less marked than, the finding in Brazil that licensing agreements between parents and subsidiaries are often used to facilitate remittances of profit on FDI[49]. If such is the case in Korea, one could hardly describe licensing agreements as playing anything other than a highly complementary role to FDI.

Nevertheless, a fairly constant 75 per cent of all licensing agreements in Korea have been signed by local firms, a significant number being the result of initiatives taken by the local licensee to gain access to foreign technology. The fact that local firms' royalty payments have grown faster than total profit remittances on FDI since the early 1970s would further suggest that on the whole licensing agreements have, after all, played considerably more than a complementary role to traditional FDI in Korea. This impression is reinforced by the fact that the ratio of royalty payments to profit remittances has been increasing, even though the figures on profit remittances include remittances from minority- as well as majority-foreign owned ventures. Given the fact that over 75 per cent of total earnings on FDI in Korea are repatriated, one might even be tempted to infer that foreign firms' earnings from licensing have grown more rapidly on the whole than their earnings on FDI over the last decade.

Lastly, an industrial breakdown of licensing agreements involving only independent Korean firms shows that a full 46 per cent are in the metal and machine industries, 19 per cent in electric and electronics, 18 per cent in chemicals and petroleum, and only about 4 per cent in textiles. These data are quite consistent with the hypothesis that the new forms of investment tend to be concentrated in the host country's major growth industries. Lack of a more detailed industrial breakdown means that the data are relatively inconclusive as regards the extent to which, *ceteris paribus,* this particular new form tends to be used more frequently in domestic-market oriented, less technically sophisticated industries. But the scarcity of agreements in the textile industry compared to other more technically sophisticated industries suggests, again, that factors other than an industry's degree of technical sophistication may weigh more heavily in determining the extent to which a new form (rather than traditional FDI) is likely to be used.

*Singapore*[50]: If Algeria lies at one end of the spectrum in terms of the degree to which new forms have been substituted for traditional FDI, Singapore lies at the other end. Since 1965, when Singapore separated from Malaysia and embarked on her strategy of export-oriented industrialisation, economic growth has been led by FDI in the country's manufacturing sector. And although wholly- and majority-foreign-owned firms have consistently received the lion's share of FDI, their dominance has been further reinforced in recent years. The limited amount of new forms of investment in Singapore – primarily joint ventures and licensing – appear to be largely complementary to the traditional form of FDI.

The stock of FDI in Singapore grew at an average annual rate of over 40 per cent from 1966 through 1973, at slightly under 12 per cent from 1973-1977, and at about 24 per cent in 1977-1979. Wholly- and majority-foreign-owned firms accounted in 1979 for only one-fifth of the number of firms in Singapore, but for over 50 per cent of gross fixed assets and employment, 64 per cent of value added, 72 per cent of output and 84 per cent of direct export sales. Their contribution to gross capital formation in manufacturing rose steadily from 45 per cent in 1966 to 86 per cent in 1972, fell back to around 74 per cent in 1973-75, and increased to 81 per cent by 1979.

Today, the major industries in Singapore are all dominated by foreign-owned firms. They are: electronics, oil refining, rig and shipbuilding, precision engineering and industrial machinery. The major investors are from the U.S., with 29 per cent of FDI stock, and Japan, with 17 per cent. The U.K., the Netherlands and Germany are also important investors, as are several developing countries, notably Hong Kong, Taiwan and Malaysia, whose investments are concentrated in textiles, clothing and metal engineering.

National ownership of industrial firms has never been emphasized by government policy in Singapore. Nor have any restrictions been placed on FDI since 1960. Only investors seeking to benefit from fiscal incentives need approach the government.

Joint ventures have received some government encouragement, more as a means by which local firms can acquire expertise and technology from foreign firms than as a method of controlling foreign investment. In the early 1970s investment incentives and choice industrial sites were sometimes used by the state's Economic Development Board to promote joint ventures, a method to which Japanese firms in particular responded. And in 1975, a Bureau of Joint Ventures was set up to help foreign investors find joint-venture partners. But the Bureau has apparently not been flooded with requests, and of those it has received, many have reportedly been from foreign investors who prefer majority ownership.

Time-series data on joint ventures (minority- and majority- foreign-owned ventures combined) show that these firms' proportion of the total number of manufacturing firms in Singapore increased from 8 per cent in 1966, to 20.7 per cent in 1975 and 19.9 per cent in 1978; the respective figures for wholly foreign-owned firms are 4.7 per cent, 12.5 per cent and 12.9 per cent. Similar trends apply to the contribution of joint ventures to total employment in manufacturing: 20.3 per cent in 1966, 35.6 per cent in 1975 and 32.8 per cent in 1978, versus 12.4 per cent, 31.5 per cent and 35.7 per cent for wholly foreign-owned firms. These figures suggest a significant increase in the role of both joint ventures and wholly foreign-owned firms since 1966 in relation to wholly local-owned firms, with joint ventures growing more rapidly up to about 1975, and wholly foreign-owned ventures more rapidly since then.

Similar data on shares of net fixed assets, value added, value of output and direct export sales partially confirm the tendency for the new and traditional forms of international investment to increase their role relative to local firms in Singapore. Locally owned firms' share of output fell from over 46 per cent in 1966, to about 18 per cent in 1975 and 17 per cent in 1978; their share of value added, which was over 42 per cent in 1966, dropped to 24 per cent in 1975 and 22 per cent in 1978. Their share of exports fell from 43 per cent in 1966 to 9 per cent in 1975 and 8 per cent in 1978. Nevertheless, their share of assets, which fell from 28 per cent in 1966 to 15 per cent in 1975, rose again sharply, to 33 per cent in 1978.

However, whereas the share of joint ventures in output, value added and export sales remained relatively constant, the share of wholly foreign-owned firms grew markedly. Thus, for example, foreign firms' share of output rose from 31 per cent in 1966 to almost 60 per cent in 1978, as compared with shares of about 23 per cent in both years for joint ventures; foreign firms' share of export sales rose from 33 per cent in 1966 to over 70 per cent in 1978, versus 24 per cent and 21 per cent for joint ventures. These data confirm the observation that the traditional form of FDI has grown more rapidly in Singapore's manufacturing sector, particularly in recent years, than have joint ventures.

Data on ownership structure broken down by industry are generally consistent with the hypothesis that the new forms are more prevalent in domestic-market-oriented industries, particularly those characterised by reasonably mature technology. They suggest that in Singapore, wholly foreign-owned firms tend to dominate such high-technology and export-oriented industries as electrical, electronics, chemical, professional and scientific equipment, and metals. Joint ventures are more common in such industries as textiles, clothing, food, wood, plastics and paper products.

Data which distinguish between minority- and majority-foreign-owned joint ventures unfortunately do not reveal any clear trend. The proportion of firms with minority foreign ownership has increased since the 1960s in such relatively low-technology industries as food and wood, but it has decreased in textiles, clothing and plastics. Among high-technology industries, minority-foreign-ownership has increased in calculators, air-conditioners and industrial machinery, but decreased in metal fabrication and transport equipment.

One factor which may help explain these figures, but which cannot be verified, is suggested by some interview data. It is that the type of joint venture in Singapore is changing. Whereas companies established in the 1960s and early 1970s, for example in the electronics-electrical industry, were commonly offshore-sourcing plants producing for re-export to multinational corporations, many recently established joint ventures are oriented towards the local and regional markets, which are growing rapidly. In other words, the pattern described above may reflect a greater degree of orientation towards regional markets in those industries where minority joint ventures have increased in recent years. This explanation would be consistent with the hypothesis that new forms are more likely to be used in domestic- (or in this case) regional-market-oriented investments, particularly those with more mature technologies. It would further suggest, again, that market orientation tends to be more important than the degree of maturity of technology.

Another factor might of course be the different, and changing, propensities of firms from different home countries to share equity with locals. Relative to firms from other countries, those from the U.S. are more likely to be wholly or majority-owned: only 6.7 per cent of U.S. firms established prior to 1970 were minority owned, as were 8.2 per cent of those established in the 1970-1978 period as a whole (although the figure rose to 17.6 per cent in 1974-1976, falling again to 5.9 per cent in 1977-1978). Japanese firms showed a slightly higher propensity to share equity prior to 1970 (10 per cent were minority owned) but a lower propensity (only 5 per cent) in the 1970s. Quite striking are the figures on joint ventures, i.e., minority- and majority-Japanese-owned joint ventures combined: whereas 90 per cent of all Japanese investments involved some local participation in the 1960s, only 39 per cent did in the 1970s. Also revealing a marked shift in the ownership structure of Japanese investment in the 1970s is the declining share of minority ventures, which fell from 11.2 per cent in 1970-1973, to 3.4 per cent in 1974-1976, and none in 1977-1978.

If Japanese investors reveal a growing use of majority- and wholly-owned firms in Singapore's manufacturing sector, investors from other Asian countries – notably Hong Kong, Taiwan and the ASEAN countries – and those from Europe reveal the opposite trend. The share of minority-owned ventures in European investments, for example, increased from zero in 1970-1973 to 5 per cent in 1974-1976 and 11.1 per cent in 1977-1978. It is also worth noting that many of the joint ventures in Singapore's industries characterised by relatively mature technologies involve firms from other developing, particularly Asian, countries.

Given the preponderance of U.S. and Japanese investment, however, the overall trend is fairly clear: minority foreign-owned ventures, though not insignificant in number, are no longer of increasing importance in Singapore's manufacturing sector. They grew during the 1960s, but since then have become less important compared to the traditional form of direct foreign investment.

As regards the use of non-equity forms of investment in Singapore manufacturing, it is unfortunate that few data have been collected systematically. Of 57 firms replying to a 1980 postal survey, 18 were wholly local-owned, eight were joint ventures (three minority-foreign and five majority) and 31 were wholly foreign owned. Of the locally owned firms, one was a pure turnkey contract and two others had licensing agreements. Of the joint ventures, one minority and one majority-foreign-owned firm had a management or licensing agreement. But of the wholly foreign-owned firms, 10 (eight of which were Japanese) had licensing agreements, two (Japanese firms) had management contracts and two others (Danish-British and Taiwanese-Japanese firms) were set up on the basis of turnkey *cum* management contracts. These findings reinforce those of earlier surveys, that in Singapore contractual arrangements are quite common in domestically oriented firms but that more often than not they accompany FDI, and are not widely used as an alternative to direct investment. They also suggest that Japanese investors are particularly prone to using such contractual arrangements in conjunction with FDI. Information derived from interviews also suggests, however, that in recent years a growing number of firms have been exploring licensing possibilities in Singapore, particularly medium-size European and U.S. firms, and particularly in such industries as industrial machinery and chemicals. It is thought that some of these firms may be interested in testing the local and regional market through licenses before undertaking FDI. There are also a number of firms, mainly European and including some well known multinationals, which have expressed interest in setting up turnkey projects and apparently prefer not to invest directly; but compared to the number of foreign investors, the number of such firms is reportedly of little significance.

To summarise, the use of new forms of investment, and particularly joint ventures, has increased in absolute terms with the rapid growth of Singapore's manufacturing sector over the years, but has never become significant compared to the traditional form of FDI on which Singapore has relied so heavily for the spectacular growth of her manufacturing industries during the 1960s and 1970s. Furthermore, since the mid-1970s the sector has become more dominated than ever by the traditional form of FDI. Singaporean firms with less than majority foreign equity which use licensing or management contracts are relatively few – reportedly accounting for less than 10 per cent of recently established firms – and most of them are relatively small and use mature technologies. Licensing agreements are more common than management and turnkey contracts, but they are usually associated with FDI, notably Japanese investment. In short, FDI is not only not becoming obsolete, it has further increased its dominance of Singapore's manufacturing sector in recent years. Contractual relationships have played a largely complementary role to FDI and do not appear to be significant as a new form of investment in their own right. It remains to be seen whether the rapid growth of the Singaporean and ASEAN regional markets will have any noticeable influence on the use of new forms of investment in Singapore.

## B. Global Trends

A comparison of findings from the ten host countries covered by our research project shows that in the majority of countries the two most important new forms of investment in the manufacturing sector are joint ventures and licensing agreements. The extent to which licensing is used as a new form in its own right or plays a complementary role to traditional FDI varies somewhat among countries, as illustrated by our comparison of patterns in Korea and Brazil; but there can be little doubt that licensing continues to play a complementary role to a significant extent.

Management contracts appear on the whole to be of limited significance in the manufacturing sector, and turnkey and product-in-hand operations appear to be of no major importance in any country covered by this study other than Algeria. International subcontracting is of some importance in Tunisia and Mexico, but in neither country does the importance of this particular new form appear to be growing as compared either to other new forms or to traditional FDI.

The importance of the new forms as a group, both relative to FDI and in terms of their role in capital formation in the manufacturing sector, varies considerably from one host country to another – as the four countries reviewed above illustrate quite well. Viewed in static terms, in no country have the new forms so completely replaced traditional FDI as in Algeria, and in all countries they have gained more importance than in Singapore. Between these two extremes probably the most accurate generalisations one can make are simply that:

1.  the new forms do play a role of considerable importance in the manufacturing sector of virtually all the countries covered by the study other than Singapore;
2.  they do not appear to be rendering FDI obsolete;
3.  like traditional FDI, they tend to concentrate in the host-country's growth industries.

Perhaps more important than static inter-country comparisons is the direction of change. Evidence from the host countries suggests that the overall tendency is a gradually growing role of new forms of investment in these countries' manufacturing industries. What little evidence we have so far collected on the use of new forms as seen from the home-country perspective[51] points to the same trend. Thus, for example, data on the ownership structure of subsidiaries of U.S. multinational firms indicate some shift toward greater use of minority ownership in developing countries' manufacturing industries in the mid-1970s[52]. These data also tend to support the hypothesis that, *ceteris paribus,* minority and fifty-fifty joint ventures are more likely to be used in industries characterised by relatively unsophisticated technology (and not highly intensive in advertising, marketing techniques or proprietary brand names) and are oriented towards the domestic market. U.S. firms investing in offshore affiliates producing for the home market appear much more reluctant to share ownership.

In the case of U.K. firms, there is some evidence of an historical trend towards increasing use of joint ventures in both developed and developing countries. Whereas this trend has been reversed in developed host countries since the mid-1960s, in developing host countries both joint ventures and non-equity forms of U.K. firms' involvement have continued to increase[53].

Among other European countries whose firms have increasingly gained importance as investors in developing countries in recent years, German, French and Italian firms have shown a relatively high propensity to use new forms, although the Swiss and the Dutch apparently less so. The growth of Japanese investment in developing countries' manufacturing industries, which really took off only in the latter half of the 1960s, has shown a very high propensity to use new forms of investment compared with firms from other countries, although the longer-term trend may be one of gradually increasing reliance on traditional FDI[54].

What conclusions can be drawn about global trends in the use of new forms of investment in the developing countries' manufacturing sector? Four points should be underlined. First, it is important to distinguish between situations where one or a combination of new forms has actually replaced or superseded traditional FDI, and those where the new forms complement or are used in conjunction with FDI. The relative frequency and importance of the latter type of situation means that, in contrast to the extractive industries, there is little systematic evidence to support the obsolescence-of-FDI hypothesis in the manufacturing sector as a whole.

Certain new forms may even lead to FDI, as mentioned in the case of Singapore. This phenomenon also appeared in the German study, for example, where certain licensing agreements were used by German firms in the machine-tool industry to explore potential markets before making equity investments. These investments often took the form of buying out the local partner[55].

Second, inter-industry comparisons within manufacturing are on the whole consistent with the hypothesis that the new forms tend to be used more frequently in industries oriented towards the host country's domestic market and characterised by relatively "mature" technologies. Even among industries whose product or process technolgies are relatively unsophisticated *per se*, equity sharing appears to be less frequent in firms which are relatively advertising-intensive or for which proprietary brand names are of critical importance. There is also some reason to suspect that the market orientation of a given investment may tend to weigh more heavily in determining the incidence of new forms of investment than either the degree of technical maturity of the industry, or the general propensity of firms from a particular home country to engage in new forms of investment.

The most important hypothesis in terms of inter-industry comparisons within manufacturing may be that both FDI and the new forms tend to concentrate in host countries' major growth industries. This tendency points to the importance of non-industry-specific factors in determining the degree to which new forms are used, and the extent to which they precede, complement or replace traditional FDI, as well as which particular new forms are used. (Noteworthy among these factors, as discussed in Chapter 4, are the host government's foreign investment policies and the host economy's overall pattern of, and potential for, growth, on one hand, and the rent-seeking nature of firm behaviour and the nature of inter-firm competition on the other.) The relevance of the fact that these same industries are often characterised by a relatively high degree of concentration will be brought out in subsequent chapters[56].

Third, evidence on the hypothesis of an emerging three-way division of risks and responsibilities in the manufacturing sector must be treated with caution. There is considerable evidence that in this sector as in the extractive industries, relations between multinational firms, international lending institutions and host countries have evolved significantly. In particular, the lending institutions are clearly more actively involved in providing financial capital to manufacturing investments in developing countries. Overall, host countries are also assuming more risks and responsibilities. But one should not jump to the conclusion that this implies a long-run tendency for the new forms to supersede FDI.

On one hand, an unknown but perhaps surprisingly large proportion of international bank lending to the developing countries' manufacturing industries actually consists of loans to majority- and wholly-owned subsidiaries of foreign companies, i.e., of "disguised" FDI. The growth of such loans undoubtedly reflects shifts by some multinational firms from heavy reliance on intra-firm funds to greater external borrowing to finance their manufacturing subsidiaries' activities; nor is it known to what extent increased debt-equity ratios are also behind such borrowing by local subsidiaries. But on the other hand, there is scattered evidence to suggest that at least in some countries international loans have been used by local partners to finance their shares of joint ventures with foreign firms. Nor is it possible to even roughly estimate the extent to which such loans have financed royalty payments on licensing agreements, fees on management contracts, etc.

In so far as new forms of investment are actually financed by international loans, furthermore, it is important to distinguish between private international bank lending and bilateral suppliers' credits, the latter often involving public institutions of the supplying firms' home country. This distinction appears to be particularly relevant for turnkey projects, which are commonly financed by large international loans. What evidence we have suggests that contrary to the extractive industries, where turnkey projects are often heavily financed by private multinational lenders (via syndicated loans, "project financing" techniques, etc.), in the manufacturing sector *per se* loans to finance turnkey plants more often than not consist primarily of suppliers' credits from the supplying firms' home countries. As suggested by the findings cited from Algeria and Brazil, such credits appear to reflect a greater degree of competition among supplying firms than is the case of projects financed by loans from the international financial market – with important implications for host and home country alike.

Finally, in looking at the longer-run trends it is important to distinguish between new forms which, from the foreign firms' standpoint are indeed investment operations, and those which are not. Algeria is the only country in this study where supplying firms used the new forms to so great a degree not as manufacturing investments but as sales operations. Here the suppliers' profits – or losses – have depended not so much on the surplus-generating capacity of the manufacturing investment *per se,* as on the pre-negotiated price of the investment operation. With the exception of Singapore, where new forms are practically irrelevant compared to traditional FDI, in most of the countries studied the new forms appear to have gained considerable importance during the 1970s as investment operations. That is, foreign firms' profits from the principal new forms – licensing and joint ventures – have usually depended at least in part on the surplus-generating capacity of the manufacturing investment project in the host country to which they have supplied resources.

The extent to which the new forms' importance relative to FDI continues to increase in the coming decade remains to be seen. A renewed emphasis on import-substituting industrial growth in many developing countries along the lines discussed in Chapter 2 might be accompanied by a renewed emphasis on traditional FDI. But it is equally conceivable that the new forms of investment will continue to gain importance in the context of an evolving division of risks and responsibilities among multinational firms, international lenders and host countries in the manufacturing sector. It is even possible, ironically enough, that whereas in the late 1960s and 1970s many developing countries pressured foreign firms to shift to new forms of investment, and not infrequently met reluctance or resistance, the 1980s may witness the reverse: host countries showing a greater interest in foreign equity investment (with varying degrees of incentives, performance requirements, etc.) while foreign firms show some reluctance, having discovered the advantages that new forms of investment can hold out.

One result may be a global tendency towards greater use of joint ventures in the manufacturing sector, as compared to traditional FDI and other new forms of investment as well. Another possibility is more vigorous growth of traditional FDI. Much will of course depend on government policies and the growth patterns and potential of individual host economies. Much will also depend on worldwide economic conditions – heavily influenced by conditions in the industrialised countries – particularly as these affect competition among and the longer-term planning horizons of multinational investors. To this subject we return in Chapter 4.

## III.  SERVICES

The services sector covers a wide variety of activities, from public utilities and infrastructure on one hand to banking, insurance, tourism or commerce on the other. Not surprisingly, evidence on the use of new forms in this sector is even more fragmentary than for the extractive and manufacturing industries. We shall therefore attempt here to provide no more than some general impressions.

The latter half of the 19th and first half of the 20th centuries witnessed substantial amounts of both portfolio and direct investment in public utilities and infrastructure. Investments were made in urban power and public transportation networks, port facilities, railroads and the like, in both the politically independent nations and the colonial territories of Latin America, Africa and Asia. However, since World War II and the political independence of many countries in Africa and Asia, private foreign investment – both portfolio and FDI – in these activities has virtually disappeared. What foreign-owned public utilities, railroads, etc. remained after independence have been largely bought out or nationalised by host governments. New foreign investment resources have come primarily in the form of public financial flows, such as official bilateral or multilateral loans, often at concessional terms. Although some of these loans have been undertaken in conjunction with private foreign investment in the extractive industries, as we saw earlier, rarely does one find private foreign investment in public utilities and infrastructure in the developing countries. In short, FDI has clearly become "obsolete" in these activities.

As for the new forms of investment used, turnkey contracts have been important in the development of nuclear power plants in a number of developing countries, including several countries which otherwise had little recourse to such contracts, like Brazil. Turnkey contracts have also been used extensively as the basis of major infrastructural investments in a number of oil-exporting countries, notably in the Gulf region where, interestingly enough, firms from a few developing countries, like Korea and Brazil, were quite successful in bidding for some very large contracts during the 1970s. The other new form to have gained considerable importance in public utilities and especially infrastructural investments in many developing countries is the technical assistance contract, which has often been used in projects involving official loans.

From the supplying firms' point of view, however, rarely if ever do such turnkey and technical assistance contracts involve an investment operation as we have defined the term. True, one often finds in these activities a certain three-way division of risks and responsibilities. But it is significant that official lenders, notably the World Bank and the regional Development Banks, often play a leading role as suppliers of financial capital, and that private firms supplying capital equipment and technical assistance[57] are almost never involved other than on an arm's-length (i.e., commercial but not investment) basis. In other words, although FDI has clearly become "obsolete" and turnkey and technical assistance contracts have gained some importance in public utilities and especially infrastructural investments, one must be careful about arguing that such contracts have globally "superseded" or replaced portfolio and FDI as forms of foreign *investment* in these activities. (One exception perhaps is where these investments are undertaken in conjunction with mining, petroleum, or other direct surplus-generating projects.) A more accurate general conclusion might be that the traditional forms of *private* foreign investment (portfolio and FDI), which played such an important role in public utilities and infrastructure in many developing countries till World War II, have since been largely replaced by public (i.e., official, bilateral and multilateral) foreign investment, whose objective is not so much to generate monetary surpluses in public utilities and infrastructure *per se,* as it is to create or augment the surplus-generating capacity of other sectors of the host economy.

International investment trends in banking and insurance have not been examined in this study, in part because the Development Centre has undertaken a separate research project on the internationalisation of banking activities in developing countries[58]. It is nevertheless worth noting that the share of total FDI stock in developing countries which is in banking apparently rose substantially during the 1970s. Without doubt, FDI is not becoming obsolete in this industry.

As for international shipping, tourism and the like, the new forms of investment appear to have played a significant role in the expansion of these industries in many developing countries. For example, management and technical assistance or service contracts are often used by developing countries' state-run airlines and shipping companies. And in the case of tourism, the rapid international expansion of a number of major private hotel chains during the 1960s and 1970s appears to have been based largely on franchising arrangements and management contracts, with relatively little FDI by the parent companies in developing countries[59].

As regards commerce, FDI in retailing and wholesaling in the developing countries in recent decades appears to have been largely associated with import-substituting manufacturing investments (i.e., used as a tool of oligopolistic competition in some domestic market-oriented manufacturing investments). One can identify some purely commercial FDI – a good example is Sears stores in Latin America – but these appear to be of rather limited and declining global importance. Nor do we have any evidence suggesting that new forms of investment are of any global significance in such activities.

Of considerable interest and potential importance for our purposes, on the other hand, are investments in developing countries by Japanese General Trading Companies (Sogo Shosha). These companies, which are active not only in international trading but also in resource extraction, manufacturing, tourism and even banking, have shown a clear tendency to retain whole ownership in their rapidly growing network of foreign subsidiaries in the commercial sector, although they are also active promoters and organisers of new forms of investment[60]. These companies are the subject of a separate study carried out in conjunction with this project[61].

# NOTES AND REFERENCES

1. In addition to the information provided in country studies carried out in conjunction with this project, the following paragraphs draw heavily from G. Barrows, *World Petroleum Agreements, 1980,* Vol. II, 1981; and U.N. doc. E/C.7/119, "Permanent Sovereignty over Natural Resources."

2. U.S. tax laws, which allowed foreign income tax payments to be credited against U.S. tax liabilities, were reportedly a key factor in Saudi Arabia's decision to impose profit-sharing and in the firms' willingness to acquiesce.

3. Competition from newer "independents" such as AGIP enabled Iran to breach the so-called Seven Sisters' resistance to host-country equity participation. (Cf. C. Fred Bergsten, et al., *American Multinationals and American Interests,* Brookings Institution, Washington D.C., 1978, p. 130, fn.)

4. As explained below, Peru relied on service contracts during the 1968-71 period, then switched to production sharing in response to growing balance-of-payments pressures.

5. The first state oil company was actually created in 1922 by Argentina (YPF). But, contrary to the cases of PEMEX and NIOC, the creation of YPF did not result in the nationalisation of foreign investment in this sector.

6. For a discussion of the use of new forms of investment in industrialised oil-producing countries (especially Norway and the U.K.) see UNCTC doc. ST/CTC/29.

7. State ownership is 100 per cent in all OPEC countries except Ecuador, Gabon, Nigeria and the United Arab Emirates, whose governments hold majority but not whole ownership.

8. For a discussion of the relative advantages of different contractual arrangements and joint ventures in the petroleum industry, see G.H. Barrows, "Special Report on World Petroleum Concessions," in *Petroleum Economist,* Oct. 1980.

9. "Oil companies generate internally up to 70 per cent of their total required financial resources. Expenditures for capital investment can, therefore, be covered largely by internal means." (U.N. ECOSOC, E/C.7/119, *op. cit.*).

10. In fact, our distinction between "firms" and "financial organisations" should be treated with caution, both because of the extent to which "firms" may rely on relatively short-term financial operations – as distinct from relatively long-term investments in physical production – as a major source of profit, and because of the extent to which "financial organisations" may become involved in direct investment activities. An interesting example of the latter is PARIBAS, which at least until its nationalisation in 1981 was a major shareholder of the Schlumberger group, which holds monopolies on a number of petroleum exploration and drilling techniques, and also held equity in the Earth Satellite Corp., which collects data for natural resource exploration. According to a recent analysis of PARIBAS' strategy, "in the petroleum sector, control by the international financial groups is achieved above all through drilling technology, geological information and all services with a high scientific, technical and financial content." (M'hamed Sagou, *PARIBAS, Anatomie d'une Puissance,* Presse de la Fondation Nationale des Sciences Politiques, 1981, p. 102.)

11. In addition to the strategy of PARIBAS cited in the preceding footnote, a good example of the role of the firms is to be found in Saudi Arabia's reliance on several major petroleum companies not only for technology and management in petroleum production but in downstream gas- and oil-related industries (e.g. petrochemicals) as well. European state-owned petroleum companies, notably Italy's ENI, France's ERAP and more recently the U.K.'s BNOC, are quite innovative in providing technical services to a number of developing countries' petroleum industries.

12. An interesting example of the growing role of state petroleum companies as purchasers, which is also an example of South-South new forms of investment, is the use of production-sharing agrreements by Brazil's Petrobras and Braspetro in Iraq, and exploration contracts in numerous countries in Latin America, Africa and the Middle East.

13. One of the most interesting illustrations of the three-way division of risks and responsibilities, and of the specific role of financial organisations, can be found in Abdallah-Khodja's description of the Algerian experience *(op. cit.).*

14. The Bank's program is reportedly designed primarily to be supplementary in nature, i.e., to assist some developing countries meet their exploration costs in association with private foreign companies. In countries where such companies are unwilling to invest in exploration, the Bank will consider providing ten-year credits to cover some of the costs. But the loans are expected to be extended on normal World Bank terms and will require a guarantee of repayment from the recipient government. The risk of unsuccessful exploration will be borne by the host country, not the Bank. (U.N. ECOSOC, E/C.7/119, *op. cit.*)

15. Examples include major investments in Peru's trans-Andean pipeline, the development of ports and pipelines in Mexico, and petrochemical plants in Saudi Arabia and other Gulf countries. Cf. J. Segal, "Long-term oil strategy succeeding", *Petroleum Economist,* 1979, pp. 369-375.

16. Historically, some 75 to 80 per cent of developing countries' mineral resources are estimated to have been controlled by multinational mining corporations through FDI based on concessions. [U.N. ECOSOC E/C.7/119]

17. See U.N. ECOSOC E/C.7/99 for a list of U.N. General Assembly Resolutions on Permanent Sovereignty over Natural Resources.

18. By 1977 some 60 per cent of developing countries' primary *copper* output was produced by majority state-owned enterprises (compared to less than 3 per cent worldwide in the early 1960s). Production in Chile, Zaire and Zambia, and one of Peru's two large mines, came under such types of control. In Mexico and the Philippines, FDI is restricted to minority positions, with private local ownership dominating (in the latter country foreign ownership limits are tied to downstream value added locally).

 In *iron ore,* over half of production in developing countries is owned by state enterprises. Brazil's state enterprise, CVRD, is the world's largest single iron-ore exporter; it dominates production in that country, although private national firms are also active in joint ventures with multinational firms (e.g., Hanna Mining Co.). In Peru and Venezuela major properties of U.S. firms were expropriated in 1975. In India the state has been largely responsible for the development of production and exports, although private national firms in Goa produce sizeable output.

 Among other minerals, *bauxite* and *tin* also reveal a substantial role of state enterprise in developing countries. Brazil's CVRD has retained majority ownership while rapidly expanding bauxite production; Guyana expropriated Alcan's facility in 1971; and in 1974, Jamaica's imposition of production levies led to renegotiation and, in 1976/77, to government assumption of 51 per cent ownership of the operations of Kaiser and Reynolds. In tin, Malaysia has taken over majority ownership through share purchases on the London Stock Exchange; and in 1978 Nigeria acquired a majority interest in most of the country's tin-mining operations.

19. For example, Exxon Minerals has acquired the Disputada de los Condes Mine, and Superior Oil is participating in the development of the Quebrada Blanca mine, both in Chile. Billiton International Metals N.V. of the Shell group is a joint-venture partner in the Cuajone copper project in Peru, in the Cerro Matoso project in Colombia and, most recently, as a partner of the NDC group in Malaysia. Amoco Minerals participates in the OK Tedi consortium in Papua New Guinea. Production sharing has also been used in the 1975 Batubaran coal contract between Shell and Indonesia, the 1976 coal contract between Shell and Colombia, and the 1976 contract between Total and Colombia. (UNECOSOC E/C.7/119)

20. G.H. Barrows, "World Legal Arrangements in Petroleum and Mining, Similarities and Differences", paper presented to DSE Conference on International Mineral Resources Development, Berlin, August 1980, p. 10.

21. It is interesting to note that with the growing division of risks and responsibilities in which multinational mining as well as engineering and construction firms are brought in not as direct investors but on a contract basis as suppliers of capital equipment, technology, etc., they presumably no longer have the same incentive to try to hold down capital costs as when they were the mine owners. See also footnote 32.

22. Considerable light is shed on this reluctance by the 1975 legal case of *Anaconda Company Iv. OPIC* (the U.S. Government's foreign private investment insurance company). The question of Anaconda's continuing control over its copper-mining operations in Chile after the host government had acquired a 51 per cent equity interest was explored in depth. The tribunal's finding included the following:

 "...the Chilean negotiators refused, because of outside political pressure, to have a "management" contract with Anaconda similar to the one already entered into with Kennecott. ... They were, however, willing to have Anaconda continue to be in charge of operations. Maintenance of adequate control was ... regarded by Anaconda as a sine qua non and the Chilean negotiators concurred. [ ...]The outcome was a complex set of documents ... designed to give Codelco the appearance or "facade" of predominance but Anaconda most of the substance of control. ... "On the evidence it is clear that from the end of 1969 to 1971, Anaconda retained de facto control in the sense that the operations continued to be carried on in the same way as before, by the same personnel – with a handful of exceptions – as before, through

67

substantially the same practical chain of command as before, and pursuant to the same plans as before."
(Reported in SKB Asante, "Restructuring Transnational Mineral Agreements", *The American Journal of International Law*, Vol. 73, 1979, pp. 351-352.)

23. The original agreement with Bouganville Copper Ltd. was renegotiated in 1974 with Cozinc Riotinto of Australia, and the Broken Hill Proprietory agreement for the exploration and development of the Ok Tedi mine was negotiated with Amoco and a German consortium in 1976.

24. Cf. UNECOSOC, 1979, *op. cit.*

25. Cf. C. Parodi and F. Gonzalez Vigil, "New Forms of Foreign Investment in Peru" in C. Oman, ed., *New Forms of International Investment in Developing Countries: the National Perspective*, Development Centre Papers, OECD Development Centre, forthcoming.

26. The Law also ordered companies to set aside 6 per cent of their annual profit for the purpose of buying shares (in the companies) on behalf of the Mine Workers' Community, up to the point where the Community had achieved 50 per cent ownership.

27. See for example the comment by Bergsten, et al., cited on [pp. 33-34] of Chapter 5. See also footnote 32 below.

28. One means of exerting downward pressure on mineral rents would presumably be to encourage long-term minerals supplies to increase. This fact, coupled with the growing substitution of FDI by new forms of investment in developing countries' mining projects, suggest that arguments that there is an insufficiency of investment in mining in developing countries must be treated with some caution. For example, one of the best known proponents of the "danger of insufficient mining investment in LDCs" argument has pointed out that a concern "which is frequently voiced by officials of international mining firms, is that *national ownership and control of mineral resources in developing countries will lead to excess capacity* and thus to lower world prices that then fail to cover the full economic costs of production. This, of course, *impairs the profitability of private mining firms* and reduces incentives to invest ..."(R. Mikesell, *New Patterns of World Mineral Development*, British North American Committee, New York, 1979, p. 16., our emphasis.)

29. M. Radetzki, "Has Political Risk Scared Minerals Investments away from the Deposits in Developing Countries?", Seminar Paper N° 169, Institute for International Economic Studies, Stockholm, February 1980.

30. M. Radetzki, "Changing Structures in the Financing of the Minerals Industry in LDCs", *Development and Change*, Vol. II, 1980.

31. An expert on project finance has recently pointed out that, "Increasingly, project finance has seen the sponsors or lead lenders encouraging the use of international agency loans [e.g. World Bank co-financing] and the multinationalisation of export credits and of participation in Eurocurrency loans with a view to spreading the political risk and hopefully thereby minimising arbitrary political actions. The process of spreading risk is certainly also helped by the internationalisation of procurement and also of the off-take arrangements," D. Suratgar, "International Project Finance and Security for Lenders", paper presented to DSE Conference on International Mineral Resources Development – Emerging Legal and Institutional Arrangements, Berlin, August 1980, p. 14. See also the comment of C. Fred Bergsten, et al., cited in Chapter 5, pp. 33-34.

32. It is at least conceivable, of course, that one factor underlying the skyrocketing of physical-capital costs in mining is the above-cited "delinking" of multinational firms' profits from mineral rents, which reduces their interest in holding down these costs. In fact, in so far as they increasingly derive their profits from supplying physical capital to host countries through turnkey contracts, and/or from serving as intermediaries in technology and equipment markets, they would presumably have an incentive to *increase* the prices of technology and equipment, which of course would be reflected in the overall physical-capital costs of mining projects. But we have no empirical evidence with which to test such an hypothesis. For a discussion of more readily identifiable factors which may explain the phenomenal rise in physical-capital costs in mining, see W.O. Gluschke, "Third World Mineral Development: Policies and Structures", paper presented to DSE Conference on International Mineral Resources Development, Berlin, August 1980, especially Appendix A.

33. "Government investment decisions with respect to the expansion of production capacities of certain minerals may at certain times be at variance with the expected growth of demand in the medium term. Also, government mining enterprises have often been less than willing to adjust output to falling price and demand conditions." Mikesell, *op. cit.*, p. 30.

34. E.A. Guimaraes, et al., *op. cit.*

35. Cf. T. Ozawa, "Japan's "Revealed Preference" for the "New Forms" of Investment: A Stock-Taking Assessment", in C. Oman, ed., *New Forms of International Investment in Developing Countries: the National Perspective*, op. cit. Ozawa explains that about 80% of Japanese ventures with equity investments in overseas minerals and oil extraction are operating either at a loss or at break-even and

paying no dividends, and that well over 90% of all profits from Japanese overseas extractive ventures are from interest on loans extended to overseas affiliates, mostly under "loan and import" contractual arrangements. See also Chapter 5 for a discussion of the "dominant buyer relationships" Japan has attained in structuring her minerals imports from developing countries.

For a broader analysis of the overseas activities of the trading companies, see K. Kojima and T. Ozawa, *Japan's General Trading Companies: Merchants of Economic Development,* OECD Development Centre, forthcoming. *Companies (Sogo Shosha),* OECD Development Centre, forthcoming.

36. D. Suratgar, *op. cit.,* p. 1

37. Even more noteworthy is the central role of Japanese General Trading Companies in organising these investments, co-ordinating production and controlling marketing operations of these firms, all of which suggest that the local joint-venture partners may have much less control of the export (as distinct from productive) operations of these firms than their status as majority owners might suggest at first glance. Cf. T. Ozawa, ibid., and K. Kojima and T. Ozawa, *ibid.*

38. The host countries covered by this study are Algeria, Brazil, India, Malaysia, Mexico, Peru, the Philippines, Singapore, South Korea and Tunisia. See C. Oman, ed., *op. cit.*

39. Drawn from Abdallah Khodja, *op. cit.*

40. Drawn from E.A. Guimaraes, et al., *op. cit.*

41. Guimaraes, et. al., report that "the main variable explaining the volume of imports associated with each project was international credit, rather than restrictions of a technological nature and/or ensuing from market dimensions." *(Ibid.)*

42. Guimaraes, et al., *ibid.*

43. Drawn from Bohn-Young Koo, "New Forms of Foreign Investment in Korea", in C. Oman, ed., *op. cit.*

44. A. Basile and D. Germidis, *op. cit.*

45. About 8 per cent of FDI stock (and 10 per cent of firms with foreign equity) is registered in free export zones.

46. The relatively small average size of Japanese investments is due largely to the numerous investments, often minority-Japanese-owned, of the export-platform type in the early 1970s.

47. A. Basile and D. Germidis, *op. cit.*

48. This last inference is perhaps a bit tenuous, particularly because the reputed higher propensity of Japanese investors to take minority rather than majority equity positions is less clear in the case of Korea than the data cited above would suggest. Measured by numbers of firms, Japan indeed had a higher proportion of minority-owned firms than any other country. But measured by value of investment, Japan had the lowest proportion and the U.S. the highest. The reason for the discrepancy is that in Korea most minority-owned Japanese firms have been very small investments, whereas the average size of Japanese wholly owned investments has been larger than that of U.S. wholly owned investments.

49. It may be recalled that in Brazil only about one-fifth of all contracts but over three-quarters of all technology payments are between subsidiary and parent companies.

50. Drawn from Pang Eng Fong, "Foreign Indirect Investment in Singapore" C. Oman, ed., *op. cit.*

51. The second phase of our research, now getting underway, is designed to provide much more comprehensive data on new forms of investment as seen at the firm- and industry-level in home countries.

52. Cf. L. Franko, "Use of Minority and 50-50 Joint Ventures by U.S. Multinationals" 1982 (mimeo).

53. Cf. Dunning and Cantwell, "Joint Ventures and Non-Equity Foreign Involvement by British Firms with Particular Reference to Developing Countries: An Exploratory Study", 1982 (mimeo).

54. Cf. T. Ozawa, *op. cit.*

55. It is also interesting to note in this regard that the data on ownership structure of subsidiaries of U.S. multinational firms suggest that once a subsidiary has been established as a minority or fifty-fifty joint venture it has more than twice the chance of ending up as a majority or 100 per cent MNC-owned subsidiary than do 100 per cent or majority-MNC-owned subsidiaries have of becoming fifty-fifty or minority-owned ventures. (Cf. L. Franko, *op. cit.)*

56. A possible exception to this last point might be the proliferation of joint ventures involving minority equity participation by small- and medium-size Japanese manufacturing firms in the textile industry in a number of Asian developing countries, notably in the early 1970s. However, one must be cautious about jumping to the conclusion that the textile industry is characterised by a high degree of price competition among independent firms, because the General Trading Companies play a central role in regulating both trade and competition among these joint ventures.

57. It should be stressed however, that the official lending agencies (e.g. World Bank) often supply technical assistance themselves.

58. See D. Germidis and C. A. Michalet, *International Banks and Financial Markets in Developing Countries*, OECD Development Centre, forthcoming.

59. Cf. UNCTC, *op. cit.*

60. Cf. T. Ozawa, *op. cit.*

61. K. Kojima and T. Ozawa, *op. cit.*

*Chapter 4*

# CAUSES OF NEW FORMS OF INVESTMENT

The preceding chapter presents an overview of what is happening in terms of the use of traditional FDI and new forms of investment in the North-South context. This chapter explores some of the reasons why the new forms of investment have grown in importance over the last ten to fifteen years.

If one were to judge exclusively from some of the business literature, one could easily conclude that almost without exception firms use new forms of investment reluctantly and only in response to host-government demands. If one were to judge from some of the literature which tends to be more critical of multinational firms, it would be easy to conclude that these firms are all-powerful and more or less unilaterally impose the particular forms of investment which best suit their purposes. Of course, both sets of arguments tend to be somewhat short-sighted and/or unidimensional, but they raise important points. In Sections I and II we review some of these points, and in Section III we develop another line of reasoning to help explain current trends in the use of new forms of investment[1].

## I. DEFENSIVE REACTION

One interpretation, which we might label the "defensive-reaction" hypothesis, regards the postwar evolution of North-South investment trends largely as a result of changes in host-governments' trade and investment policies. The rapid growth of FDI in manufacturing during the 1950s and 1960s is explained as primarily a defensive reaction by leading industrial firms of the more industrialised countries, especially the U.S., that sought to gain or retain access to foreign markets in the face of trade barriers increasingly imposed by host governments pursuing import-substituting industrialisation. Analogously, the move by multinational firms since then towards greater use of reduced- or non-equity forms of investment in both manufacturing and extractive industries is seen as an essentially defensive reaction, as these firms seek to retain or ensure access to markets and/or sources of raw materials in the face of host government restrictions on foreign ownership, increasing risks of expropriation or nationalisation and, more generally, a deteriorating "investment climate" due to increasing nationalism and state intervention in developing countries.

The defensive reaction hypothesis holds, in other words, that the new forms of investment represent little more than a "second-" or even a "third-best" strategy for firms trying to achieve what under "free market" conditions would largely take place through arm's-length exports and imports in a context of competitive world markets[2].

Furthermore, as world markets are felt to be quite "imperfect" – that is, neither highly competitive nor very free – this interpretation would suggest that responsibility for such "imperfections" lies primarily with the growth of State intervention, particularly, though not exclusively, in the developing countries[3], rather than, say, with the monopolistic advantages possessed by firms or the oligopolistic nature of inter-firm competition.

There are of course important theoretical reasons for questioning this interpretation, especially its assumption of competitive markets in the absence of government intervention, as brought out for example by the industrial-organisation analysis of the importance of firms' monopolistic power in explaining FDI, a point to which we return in Section III of this chapter. But the "defensive reaction hypothesis" does focus attention on two points of considerable importance in explaining trends in firms' use of new forms of investment: the role played by host-government policy; and the importance of foreign business executives' perceptions of a given country's "investment climate", regardless of how subjective those perceptions may sometimes be[4]. It also serves to highlight the fact that the success of host-government policies designed to favour the use of new forms over traditional FDI depends on the willingness and ability of foreign firms to accommodate rather than simply pull out or refuse to do business.

As regards the role of host government intervention, the evidence strongly suggests that the wave of changes which occurred in a number of developing countries' foreign investment policies during the late 1960s and early 1970s were indeed of decisive importance in bringing about the growth during the same period of new forms of investment in these countries[5]. (Virtually all the countries covered in our study except Singapore witnessed some such policy changes.) These policy changes included, with widely varying degrees of scope and emphasis: the establishment of government boards for screening and registering foreign investments, the imposition of local-integration and export-performance requirements, limitations on profit remittances, the demarcation of sectors or industries where foreign investment is forbidden or restricted, the control of foreign takeovers of local firms, the restriction of foreign equity to minority positions, etc. There can be little doubt that such policies, which generally aimed not to discourage foreign investment but to regulate its entry and behaviour, and which often involved incentives and guarantees as well as restrictions and regulations, were a major cause of the shift to greater use of new forms in general, and minority joint ventures in particular, during the late 1960s and early 1970s.

In support of the defensive-reaction hypothesis one might also cite numerous declarations by multinational business executives lamenting a general deterioration of the "investment climate" in developing countries during this period. They decried increasing political instability, rising nationalism, and "anti-imperialist" or even explicitly anti-multinational-enterprise rhetoric, impressive increases in expropriations – primarily though not exclusively in the extractive industries[6] – contract renegotiations and threats of expropriation. Added to this was the plethora of government regulations mentioned above, which foreign business executives often pointed to as an important manifestation of this deterioration[7]. There is also widespread agreement both within and outside the international business community that the bargaining power of the developing countries as a group tended to increase during this time – even if many of the chips remained in corporate hands. In the case of the raw materials industry, the "obsolescing bargain" theory[8] illustrates why host countries are apt to improve their bargaining position quite rapidly once a direct investment has been made. And in manufacturing industries, the stagnation of growth in the OECD region, combined with sustained growth of markets in a number of developing countries, has given added strength to the bargaining position of host countries with large and attractive markets.

Aside from the theoretical considerations raised by the industrial-organisation paradigm (and discussed below), however, there are a number of empirical reasons for doubting the ability of the "defensive-reaction" hypothesis to adequately explain trends in the use of new forms of investment. First, if one looks at what is undoubtedly the most spectacular manifestation of the increased bargaining power of developing countries during the 1970s, namely the increase of petroleum prices and the widespread nationalisation of oil production by the OPEC countries, one finds not only that the multinational petroleum companies do not seem to have suffered in terms of profitability, but that the vastly increased revenues of the oil-exporting countries in turn created highly lucrative new investment opportunities in the form of turnkey and management contracts, licensing agreements and joint ventures, among others. True, the form of these investments reflects host-government policy as well as decisions by foreign suppliers. But the point is that many foreign suppliers, including some of the major petroleum firms whose assets were nationalised, took advantage of these opportunities and can hardly be characterised as behaving in terms of a purely defensive reaction.

Nor does the cross-sectional evidence clearly support the hypothesis of a correlation between the growing use of new forms of investment relative to traditional FDI and a deterioration in the "investment climate" in a given country. Of course, if one defines "favourable investment climate" to mean simply the absence of host-government regulations and the predominance of laissez-faire policies highly amenable to traditional FDI, and significant state intervention is associated with a deteriorating or "unfavourable" investment climate, there appears to be some correlation between the latter and the growing use of new forms of investment. Many of the new forms were first developed internationally in the context of East-West relations[9], and one of the first developing countries to actively pursue certain new forms as an alternative to FDI, Algeria, was indeed characterised by a high degree of centralised state control, considerable nationalist and "anti-imperialist" rhetoric, and the like. But one also finds a growing use of new forms of investment in such countries as Brazil and Korea, whose investment climate was generally considered both good and improving during the late 1960s and 1970s, precisely at the time when the new forms were of growing importance there.

It is also striking that in such countries covered by our study as Brazil, Mexico, the Andean Group (which includes Peru), Korea, Malaysia, the Philippines and India, which by the early 1970s had all adopted policies to regulate FDI, there occurred – contrary to what one would infer from the defensive-reaction hypothesis – substantial inflows of traditional FDI, as well as a greater use of new forms. Empirical support for the idea that government intervention may not lead to a decline in FDI is found, for example, in a recent study showing a positive correlation between the size of the government sector and the inflow of private foreign investment[10]. Other studies have also pointed out that host-country regulations may even have encouraged the inflow of foreign investment capital. One often sees reference to the data on FDI in Mexico, for example, which show a stagnation during the early 1970s and renewed vigor subsequent to the introduction of regulations on foreign investment in 1973.

Eduardo White has recently lent further support to the idea that state intervention does not necessarily discourage foreign investment. He cites two counter examples, Argentina and Chile, which considerably relaxed controls on foreign investment with the explicit intention of encouraging investment and technology flows[11]. He does not see the disappointing results of these deregulating experiences over the last decade as suggesting that open door policies are a discouragement to foreign investors. But he concludes that the overall state of the host economy and the worldwide business cycle are more important than the regulatory or incentive-oriented nature of host-government investment policies *per se*. He adds, and his point sheds much light on the limits of the "defensive-reaction" hypothesis:

"the experience of the main host developing countries seems to indicate that, contrary to the traditional concept which identifies a "good investment climate" with free-market and laissez-faire policies, attractive investment conditions include a good share of government interventionism and regulations. In other words ... TNCs [transnational corporations] were attracted by policies of economic growth which involved a high degree of market intervention, such as a significant level of tariff protection, reserved markets, subsidised local capital, wage controls, export and import subsidies and government procurement policies, without mentioning the availability of risk-minimising state partners for huge investment projects. "The cases of Argentina and Chile are helpful in illustrating the effects of certain liberalisation policies on the investment strategies of TNCs. In both countries, the recent de-regulation of TNCs was just an aspect of a global transformation experiment which involved the dismantling of tariff barriers, the liberalisation of the capital markets, the elimination of subsidies and the overvaluation of local currency as the main stabilisation instruments. As a result of the upsurge of import competition and the clearly recessionist effects of such policies, sooner or later it became nearly impossible for industrial firms, including TNCs' subsidiaries, to plan future investments for constantly shrinking domestic markets. Thus many of the TNCs' subsidiaries were transformed into export outlets for the production of companies abroad, or, more significantly, into financial centres for exploiting the high profit opportunities offered by the combination of a fixed exchange rate with extraordinary positive interest rates in the domestic market, much higher than those prevailing in the international markets. Short-term capital flows through intra-company loans replaced in this manner direct investment."[12]

Nor does the evidence suggest a clear temporal correlation since the mid-1970s between trends in host-government regulation of FDI and trends in the use of new forms of investment in the developing countries as a group. On the one hand, there has been a tendency to adopt more flexible and on the whole somewhat more liberal policies towards FDI in a number of developing countries which had previously introduced regulatory policies[13]. On the other hand, evidence from these countries suggests that on the whole the use of new forms of investment has continued to grow. It remains to be seen, of course, whether there exists a time lag between these policy changes and their impact on investment forms, which might lead to a declining importance of new forms relative to FDI in the coming years. But the evidence now available on trends in investment regulatory policies and businessmen's perceptions of the "investment climate"[14], on the one hand, and trends in the use of new forms of investment on the other, cannot be adequately explained by the defensive-reaction hypothesis, especially since the mid-1970s.

It is also worth noting that regulatory measures introduced by some host governments, particularly those aimed at controlling or limiting profit remittances by multinational firms on FDI, may actually have induced firms to pursue strategies or introduce measures which are incompatible with equity sharing. For example, certain techniques introduced by multinational firms as a defensive reaction to host-government exchange controls, such as "netting" and "parallel loans"[15], may have strengthened rather than weakened some firms' strategic interest in retaining full ownership of their foreign investment operations. Firms seeking to avoid taxation and/or to circumvent restrictions on profit remittances may also prefer to retain 100 per cent ownership so as to facilitate transfer pricing. In short, under certain circumstances the logic of the defensive reaction hypothesis would imply a movement away from new forms towards greater reliance on traditional FDI, or at least a reinforcement of the latter, rather than the other way around.

## II. STRATEGIC INITIATIVE

An alternative interpretation, which is virtually the converse of the defensive-reaction hypothesis, and which might be labelled the "strategic initiative" or "offensive" hypothesis, would regard the evolution of North-South investment trends as being at least in part the result of spontaneous or strategic initiatives taken by the international business community. To begin with, this interpretation would point out that the rapid growth of direct foreign manufacturing investment in developing countries in the 1950s and 1960s was and still is, for that matter, often the result of large industrial or commercial firms taking advantage of opportunities for profitable investment created by import restrictions and other policies implemented by many developing countries in their pursuit of import-substituting industrialisation. These host-government policies may be seen, in other words, not so much as leading to purely defensive reactions on the part of foreign firms, as creating conditions – e.g., through these policies' impact on the distribution of income within the host economy – which contribute to increasing the profitability of direct manufacturing investment, foreign as well as local, in these countries. This interpretation would also suggest, in sharp contrast to the defensive-reaction hypothesis, that in some cases there may exist an important convergence or overlap of interests between foreign as well as local investors and the host-country's government, such that the regulatory policies of the latter may not necessarily run counter to, or even always be designed independently of the direct influence of, major foreign investors.

In seeking to explain the growing importance of the new forms of investment since the late 1960s, the strategic-initiative hypothesis suggests that whereas conditions prevailing in the colonial territories and independent developing countries in the immediate postwar period were not generally conducive to forms of foreign investment other than those based on whole- or majority-ownership, important structural changes brought about by political independence and/or induced by periods of rapid economic growth during the 1950s and 1960s in developing countries in turn helped to create, particularly since the late 1960s, new or expanded opportunities for foreign business involvement to which the new forms of investment are sometimes better adapted, from the foreign-investor's as well as the host-country's viewpoint, than traditional FDI.

These structural changes are generally reflected in, but run deeper than, the unequal sectoral growth rates that often show up in a country's national accounts in the form of a relative increase of industry and services and a decline of agriculture as a proportion of GDP. They would include, for example:

a) the "freeing" or expulsion of large numbers of peasants from traditional agriculture and of artisans from traditional handicraft industries, and the concomitant emergence and growth of an urban-based wage-labour force available for employment by investors of capital in the "modern" sector,

b) the decline of economic and political power of certain traditional élites (e.g., a "feudalistic" or colonial-based land-owning "oligarchy") often antagonistic to modernisation, and the concomitant consolidation of economic and political power by the local "bourgeoisie" – various groups of industrialists, merchants, bankers, etc. – and

c) significant expansion of urban-based markets for durable and non-durable consumer goods, industrial inputs (i.e., raw materials, intermediate goods, technology, etc.) and, eventually, infrastructure to support the expansion of both private industry and the public sector.

Such structural changes may be reflected, particularly during critical periods of local power consolidation requiring some mobilisation of political and social forces within a developing country, in relatively aggressive, "nationalistic" attitudes – occasionally even "anti-imperialist" rhetoric – by local élites vis-à-vis their counterparts in the industrialised countries and the international business community. But it is equally true that such structural changes also often reflect, and further contribute to, the spread and consolidation of "Western" patterns of behaviour, as expressed for example in terms of demand for products ("consumption patterns"), business managerial and organisational techniques, styles of inter-firm and international negotiation, etc. All of these may play a vital role in creating and/or expanding the opportunities in these countries for foreign investment.

In other words, if the political instability, nationalistic attitudes and increased state intervention which often accompany these structural changes result in greater risk and/or costs for foreign firms of "internalised" or intra-firm capital flows to developing countries as is the case with traditional FDI, they may also serve in the longer run both to create the possibilities for and reduce the "transaction" costs of such flows when "externalised" or when new forms of investment are used. We shall return to this point below.

Furthermore, and of particular importance in explaining the growing use of new forms of investment, the consolidation of power by and growing "maturity" of local élites in recent years may have laid the foundation for a new division of risks and responsibilities – as hypothesised in Chapter 2 – in which foreign firms and international lenders can increasingly rely on the local business community and/or public sector of the host country to assume a number of important risks and responsibilities involved in international investment. One well known example is of course the responsibility for labour relations, especially the task of holding down local wages and containing labour "unrest", which can be a very ticklish problem for managers of wholly or majority-foreign-owned firms. By investing in firms with majority local private or public ownership and/or using contractual forms of investment, foreign investors can often shift the responsiblity of labour relations to their local partners, who are often more efficient in these tasks than even the most ruthless expatriate manager could hope to be.

Another interesting example of responsibilities which may increasingly be left to local partners is the realm of commercial operations in which mass advertising is unimportant but intimate knowledge of the local clientele is. Such might be the case, for example, of spinning and weaving firms whose output is sold primarily to wholesalers or retailers and apparel manufacturers, but not to individuals. For such firms commercial success depends on a carefully developed and continually renewed commercial network requiring an intimate knowledge of customers and a feeling for which ones should get credit, which are too risky, etc. It is not surprising that in Brazil's textile industry, to cite only one example, joint ventures have reportedly become increasingly popular among foreign firms interested in breaking into the local market[16].

Another very important set of examples is where the local firm assumes not merely such aspects as labour relations or marketing, but responsibility for the overall investment decision and financial risk. One case would be the not infrequent situation where a licensing agreement is used by a licensor as a means to get his foot in the door of an important market without committing substantial resources to, or incurring financial risk in, the investment project itself. Here licensing, or a management contract or franchise, may be the best or only means for smaller firms or those with limited financial or managerial resources, for example, but which have unique technological, managerial or marketing know-how to enter a foreign market[17]. In others such a strategy may be used to "test the terrain" and, if the operation proves successful, the local licensee may subsequently be absorbed by the licensor, or a joint venture may be created[18]. One very important implication of such new forms of investment, in other words, is that firms may get considerably greater *leverage* on their intangible assets – technology, management know-how, etc. – than they would from traditional FDI.

Another case obeys a slightly different logic in that production is for the market of the home rather than the host country. International subcontracting may be used by firms to avoid the cost of expanding production capacity, thereby shifting to subcontractors in the host country at least part of the risk associated with fluctuating demand conditions in the home or world market[19].

Lastly, there is the case, which has involved a large volume of capital in recent years, where the decision to invest and the financial risk are assumed by the host country at least partly because of foreign firms' refusal or reluctance to undertake the project *as an investment operation.* The cause of such refusal/reluctance to invest, quite aside from host countries' insistence on full or majority local ownership, may be foreign firms' inability to assess the expected profitablity[20] and/or, more frequently perhaps, their view that a given project is not likely to be viable as an investment project in its own right. This is frequently the case in a number of basic industries, such as steel or petrochemicals, which are plagued by worldwide overcapacity. In such cases, a foreign firm's involvement in the project reflects the host-country partner's ability to pay, which in turn often depends on the host country's oil or other export revenues and/or its ability to borrow on international financial markets, rather than the long-run surplus-generating capacity of the investment project *per se.* As a result, many of the new forms take on the logic *from the foreign firm's standpoint* not of an investment project but of a *sale* of plant and equipment, services, etc.

One example of this phenomenon might be a turnkey plant in an industry characterised by significant economies of scale but operating in the host economy under conditions of high local costs and limited local demand, such that the plant is not viable as an investment project in market terms, but which is undertaken by the host country for, say, internal political reasons[21]. Another example might be a mining project which foreign mining companies are unwilling to develop through FDI but which the host country wishes to undertake either as a vital source of foreign exchange or again, for internal political reasons[22]. Under such circumstances foreign firms may be brought in through various new forms: licensing and management contracts, turnkey contracts both for the mining project itself and accompanying infrastructure, subcontracting, etc.[23]. Rather than relying on mining rents *per se* as their principal source of profit as would normally be the case of traditional FDI, the supplying firms may be seen as selling goods and services to the host country for a more immediate payoff, and/or seeking to profit from downstream rents, for example through marketing. While financing for such projects may come from the international financial market in the form of "sovereign loans" or "project finance" and/or credits from the supplying firms' home countries, much of the investment risk is effectively assumed by the host country. In some cases it may even end up subsidising production when ore prices fall in world markets, rather than curtail production, because of the need to sustain the inflow of foreign exchange.

A third example is where turnkey cum technical-assistance contracts are signed between producers of machinery and equipment, notably European firms, and host-country firms selling in the local consumer-goods market. Such arrangements appear to be quite common in a number of NICs and middle-income developing countries, particularly those with a relatively dynamic local business community, whose consumer-goods markets are growing rapidly; they are often used in industries where the role of mass advertising and brand image make direct foreign investors relatively reluctant to share ownership with local partners. The contractual arrangements reflect the fact that the foreign suppliers of capital equipment and technical assistance are normally not producers of the consumer good even in their home markets and therefore would have no competitive basis for undertaking direct investment in the production of consumer goods in the host economy. Rather, these producers of capital goods extend to developing countries a market for capital goods they have developed in their home economies – capital goods which may embody rather sophisticated process technology and often constitute the basis on which the local firm, having acquired the technology on a turnkey cum technical-assistance basis, competes in the local market with foreign-owned firms with established brand names, large advertising expenditures, etc.[24].

The most spectacular examples of this case are undoubtedly the multi-million and billion-dollar turnkey projects undertaken in a number of oil-exporting countries, whose large export revenues and desire to achieve rapid industrialisation – and to accelerate the process of structural modernisation, as illustrated so well by the Algerian experience – created during the 1970s numerous lucrative business opportunities for foreign firms. That the primary mode of realisation of these projects has been turnkey contracts in particular, and new forms in general, certainly reflects in part the host countries' desire to retain full or majority local ownership. But it also clearly reflects the strategic approach to these projects by foreign suppliers as *sales,* not investment, operations in many cases. More recently, a number of developing countries have begun providing major incentives – fiscal, financial, long-term petroleum-supply contracts, etc. – and/or exerting considerable pressure on the supplying firms to take minority equity positions in these projects, that is, to approach them as *investment* rather than purely sales operations.

To conclude, an interesting implication of the strategic-initiative hypothesis is that the new forms of investment may allow foreign firms to invest in new activities or capitalise on business opportunities in those countries which would have been relatively inaccessible or unprofitable under traditional FDI. Insofar as the new forms of investment reflect a new international division of risks and responsibilities in the organisation of production and capital formation in developing countries, made possible in part by the ongoing structural changes in these countries, the strategic-initiative hypothesis would also imply, contrary to the defensive-reaction hypothesis, that the new forms are not merely replacing but actually complementing and expanding the possibilities offered by traditional FDI for profitable investment in the developing countries. By combining the particular strengths of the local and international business and financial communities, the new forms of investment in developing countries may even constitute a necessary, if not sufficient, condition for the continued expansion of the sphere of investment and accumulation worldwide. To this far-reaching hypothesis we shall return in Chapter 5.


## III. THE CHANGING GLOBAL INVESTMENT ENVIRONMENT

Useful as the "defensive-reaction" and "strategic-initiative" hypotheses may be at the conceptual level in helping to clarify possible alternative explanations for why multinational firms are apparently using the new forms of investment more now than prior to the late 1960s, these hypotheses are virtually impossible to test empirically. True, one can find important bits of empirical evidence which appear more consistent with one hypothesis than another, such as the numerous minority-foreign-owned joint ventures established in Korea's free export zones where there are no host-government constraints on foreign ownership (which hardly seem consistent with the defensive-reaction hypothesis). But if one addresses the question of why new forms have taken on increasing importance to the managers of the firms themselves, one is likely to be told, in effect, that firms are adapting to a changing international investment environment calling for both defensive measures and strategic initiatives. One is also likely to find that the relatively subjective elements of individual firms' management philosophies and individual managers' perceptions strongly influence the extent to which a given management decision is seen by the firm itself as a defensive measure or a strategic initiative.

For our purposes, therefore, another useful approach might be to identify some of the most important "objective" factors, that is, those which depend neither on individual firms' management styles or philosophies nor on individual managers' perceptions. In looking at firms' use of or involvement in new forms of investment as a response to mounting pressures, the most useful distinction might be that between those pressures which emanate from or depend largely on the host countries themselves, and those which do not. In other words, pressures exercised on foreign investors by some developing-country governments are emphasized by the defensive-reaction hypothesis, and new possibilities created by the structural evolution brought about in these countries (government policies reflecting or representing one aspect of this evolution) are emphasized by the strategic-initiative hypothesis. Such factors have undoubtedly been of critical importance in the growing use of new forms of investment, but one should not ignore factors which are less endogenous to host countries. A third hypothesis – which might be labelled the "changing global investment scenario" hypothesis – would focus less on changes occurring in the developing countries *per se* than on factors underlying changes in the international investment scene as a whole.

Among these factors, two categories appear to be of particular importance. One is the evolution of economic conditions in the major industrialised countries – considered both collectively and individually – which is important because these countries play a predominant role in the world economy and hence the global investment scene, and also because these countries are the home countries of the principal multinational investors. The second is the dynamics of firm behaviour and of worldwide inter-firm competition. In reality of course these factors are hardly independent of one another. The growing interdependence of national economies in the OECD region, not to mention in the North-South context, means that changing economic conditions in one country affect those in another. The dynamics of firm behaviour and of inter-firm competition are also of course closely related. And changing economic conditions in the industrialised countries, collectively and individually, influence firm behaviour and the dynamics of inter-firm behaviour, just as the latter clearly influence the former. Nevertheless, to simplify our discussion, we shall address these factors separately.

## A. The Home Countries

### i) Global Conditions

Among the first category, perhaps the single most important factor has been the economic slowdown in the OECD region as a whole, as reflected in stagnating investment and declining productivity growth[25]. This slowdown combined with the breakdown of the Bretton Woods system of fixed international currency exchange rates, on the one hand, and the rising global rates of inflation and interest characteristic of the 1970s on the other, have all led to growing uncertainty and perceptions of risk on the part of many business managers. These perceptions have in turn been accompanied by growing tendencies on the part of many firms to minimise the risk of exposing long-term investment capital, and to seek to maximise their leverage on the capital which they do invest. Firms have also tended to focus on relatively short-term financial returns and, more generally, to shorten overall investment planning horizons considerably[26]. In and of themselves, the economic slowdown, inflation and instability of exchange and interest rates which have plagued the OECD region as a whole during the past decade probably induced greater use of new forms of investment because of the risk-reducing, or risk-shedding, and leverage-increasing advantages they offer to firms compared with traditional FDI.

At the same time, rates of growth have been stronger in a number of "NICs" and middle-income developing countries than in the industrialised countries as a group, and there has been a phenomenal expansion of investment demand in a number of oil-exporting countries. The size and dynamism of these developing-country markets – a key factor behind the increased bargaining power of developing countries (alluded to in Section I) – undoubtedly induced many firms based in industrialised countries to seek profitable investment opportunities in developing countries more actively than would have been the case had economic conditions in the OECD region been more buoyant. As a result, the inclination by numerous firms to shorten investment planning horizons, to seek maximum leverage on and minimum exposure of long-term investment capital, and to emphasize relatively short-term financial returns over long-term productive investments, have undoubtedly been accompanied by firms giving greater attention, independently of host-government pressures or regulations, to developing possibilities for licensing their technologies, supplying capital equipment in the form of turnkey contracts, etc. – in short, to using new forms of investment rather than traditional FDI – than otherwise would have been the case.

Another important and closely related factor has been the phenomenal expansion of offshore financial markets in general, and that of the Euro-currency markets in particular[27]. The relatively short-term nature of the bulk of deposits in these markets and the banks' subsequent need to create relatively short-term assets have undoubtedly been a contributing element to the shortening of investment planning horizons. The large and rapidly growing volume of these markets has undoubtedly reinforced the emphasis on the purely financial logic of international investment decision making[28]. But equally important, it has also made possible the division of risks and responsibilities between firms and banks, as can be seen by the phenomenal growth during the 1970s of "sovereign loans" and later of "project loans" to developing countries. In the past few years the substantial increase in interest rates in these markets also probably reinforced the tendency for firms to minimise long-term equity investments: firms without surplus capital hesitated to borrow to undertake new investment, and those with surplus financial capital often preferred to place it in the financial markets. This no doubt also increased their propensity to use new forms of investment.

### ii) Conditions in Individual Home Countries

Another set of factors reflects changing economic conditions in specific investors' home countries. One factor is the structural shift in the balance of payments situations of a number of industrialised countries which occurred in the late 1960s and early 1970s. That is, just as the predominance of FDI in the 1950s and 1960s may be seen as a reflection of the combined influences of the international strength of the U.S. dollar, at a time when the European and Japanese economies were absorbed in reconstruction, and the marked preference of U.S. firms for retaining whole or majority ownership of their foreign investments, so might it be argued that the crisis of the dollar and the appearance or reinforcement of structural balance-of-payments surpluses in Japan and Germany, on the other, both of which occurred in the late 1960s/early 1970s, explain at least in part the importance gained by the new forms of investment at this time.

As regards the crisis of the dollar, the explosion of the U.S. balance of payments deficit led the U.S. government to restrict capital outflows from the U.S., including direct foreign investment, during this period[29]. The restrictive measures may have pressured U.S. firms investing abroad to devise strategies involving reduced outflows of financial capital and increased leverage on assets, and/or greater reliance on non-U.S. sources of financial capital, especially Euro-market and host-country sources of funds. One logical result of these restrictive measures was a greater incentive for U.S. firms to "unbundle" the traditional FDI investment package and use various new forms in order to increase their leverage on financial and other assets (such as licensing for technology, etc.), and to share ownership with local partners as a means to facilitate access to local sources of finance. Another result of these measures, reinforced by the lower interest-rate margins in Euro-markets during the early 1970s, was undoubtedly a tendency for U.S. firms to rely less on intra-firm loans and other intra-firm sources of funds, and turn to external sources of financial capital, notably the Euro-market, to finance their foreign investment activities[30]. In some cases this shift in firms' financial strategies took the form of wholly/majority-U.S.-owned subsidiaries in developing countries borrowing directly from international financial markets; in others it helped bring about the three-way division of risks and responsibilities and a greater use of new forms of investment in developing countries by U.S. firms.

It was also precisely in the late 1960s and early 1970s that Japan began showing major balance of payments surpluses and some European economies, notably Germany, saw theirs reinforced, thereby creating or strengthening conditions favorable to foreign investment by firms based in those countries. Japan was even led to reverse her postwar policy of discouraging foreign investment[31]. Since European and Japanese firms appear on average to use new forms of investment more than do U.S. firms[32], it could be argued that the growing importance of the new forms since the late 1960s/early 1970s is in part simply a reflection of the rapid increase in the role of European and especially Japanese investment, and the corresponding decline of U.S. investment, as a proportion of total foreign investment in developing countries.

This hypothesis raises the question of why European and Japanese firms show a somewhat higher overall propensity to use new forms than do American firms. This question leads directly to the second category of factors cited above, namely the role of firm behaviour and inter-firm rivalry. One hypothesis, in other words, is that a greater willingness to share equity, to license technologies and, more generally, to use new forms of investment is a strategy commonly used by "newcomers" or "outsiders" trying to establish themselves in new markets. Depending on competitive conditions in a given industry, this can increase pressure on the "majors", notably U.S.-based multinationals, to follow suit. To this hypothesis we shall return below.

But in looking at the propensity of European and Japanese firms to use new forms of investment, other home-country factors should be mentioned at this point. The postwar pattern of capital formation and industrial integration in Europe, particularly since the formation of the European Economic Community, has been characterised by considerable firm specialisation and intra-industry integration across national frontiers. One result has been the development of a number of relatively specialised capital-goods producers which supply final-goods producers with machinery and equipment on a national or even Community-wide basis. Many of these capital-goods producers are small- to medium-size firms whose financial and/or managerial resources are often insufficient to support strategies of internationalisation based on traditional FDI. However, since the late 1960s various new forms – notably licensing and the turnkey cum technical-assistance contracts – have proved effective as a means for them to extend their markets to a number of developing countries, especially the more rapid industrialisers. The specific nature of industrial capital formation and integration in postwar Europe may, in other words, help explain why some European firms, notably in capital goods industries, have been relatively active users of certain new forms of investment in developing countries.

As regards Japan, the "industry restructuring" model developed by Kojima and Ozawa[33] refers to a number of home-country factors which may be of major importance in explaining the "revealed preference" of Japanese investors in using various new forms of investment in developing countries, both in the extractive industries and some manufacturing industries. These factors include Japan's heavy reliance on imported petroleum and other primary products to feed her fast-growing industry; increasing home-country demands for environmental protection, which create new constraints on pollution-prone resource-transformation (e.g. smelting) and manufacturing industries; and rapid growth-induced increases in labour costs which have sharply limited profit margins in relatively "mature" industries, on the one hand, and rapid increases in Japan's technological capacity and capital stock which have created the conditions necessary for the restructuring of the economy towards more technology- and capital-intensive industries, on the other. As regards foreign investment by Japan's manufacturing firms, Ozawa explains:

"As their home-based production deteriorates as a result of changing factor endowment, some of them may succeed in shifting to higher value-added lines of product by upgrading corporate technology, but many of them may also choose to relocate themselves in more labour-abundant or more resource-abundant (and environmentally congruous) developing countries. Since many investors are small to medium enterprises, their capital resources are somewhat limited. Moreover, since their technology is not new, the appropriability of such technology is low. As a consequence, the enterprises themselves are not interested in setting up wholly or majority-owned ventures... Minority-owned joint ventures are usually the most appropriate modes of operation[34]".

Thus, Japanese industry has so far transplanted to developing countries such low value-added manufacturing activities as textiles, footwear, apparel, toys, electric household appliances, and labor-intensive intermediate products, mostly in the form of joint ventures in which Japanese investors willingly held minority interests[35].

And as regards Japan's overseas investment in the primary sector, Ozawa clarifies the situation as follows:

"Japan, being natural-resource-indigent, is particularly active in accepting whatever demands are made by host countries about forms of investment as long as the social benefits (if not the private benefits) of securing overseas resources are greater than the private costs of such operations. As a result, a variety of government subsidies are provided to share the costs with private Japanese investors. Besides, the social costs of running resource-based industries (such as smelting) in Japan have risen to such an extent that Japan is now eager to transfer resource-processing activities overseas, so long as secure supplies of processed resources are assured. Japanese industry is, in fact, taking the initiative to work out new forms of operations, such as "loan-and-import" contracts, production sharing, and provision of economic aid for the infrastructures needed for extractive and processing ventures. (...)

"In order to secure oil supplies Japan is also assisting many oil-rich countries to set up social-overhead facilities (such as utility plants, desalination plants, telecommunications networks, schools, and residential and shopping centers) as well as resource-based manufacturing complexes (such as petrochemical complexes and integrated steel mills). These ventures are carried out under a variety of new forms, including turnkey operations, management and marketing contracts, and gradual divestment."[36]

Ozawa further explains that Japanese foreign ventures in minerals and oil extraction commonly use the "loan and import" approach to securing access to vital raw materials, whereby Japanese importers of raw materials extend concessionary long-term loans to host-country extractive firms in exchange for assured and, they hope, favourable long-term supply contracts[37]. Not only does this strategy provide the host-developing-country firms with two key components of an "unbundled" foreign investment package unaccompanied by foreign ownership, namely financial capital and access to world export markets, it also is attractive to Japanese firms wary of sinking large sums of direct investment capital in foreign extractive ventures. He also stresses that about 80 per cent of Japan's overseas ventures in the extractive industries operating with majority or 100 per cent equity are unprofitable as individual ventures, operating either at a loss or breaking even. Thus, while it is the interest paid on loans under the "loan and import" arrangements that currently constitute the major source of direct income from these investments[38], the primary goal pursued by Japanese investors is a secure supply of resources, with such interest income constituting only a secondary or incidental receipt.

The Japanese experience with new forms of investment is certainly of great importance for our understanding of worldwide investment trends, if for no other reason than because of the pressures exerted by Japanese firms on those of other countries to follow suit. But one wonders how applicable as a home-country factor the "industry restructuring" model is to countries other than Japan in trying to explain the use of new forms of investment in developing countries. One could argue, for example, that a country like Germany is just as indigent as Japan in many raw materials needed to feed her fast growing industry. But German extractive firms have not shown a comparable willingness to use new forms of investment. One characteristic which may be rather unique to Japan is the widely discussed but apparently poorly understood relationship between private enterprise and the public sector, which provides the foundation for firms to undertake ventures where such social benefits as securing access to raw materials for the home economy transcend the private benefits of individual investment projects or even of individual investors. A second and closely related characteristic is undoubtedly the role of Japan's leading trading companies in internalising the externalities to be derived from Japanese foreign investment, new forms as well as traditional FDI.

Nonetheless, the industry-restructuring model does serve to highlight a number of points related to overall, changing economic conditions in investors' home countries, which may help explain global trends in the use of new forms of investment. One is the rapid increase in labour costs, which may encourage a country's relatively labour-intensive firms in "mature" manufacturing industries to relocate in lower-wage developing countries. As Ozawa points out[39] this pattern seems to fit quite well a number of Asian countries – for example Korea and Singapore – whose governments have recently begun pursuing industrial restructuring policies and some of whose firms are gaining importance as investors in other developing countries. In partial contrast to the Kojima-Ozawa model, many of these "third world multinationals" appear, by local standards at least, to be among the larger firms. But even more important, the available evidence suggests that these firms rely very heavily on various new forms of investment in their overseas ventures in developing countries[40].

The model also serves to highlight the central importance of differential rates of national capital accumulation and the accompanying development of national techno-logical capacity in different home countries. In any given country, and quite aside from the balance of payments factor mentioned previously, these factors may create both pressures on, and the conditions necessary for, local firms to expand internationally through foreign investment. To the extent that the technological lead of the U.S. economy in the postwar period, which benefitted U.S. firms in their global expansion, is diminishing relative to other home economies (notably Japan, and some European countries), and to the extent that firms from the latter countries pursue strategies involving the use of new forms of investment, the closing "technological gap" may in turn lead U.S. firms to increase their use of new forms of investment as well. It is equally conceivable, however, that with the closing of the technological gap, the trend will be for the "latecomers" to turn increasingly to traditional FDI as their foreign investment activities expand into more technologically sophisticated industries. The overall trend will of course be strongly influenced by industry-specific and host-country-specific, as well as home-country-specific, factors. But just as overall trends in capital accumulation and technological development in a given home country are as much a result as a cause of firm behaviour and the nature of inter-firm competition, so must the dynamics of firm behaviour and inter-firm competition be seen as fundamental to understanding trends in the use of new and traditional forms of international investment in developing countries.

## B. The Companies

### i)  Firm Behaviour

By way of introduction to our discussion of the dynamics of firm behaviour and inter-firm competition in explaining why firms use new or traditional forms of investment, let us first briefly look at what the massive literature to come out in recent years on international production and the multinational enterprise has to offer by way of explanation of foreign investment in general[41].

To begin with, there is virtually unanimous agreement among students of the multinational firm that the rapid growth of FDI in the postwar period cannot be adequately explained by portfolio theories of investment based on neoclassical assumptions of competitive factor markets within countries and product markets internationally. Rather, the consensus is that the growth of FDI must be understood as the result above all of so-called market-structure imperfections and the monopolistic advantages possessed by international investors both at home and abroad. These firm-specific advantages – seen primarily as "intangible assets", such as patented technology, differentiated product or brand image, marketing skills, etc. – both encourage growing firms to internationalise their activities (e.g., in order to avoid undercutting monopoly rents and/or upsetting a potentially unstable oligopolistic equilibrium at home) on the one hand, and are what allow them to successfully compete abroad with local firms (whose superior knowledge of local conditions would otherwise give them a competitive edge) on the other[42].

The essence of foreign investment and the internationalisation of production in general is thus understood not as the transfer of financial capital, but as the internationalisation of firms' *control* over the organisation of production and/or distribution. "Market imperfections" are seen as providing firms with the incentive to bypass markets and capitalise on – "internalise"[43] – the rent-generating possibilities created by these imperfections through hierarchically controlled means, that is, through international *investment* rather than exports. These conclusions are, we believe, applicable on the whole to new forms of investment just as they are to traditional FDI.

Of crucial significance for our purposes, however, is the fact that much of the literature seeking to explain the growth of multinational firms and international investment focusses only on traditional FDI, in which the internationalisation of firms' *control* is accompanied by an internationalisation of *ownership* rights over investment projects. Nowhere in the literature have we found an explicit argument that the control required by firms to appropriate rents from their monopolistic advantages through foreign investment must be based on the firm's ownership of the investment project itself, as distinct from its "intangible assets", but the new forms are rarely considered in any depth in their own right[44].

84

One reason for this "omission" appears to be an assumption by many authors that the monopolistic advantages derived by investors from their intangible assets, which are the *sine qua non* of foreign investment, require at least majority ownership of the *tangible* assets and output, which in turn embody the intangible assets from which the rents are derived[45].

Thus, for example, one author who recognises the growing importance of what we call "new forms of investment" but who argues that traditional FDI is inherently superior, makes the revealing statement that, "There is no "market" for proprietory information in the generally accepted use of the term. There are no homogeneous products being priced; indeed there is no price per unit of knowledge. The "market" does not exist... Instead all we observe are the results of specific deals."[46] The author's point in making this observation, which in itself we find correct, is basically that relative to FDI, the new forms of investment are characterised by significant transaction and enforcement costs – those which a firm incurs in finding a suitable local partner, negotiating, monitoring and enforcing an agreement, etc. – and by significant risk that a firm's monopolistic advantages will be dissipated. He sees traditional FDI as minimising or avoiding these costs and risks.

Given our interest in explaining the growing use of new forms of investment in the North-South context, the author's comment serves, first of all, to highlight the distinct possibility that in many developing countries the transaction and enforcement costs associated with new forms of investment may in fact be decreasing, and/or those associated with traditional FDI at least in some cases may have increased since the 1960s[47]. The potential significance of the point brought out by the strategic-initiative hypothesis regarding the consolidation of power by, and "Westernisation" or "modernisation" of managerial and negotiating styles of local elites in many developing countries – which may be reducing the costs of finding suitable local partners, of negotiation, enforcement, etc. – should not be underestimated in this regard. Also, the substantial improvements in infrastructure and especially communications networks both within some developing countries and internationally in recent years may have substantially reduced costs of monitoring, etc., and thereby facilitate parent-company control of worldwide operations even in the absence of full or majority ownership of operations in some host countries[48]. Nor should one discount the possibility that transaction and enforcement costs associated with traditional FDI may have increased significantly since the 1960s (as brought out by the defensive-reaction hypothesis) due, among other things, to host-government pressures for renegotiation and imposition of performance requirements. In short, whereas the importance of transaction and enforcement costs associated with foreign investment have led some authors to argue for the inherent superiority of traditional FDI, the nature of their change over the last decade or so may in fact be one reason why new forms of investment are becoming increasingly more viable, or less unattractive, compared to FDI, in the North-South context. They may also be one reason why contractual arrangements in general, and bilateral investment treaties in particular[49], appear to be gaining importance in the North-South context as well – a point to which we return in Chapter 5.

Secondly, by focussing on the highly "imperfect" nature, or practical non-existence, of markets for firms' intangible assets, the observation cited above also serves to highlight the all-important role of barriers to market entry in explaining foreign investment[50]. One extremely important implication of this observation, and of the literature on FDI in general, is that just as is the case with traditional FDI, the *new forms of investment cannot be understood in the absence of monopoly power*[51].

Whereas the above-cited author, and many others, recognise the central importance of firms' monopolistic advantages in explaining foreign investment, they generally portray these advantages as primarily the result of "natural" market imperfections reflecting the public-good nature of knowledge (knowledge being defined broadly to cover most firm-specific "intangible assets", such as technology, management and marketing know-how, and the like)[52]. Given our interest in considering firms' potential for creating or maintaining rent-creating monopolistic advantages in the absence of full and exclusive ownership rights over a foreign investment project, however, the distinction between "natural" and firm-created barriers to entry – which may exist even in the absence of ownership rights on the one hand, and of "natural" market imperfections on the other – becomes critical. In other words, to the extent that a firm can create barriers to entry and/or appropriate rents from its "intangible assets" without having to establish property rights over an investment project, a new form of investment may be just as effective as FDI for purposes of rent appropriation. It may even be preferable, to the extent that fewer funds or other "tangible" assets must be committed, that is, to the extent that the firm can achieve greater leverage on its intangible and/or tangible capital.

In the case of horizontal foreign investment, i.e. international investment in the same product line, trademark or brand image is a classic example of firm-created barriers to entry. Thus, in the hotel industry, franchising may be the most cost-effective means for a hotel chain to capitalise on its firm-specific monopolistic advantages[53]. And in the case of undifferentiated products, like raw materials or "mature" price-competitive manufacturing industries, firms' pursuit of monopolistic advantages may lead to high concentration through vertical (upstream) integration and/or the establishment of exclusive "internalised" (downstream) global marketing networks[54]. In both cases economies of global integration, not to mention firms' monopolistic advantages in their home-country markets, may constitute effective barriers to entry such that ownership of production by firms in the host country is not required for appropriation of monopoly rents[55].

Thirdly, the crucial role of information and technology in explaining foreign investment has also led some authors to develop the notion of "industry technology cycle", sometimes referred to as the appropriability theory[56] – and not to be confused with the concept of "product life cycle" discussed below. Because sophisticated or rapidly changing technologies generally constitute more effective barriers to entry and thus offer greater rent-appropriating potential than do simple or standardised technologies, these authors see a strong incentive for the economic system as a whole to generate sophisticated technologies – in some cases to the detriment of users' needs, notably those of developing countries. And because intra-firm channels are considered to constitute the most effective and profitable means of information transmission, with the fundamental characteristic of young industries being the rapid creation of new information, this approach sees the optimum size of firms increasing as an industry develops. Thus, there is a tendency for FDI to result in takeovers of local firms rather than "green-field" or "de novo" investments, in part because takeovers and mergers serve to maintain or reinforce barriers to entry by absorbing the most likely local competitors. One possible implication of this interpretation, particularly under conditions of high capital costs and/or host-government pressures to limit foreign ownership, is that joint ventures with local firms are a predictable outcome of international expansion by firms in a young, growing industry.

As the period of intensive innovation runs its course and the creation of information decelerates, an industry reaches maturity and, according to the appropriability theory, the optimum size of the firm decreases. Moreover the efficiency and profitability of licensing – or other new forms of investment, depending on the specific industry – increase in relation to FDI in the international expansion of firms' rent seeking activity. In other words, the industry-technology-cycle hypothesis predicts an increasing use of new forms of investment, especially licensing, as industries mature. This prediction is certainly not inconsistent with the general trends we described for the manufacturing sector in Chapter 3[57].

It does not however explain them fully. Another interpretation, which stands in partial contrast to the industry-technology-cycle hypothesis, points out that new forms of investment may proliferate as firms in maturing industries tend to substitute greater reliance on competitive advantages in international trade and access to capital markets for those in local production and marketing in host countries, on which they may have relied more heavily in the 1950s and 1960s. Rather than witnessing a decrease in the optimum size of firms, some maturing industries may witness just the opposite, as economies of scale in worldwide distribution and finance replace technological advantages in production and/or local marketing in host countries. As developing countries' need for access to industrialised countries' markets has not declined in most raw materials industries and has significantly increased in many manufacturing and some service industries – not to mention the developing countries' need for access to international financial markets, supplier's credits and the like – there is good reason to think such a trend has indeed accelerated since the late 1960s. Thus, new forms of investment may be increasingly used, not because of a decreasing optimum size of firms in mature industries as predicted by the industry-technology-cycle, but on the contrary, because of the important monopolistic advantages to be derived from economies of scale in international trade and finance.

The growth strategies pursued by many of Japan's leading trading companies appear to be a good illustration of this last interpretation. The monopolistic advantages of these firms undoubtedly originated in their home market, but the leading trading companies appear to be rapidly expanding those advantages internationally. Moreover, while they rely heavily on traditional ownership rights in setting up their own branch offices abroad as they internalise international transactions on a global scale, they simultaneously play a leading role in promoting and organising new forms of investment in developing countries, usually bringing in Japanese manufacturing and raw-materials firms and taking an active role themselves as joint investors, providers of loans, buyers of products, brokers of technology and "suppliers of all other conceivable business services"[58].

### ii) Inter-firm competition on a global scale

Useful as the market-imperfections/monopolistic-advantages paradigm is in explaining why firms may use FDI rather than exports as a vehicle for international expansion, we have seen that it does not go far enough to explain why firms may use new forms rather than traditional FDI. One reason is that many authors assume that traditional FDI is inherently a "first-best" solution because of firms' need for ownership of the tangible assets and output of an investment project in order to ensure maximum appropriation of the rents generated by the "intangible assets" in which the firms have monopolistic advantages.

A second reason for this limitation, we believe, is that the literature tends to focus on the *monopolistic* advantages possessed by firms, but gives relatively limited attention to analysing the specific *oligopolistic* nature of inter-firm rivalry and interdependence on a global scale. While the role of firm-specific monopolistic advantages is necessary to understand the growth of both new forms of investment and traditional FDI, the dynamics of competition among firms internationally appear to be of major importance in understanding the growing use of new forms of investment, as distinct from traditional FDI.

Probably the most widely known interpretation to focus on the interdependence of firms competing internationally, within a given industry, is Vernon's "product life cycle" hypothesis[59]. He sees firms reacting to the threat of losing export markets as their product "matures", that is, as the barriers to market entry weaken and the product's technology becomes more widely disseminated and "standardised". Firms shift from a strategy of servicing foreign markets, and capturing rents derivable from the technology embodied in the product, to FDI in order to capture the remaining rent derivable from the products' development. The hypothesis makes no predictions, however, as regards the use of new versus traditional forms of foreign investment.

More recent analyses highlight the key role of inter-firm competition in a context of oligopolistic interdependence and focus on such phenomena as the "follow the leader" strategy, where the investment moves of one firm trigger similar moves by other leading firms in the industry, and the "exchange of threats" strategy, where oligopolistic competitors imitate each other by establishing subsidiaries or affiliates in each other's markets[60]. The "follow the leader" and "exchange of threats" hypotheses were originally formulated to explain firms' overseas expansion through FDI, not through new forms of investment. However, since the internationalisation of oligopolistic competition during the 1970s increased pressures on firms to take investment positions in numerous markets at a time when capital costs were rising and cash-flow problems were mounting due to depressed conditions at home, these hypotheses may help explain why many firms turned increasingly to joint ventures and other new forms of investment in association with the local business community, on the one hand, and to increased borrowing on international financial markets on the other. That is, firms whose resources are stretched thin may be turning to new forms of investment in developing countries as a defensive reaction not to host-government policies but to inter-firm competitive pressures in a context of international oligopoly.

These trends have probably been accentuated by the perceptible shift in the very nature of international oligopolistic inter-firm rivalry over the last decade or so, from one dominated by local competition in individual host and home countries to a globalisation of inter-firm rivalry in many industries[61]. One reason for this shift has of course been the dramatic increase in corporate players entering the foreign investment scene, including not only private European and Japanese firms and state-owned enterprises previously restricted to their domestic markets, but private and state enterprises based in developing countries as well. Many of these "outsiders" or "newcomers" have used new forms of investment as a competitive strategy to establish positions in foreign markets, bringing pressure to bear on the "majors" in some cases to follow suit[62].

This globalisation of oligopolistic inter-firm rivalry, combined with the economic slowdown which has plagued the OECD region as a whole, has been accompanied by growing strategic emphasis in some industries on cost reduction, including some industries which had previously relied on product differentiation as a competitive strategy. One result has of course been an increasing use, notably by U.S.-based firms in the electronics and textile industries, not of industrial restructuring as described in the Kojima-Ozawa model for Japan, but of international subcontracting with firms in a number of Asian and Latin American developing countries. These strategies seek to reduce costs both by taking advantage of significantly lower wage rates in the host countries and by reducing the capital costs of expanding capacity at home – a significant factor in times of depressed or fluctuating demand conditions. Whether this particular new form of investment will continue to gain importance is somewhat doubtful, however, because of more recent tendencies (notably in the semi-conductor industry) to introduce robots and other types of highly automated production, accompanied by a relocation of production back to the home country[63].

Another trend which has characterised the globalisation of oligopolistic competition and increased emphasis on cost reduction has been the tendency towards global rationalisation of operations, as exemplified by Ford's global production strategy. Since even minor conflicts with local partners could disrupt a firm's global operations and since host governments welcome such export-oriented foreign investment, often with generous incentives[64], it is widely believed that firms pursuing global rationalisation strategies will be extremely averse to using new forms of investment or even taking on minority local partners[65]. In other words, global rationalisation strategies which seek to reduce costs in a context of global oligopolistic competition presumably work against the use of new forms of investment. However, a recent study of the global-product managerial systems introduced by many U.S. firms during the 1970s shows that firms that introduced such systems have relatively high levels of ownership-sharing and licensing:

> "In most companies, the change to a global product organisation has significantly reduced the scope of international commitment. Attention shifts from reliance on investment to emphasis on licensing. Global product companies view licensing more favourably than other forms of investment[66]."

Be that as it may – and it should be stressed that the authors are not addressing the issue of investment in developing countries *per se* – it does not appear that the globalisation of inter-firm oligopolistic rivalry is necessarily going to be accompanied by massive redeployment of industry from the industrialised to the developing countries, either through new forms of investment or via traditional FDI.

In sum, if the growing use of new forms of investment reflects the internationalisation of firms' *control* over the organisation of production and/or distribution in order to appropriate rents from their competitive advantages, particularly in "intangible assets", the extent to which new forms supersede traditional FDI as the dominant strategy in the North-South context will depend upon the dynamics of oligopolistic inter-firm rivalry in an increasingly globalised competitive framework. These competitive dynamics will in turn influence and be influenced by such factors as differential rates of capital accumulation and technological development in firms' individual home countries and, perhaps more than ever, growth-cycle trends in the world economy as a whole. The tendency for those responsible for investment decisions to react to risk and uncertainty by shortening their investment time planning horizons and by seeking to avoid the risks of longer-term engagements in productive investment in favour of shorter-term portfolio-type investment strategies may prove crucial in this regard.

As we have seen, the growing use of new forms has reflected a certain intensification of inter-firm rivalry internationally which accompanied the economic slowdown of the OECD region as a whole. In the 1970s many "newcomers" entered the multinational investment scene, and there was a globalisation of oligopolistic structures. Meanwhile, the economies of a number of capital-surplus oil-exporting countries soared. However, a stabilisation of oligopolistic competition and a levelling-off of oil exporters' revenue surpluses may reveal the growth in importance of new forms of investment to have been a relatively transitory phenomenon. Much will depend on whether at least some of the new forms of investment have proved to offer longer-run advantages, compared to traditional FDI, both as a means for firms to extend their control of production and/or distribution internationally and as a means for local elites in host countries to internationalise their economic bases as well. To the latter point we shall return in Chapter 5.

# NOTES AND REFERENCES

1. This chapter draws extensively from secondary sources. Many of the arguments and "conclusions" presented here will serve as hypotheses to be tested and refined in the second phase of the Centre's research, which will generate more primary data at the level of individual firms and industries.

2. It would be consistent with this approach to argue that "free markets" are "first best" not only from the firms' point of view but in terms of international economic "efficiency", and hence from the host countries' standpoint, in a Pareto-optimal sense, as well.

3. In a paper on "Increasing Private Investment in Developing Countries: the Impediments and the Outlook" prepared by the North-South Institute for the OECD's Business and Industry Advisory Committee on Development (February 1980), J. Adams points out that certain trade and fiscal policies pursued in industrialised countries may constitute important market imperfections, and that "home country restrictions and continuing pressures to impose them remain one of the more serious potential impediments to foreign investments." (p. 15)

4. On the subject of executives' perceptions Adams thus comments that, "For the most part, the concept of an impediment to investment is a relative one. The perception of the degree of hindrance presented for example by certain government policies, by structural economic problems, or by political uncertainty, will often vary significantly from one potential or actual investor to another. One investor's impediment is another's inconvenience. Underlying these variations are distinct subjective and objective appraisals of the investment climate, and different perceptions of the expected rate of return on capital invested." (*Ibid.*, p. 2)

5. See Eduardo White, "Evolution and Recent Trends in Host Developing Countries' Policies vis-à-vis TNCs," paper prepared for UNCTC, Buenos Aires, April, 1982. White points out that these policy changes occurred rather "suddenly" and in only about 20 developing countries, while the majority of developing countries maintained traditional open-door policies. But, he notes, "the international repercussion of a trend which involved not much more than 20 countries is explained by the fact that such countries were the markets for about two-thirds of the overall participation of TNCs in the developing world, and were considered as the main areas of attraction for the future. They were the largest, most advanced, fast growing and semi-industrialised countries and sub-regions of Latin America and Asia." (pp. 4-5).

6. Data on nationalisations and expropriations in natural resource extraction by developing countries through 1976 are presented, for example, by D.A. Jodice, "Sources of change in Third World regimes for foreign direct investment, 1968-1976," in *International Organization*, Vol. 34, No. 2, Spring 1980.

7. The U.N. General Assembly's declarations on permanent sovereignty and the initiation in various U.N. bodies in the early 1970s of the sometimes acrimonious debates and negotiations on international codes of conduct for transnational corporations and technology transfer undoubtedly reinforced these perceptions of a deteriorating investment climate in the developing countries.

8. Cf. R. Vernon, *Sovereignty at Bay: the Multinational Spread of U.S. Enterprises,* (New York: Basic Books, 1971), pp. 46-53.

9. See e.g. C.H. MacMillan, "Trends in East-West Industrial Co-operation", *Journal of International Business Studies,* Fall, 1981.

10. F. Root and A. Ahmed, "The Influence of Policy Instruments on Manufacturing Direct Investment in Developing Countries", in *Journal of International Business Studies,* Vol. 9, Winter 1978.

11. See White, *op. cit.*, pp. 49-50.

12. *Ibid,* pp. 52-53

13. Among the countries in our study, such has clearly been the case in Peru and the Philippines, and most recently in India, Korea and Algeria. It is also interesting to note the movement towards more flexible policies on FDI since the mid-1970s in a number of socialist countries. Such has been the case, e.g., of Rumania and Hungary in the North and of Angola, Mozambique, Guyana and Vietnam in the South. Another interesting example is the "Law on Joint Ventures using Chinese and Foreign Investment" promulgated by the People's Republic of China in 1979.

14. Interviews with a number of business groups indicate that in general the investment climate in developing countries is seen by business as having improved on the whole in recent years.

15. Cf. "Ways to Beat Exchange Rules", *Business Week*, 26 October 1981.

16. Cf. P. Evans, *Dependent Development* (Princeton U.P., 1979) p. 135. This author also focusses considerable attention on the broader role which local élites may play in integrating foreign capital into the host economy, especially into what he calls the "solidary nonmarket ties among economic élites". He argues that "foreign groups with partners embedded in the local social structure have a special competitive advantage over those which lack such partners. The industrial order overall requires the existence of such integrative roles. When the roles are performed by individual members of the local bourgeoisie, these people are in a position to demand a share of the returns that accrue from cooperation. When integrative roles are played by owners of large-scale capital, they can go beyond that and participate not just in the returns but in shaping the process of accumulation." He also points out that this "integrative role" may be an important source of bargaining power for local élites in their dealings with foreign investors, "at least in so far as the role is self conscious." (pp. 162-163)

17. See for example Business International Corp., *International Licensing*, 1977; and F.J. Contractor, *International Technology Licensing* (Lexington: D.C. Heath and Co., 1981).

18. German firms reportedly use this technique with some frequency. Cf. C. Pollak, *op. cit.*

19. See Ghorbel, *op. cit.*

20. Conditions of high uncertainty do not always lead firms to shy away from investment opportunities or to prefer new forms, of course; it depends on the type of uncertainty. For example, if the likelihood of recovering initial investment is reasonably high, with considerable uncertainty as to whether returns will be simply normal or, say, 1000 per cent during normal payback period, then a firm may show great reluctance to even share equity. That is, in order to reap maximum benefits from such a potentially "explosive" business opportunity in a developing country, such uncertainties as these may lead firms to prefer the traditional form of FDI.

21. Such was reportedly the case, to cite only one notorious example, of an auto plant sold several years ago to Egypt by Fiat.

22. An interesting example here might be the Peruvian experience with its Cerro Verde mine (Cf. Gonzalez Vigil and Parodi, *op. cit.*).

23. The major international mining companies are not infrequently involved in these projects. But as Abdallah-Khodja pointed out for the Algerian case, whereas under traditional FDI engineering firms are often subcontractors for mining operations, under turnkey contracts the relationship is often inverted, with engineering firms playing the leading role and mining firms involved as subcontractors.

24. An interesting example is the Peruvian crackers and cookie industry, where in the early 1970s a number of medium-size wholly Peruvian owned firms acquired relatively sophisticated continuous-process technology from Swiss and Italian equipment producers on a turnkey-cum-technical-assistance basis. These Peruvian firms competed directly with a couple of larger wholly foreign (U.S.) owned firms using more standardised technology. The Peruvian owned firms reportedly competed quite successfully during the relatively expansionary period of the Peruvian market in the early 1970s, although with the severe downturn of the economy in the mid-1970s a number of the Peruvian-owned firms were apparently forced out of business.

25. Cf. "Investment and Productivity: A Business View", Position Paper of the Business and Industry Advisory Committee to the OECD, April 1980.

26. For a criticism of U.S. business management tendencies to overemphasize short-term financial returns see for example R. Hayes and W. Abernathy, "Managing our way to economic decline," in *Harvard Business Review*, July-August 1980; and "The Money Chase", in *Time*, May 4, 1981.

27. See for example P. Wellons, *Borrowing by Developing Countries on the Eurocurrency Market*, OECD Development Centre, 1977.

28. Cf. E.L. Versluysen, *The Political Economy of International Finance* (Westmead: Gower, 1981).

29. In 1965 U.S. banks were given "voluntary" ceilings, monitored by the Federal Reserve, on their loans to non-resident entities. A second set of voluntary restrictions was designed to curtail direct overseas investments by U.S. corporations. In January 1968 these restrictions, renamed "Foreign Direct Investment Program" were made mandatory and specific quotas were put on the transfer abroad of net direct investments, financed from U.S. sources, by non-financial organisations. Cf. *The Banker*, London, March, 1973, p. 252.

30. "Voluntary" and mandatory restrictions ... provided a strong incentive for U.S. corporations to seek offshore finance for their international expansion." "Euro-currency loans are often cheaper for the borrower than comparable facilities obtained in domestic markets. This is due to the fact that lending

margins – the difference between the lender's cost of funds and the interest rate charged to the borrower – are often smaller than in domestic banking." E.L. Versluysen, *op. cit.,* pp. 24, 40.

31. Japanese outward investment rose from a relatively insignificant $275 million in 1967, to over $2 800 million by 1977, with over half of total foreign investment going to developing countries (data cited from Y. Tsurumi, *The Japanese are Coming,* Cambridge, Mass., 1977).

32. Franko, *op. cit.,* reports that of almost 800 subsidiaries established by European (non-U.S. parent) firms in developing countries in the early 1970s, 34 per cent were wholly-owned and another 32 per cent majority-owned, whereas figures for U.S. firms' subsidiaries were 57 per cent wholly-owned and 19 per cent majority-owned in the same period. Comparable figures for U.S. firms' subsidiaries established in the mid-1970s are 48 per cent wholly-owned and 14 per cent majority-owned, suggesting a shift by U.S. firms to somewhat greater use of minority-owned ventures in the mid-1970s as compared to a few years earlier, but still a greater use of wholly-owned subsidiaries than European and especially Japanese firms. See also T. Ozawa, op. cit., for a discussion of Japanese firms' "revealed preference" for new forms of investment.

33. Cf. K. Kojima, *Direct Foreign Investment: A Japanese Model of Multinational Business Operations* (London: Croom Helm, 1978); and T. Ozawa, *Multinationalism, Japanese Style: The Political Economy of Outward Dependency* (Princeton University Press, 1979).

34. Ozawa, *op. cit.,* pp. 29-30.

35. *Ibid.,* p. 33.

36. *Ibid.,* pp. 34-35.

37. Thus, for example, in 1978 approximately 50 per cent of the copper ore and 30 per cent of the iron ore Japan imported were obtained under the loan-and-import arrangement. (*Ibid.,* p. 10)

38. Japanese overseas ventures in the extraction of minerals and oil reportedly derive about 94 per cent of their profits from interest on loans extended to overseas affiliates. (*Ibid.,* p. 9)

39. *Ibid.,* p. 30

40. The second phase of our research will also examine the strategies of outward investment pursued by firms from some developing countries. For an analysis of "third world multinationals", see for example K. Kumar and M. McLeod (eds.), *Multinationals from Developing Countries,* D.C. Heath and Co., Lexington, Mass., 1981; and L.T. Wells, *Third World Multinationals: The Rise of Foreign Investment from Developing Countries* (MIT Press, forthcoming).

41. For a survey of some of this literature see, e.g., A.L. Calvet, "A Synthesis of Foreign Direct Investment Theories and Theories of the Multinational Firm," in *Journal of International Business Studies,* Spring/Summer, 1981.

42. The crucial importance of firms' monopolistic power in explaining FDI was first brought out by Stephen Hymer in his seminal thesis of 1960, and since developed by many others. Cf. S. Hymer, *The International Operations of National Firms : A Study of Direct Foreign Investment,* MIT Press, 1976.

43. Cf. the literature on "internalisation" as a sweeping theory of FDI, especially J.C. McManus, "The Theory of the International Firm", in *The Multinational Firm and the Nation State,* edited by C. Paquet, (Collier-Macmillan, Toronto, 1972; and P.I. Buckley and M.C. Casson, *The Future of the Multinational Enterprise,* Macmillan, London, 1976.

44. A notable exception is the recent work of John Dunning. See e.g., J.H. Dunning, "Non-equity forms of foreign economic involvement and the theory of international production," University of Reading Discussion Paper No. 59, February, 1982. Also, for an analysis of licensing, see P. Buckley and H. Davies, "The place of licensing in the theory and practice of foreign operations," University of Reading Discussion Paper No. 47, November 1979; and F. Contractor, *International Technology Licensing,* D.C. Heath, Lexington, 1981.

45. For a clarification of why we question the strength of this assumption, see Section III of Chapter 1.

46. A. Rugman, *Inside the Multinationals: the Economics of Internal Markets,* Croom Helm, 1981, p. 70.

47. In a static context Dunning illustrates this point well: "Suppose the main ownership advantage of a firm is its superior management facilities. If, in a management contract, a firm can fully appropriate the economic rent of this asset (which implies the buyer is willing to pay at least the price which the seller knows it is worth) and it can protect (through the terms of the contract) the dissipation or misuse of the techniques and information provided, then why should it prefer direct investment to a management contract? A similar question may be asked where the ownership advantage is a trademark; it may be perfectly possible for a firm to fully exploit its economic rent by way of a franchising agreement. In these instances, it is postulated that control to protect the assets can be written into a contract and that the overall benefits are at least equal to profits on any equity investment (after discounting for risk)." J.H.

Dunning, "Non-Equity Forms of Foreign Economic Involvement: the Theory of International Production," University of Reading Discussion Paper No. 59, February, 1982, p. 14.

48. Recent analyses of transborder data flows and business strategies undertaken at both the United Nations and OECD are also of some interest here.

49. See A. Gourdain Mitsotaki, "Les Accords Intergouvernementaux Relatifs aux Investissements", *op. cit.*

50. The relatively firm-specific monopolistic advantages which constitute barriers to entry and may induce those possessing or seeking to create them to undertake foreign investment include, among others, technological advantages from patents, large R&D budgets (sometimes publicly subsidised), economies of scale (i.e., decreasing costs) in production, etc.; and marketing barriers through vertical integration product differentiation, multiproduct differentiation, brand image, multiproduct economies of scale in advertising and/or distribution, etc.

51. "It is essential to recognise that each MNE is a monopolist in its use of knowledge (or some other firm-specific advantage). Otherwise the MNE does not need either an internal market (FDI) or a contractual arrangement. When there is no monopoly in knowledge then a regular market suffices." Rugman, *op. cit.*, p. 71.

52. Authors using the expression "natural market imperfections" generally refer to three well known causes of "market failure": externalities, public goods, and decreasing-cost industries (sometimes referred to as natural monopolies). Cf. H. Johnson, "The Efficiency and Welfare Implications of the International Corporation" in C. Kindleberger (ed.), *The International Corporation*, MIT Press, 1970.

53. See Dunning's comment cited in footnote 47 above.

54. Referring to firm-created barriers to entry in primary exports, Diaz-Alejandro has pointed out that vertically integrated firms "routinely erect and protect barriers to entry, including hoarding mineral deposits, limiting technological diffusion and establishing exclusive market networks." (C. Diaz-Alejandro, "International Markets for Exhaustible Resources: Less Developed Countries and Transnational Corporations," Yale University Economic Growth Center Paper No. 256, 1976, p. 14.)

55. Particularly relevant in this regard are the global marketing networks and involvement in new forms of investment by Japanese Trading Companies. See Kojima and Ozawa, *op. cit.*

56. See in particular S. Magee, "Multinational Corporations, the Industry Technology Cycle and Developlent," *Journal of World Trade Law*, July/August, 1977.

57. Thus, for example, Ozawa uses the industry-technology-cycle approach in conjunction with his industry-restructuring model to explain some of the new forms of investment in developing countries by Japanese firms, notably the small and medium size firms in relatively mature industries. (Ozawa, *op. cit.*, pp. 25-32)

58. Ozawa, p. 36; See also Kojima and Ozawa, *op. cit.*

59. Cf. R. Vernon, "International Investment and International Trade in the Product Cycle," *Quarterly Journal of Economics*, May, 1966.

60. See for example, F.T. Knickerbocker, *Oligopolistic Reaction and Multinational Enterprise*, Harvard University Press, 1973.

61. See for example, W.H. Davidson and P. Haspelagh, "Shaping a Global Product Organization" in *Harvard Business Review*, July-August, 1982.

62. Franko points out for example that, "As whole sectors of industry mature, and as technology, knowhow and access to world markets diffuse over time, even industry leaders find themselves compelled by competition to offer joint ventures (and sometimes minority ventures or other "new forms") to countries whose governments insist on them... For example the Brazilian Government rejected a bid by IBM to produce mini-computers in a 100 per cent owned facility in the late 1970s and accepted Japanese and European minority joint ventures and licensing agreements instead. One result was an undramatic but palpable shift to a more flexible stance toward shared ownership, or other non-equity forms of cooperation on the part of IBM in countries such as Nigeria and Saudi Arabia. A similar evolution had occurred earlier in the automobile and oil refining and extractive industries where, after rejecting or resisting joint ventures in the 1950s and early 1960s, industry leaders such as General Motors and Exxon subsequently adopted a more accommodating stance. This occurred after "outsider" competitors gained exclusive access to particular markets or raw material sources, and thus gained world market share by offering ownership participation to local partners whose governments insisted on it." (Franko, *op. cit.*, pp. 22-23)

63. See for example D. Ernst, "Restructuring World Industry in a Period of Crisis – the Role of Innovation", UNIDO Working Paper on Structural Changes, Is.285; and L. Nowicki, "La Crise et les nouvelles stratégies d'investissement à l'échelle internationale" (mimeo, 1982).

93

64. See e.g. R. Cohen, "Internationalisation of the Auto Industry and its Employment Impact," SAE Technical Papers Series No. 820445, February 1982, cited in Nowicki, *ibid*, pp. 16-17.

65. Cf. J.M. Stopford and L.T. Wells, Jr., *Managing the Multinational Enterprise*, (New York: Basic Books, 1972), especially pp. 113-117.

66. Davidson and Haspeslagh, *op. cit.*, pp. 128-129.

*Chapter 5*

# CONSEQUENCES OF THE NEW FORMS

There can be little doubt that most multinational investors and developing countries perceive a common interest in promoting the international transfer of tangible and intangible productive resources. Nevertheless, tension in North-South investment relations in recent decades appears to stem from a perception by many developing countries that important divergencies of interest exist between host countries and foreign direct investors. For example, tensions often arise over the degree to which multinational firms promote or inhibit exports by their manufacturing subsidiaries in developing countries; over the extent to which they rely on local firms versus imports for necessary inputs; over multinatonal firms' use of transfer pricing; over the extent to which they bring in new financial capital or absorb local sources of funds; and over the extent to which they promote technology transfer and/or undertake R&D expenditures locally.

According to some, these conflicts reflect a partial contradiction between the "nationalist logic of accumulation" pursued by host-country élites and the logic of global profit maximisation and accumulation pursued by multinational firms[1]. To assess the implications of new forms of investment, then, one approach might be to try to identify the implications of new forms, relative to FDI, in accordance with the "logic of national accumulation" on the one hand, and with the "logic of global accumulation" on the other. Most importantly, they might be assessed in terms of the actual or potential advantages and disadvantages offered by new forms of investment in reconciling the two "logics" of accumulation.

Another approach might take as its point of departure the idea that it is difficult to identify two distinct "logics" of accumulation, but that within the logic of capital accumulation at the national or global level, conflicts of interest are bound to emerge among parties and groups competing for control over rents and profits in a short- to medium-term perspective and, in the longer-run, for control over the process of capital formation and the creation of profitable investment opportunities. If, as pointed out in Chapter 4, both traditional and new forms of foreign investment are best understood as the international extension by individual multinational firms of their control over production and/or marketing in order to appropriate rents from their firm-specific monopolistic advantages, it may similarly be argued that the interest shown by many developing-country élites – firms, private groups, governments – in "unbundling" FDI and in using new forms of investment is best understood as a reflection of their seeking to establish and/or take fuller advantage of their group-specific advantages to appropriate rents and to eventually increase their control over the process of investment and accumulation. It is logical that, as nationalist attitudes in the host country can reinforce local élites' group-specific advantages in their dealings with non-nationals, they should pursue a "logic of national accumulation".

Indeed, it has been argued that the group-specific advantages of host-country élites are primarily political in nature[2]. But there is no reason to think that their interests are intrinsically more confined to the national economy or more nationalistic than those of foreign investors – as the growing importance of "Third World multinationals" in recent years seems to confirm. The difference, of course, is that whereas the monopolistic advantages of multinational firms tend to be more technological and/or world-market and hence non-national in character – perhaps reflecting the greater advancement of capital formation in their home countries – the advantages of host countries tend to be more national in character. And, as a result, host-country élites often tend to be more sensitive than foreign investors to such "national" objectives as employment, development of local technological capacity or balance-of-payments equilibrium, at the very least in order to consolidate their social, political and economic bases of power, which are also their group-specific advantages when dealing with foreign investors.

Whether or not the implications of new forms of investment are assessed in a framework of two distinct "logics" or "the" logic of accumulation, then, the central issue may usefully be phrased, at a more concrete level, in terms of the relationship between *ownership* and *control* of investment and capital formation in developing countries. What the new forms have in common and, by definition, what distinguishes them from traditional FDI, is of course that ownership is not foreign but majority or wholly local. But the question is, does this partial or complete shift of ownership from foreign investors to their host-country partners imply an equivalent shift to the latter of effective control? Whereas foreign investors traditionally felt that ownership was necessary to ensure effective control, the new forms of investment offer the distinct possibility of a separation of ownership and control.

For individual host countries, the question may be expressed in terms of the actual or potential advantages and disadvantages offered by new forms, compared with FDI, as regards certain developmental, structural or even balance-of-payments objectives. These objectives might include, for example, enhancing local firms' access to and/or competitiveness on world export markets as well as their competitiveness at home (both of which may have important structural as well as employment and balance-of-payments implications); increasing the volume and local share of rents derivable from the country's extractive industries; reducing foreign investors' scope for transfer pricing; and controlling their absorption of local savings and/or external indebtedness. Other objectives could be: favouring the development of local technological capacity and/or the transfer of "appropriate" technologies; increasing the development of local entrepreneurship and management skills; limiting the degree of concentration and/or increasing price competition in the local economy (which may again have far-reaching structural implications); promoting regional integration and/or co-operation among developing countries; and minimising the cost to the host country of gaining access to foreign technology and investment resources.

The question could also be usefully phrased in broader terms: to what extent do the new forms of investment contribute to more effective control by the State and/or the local private sector so as to make development planning and/or implementation of industrial policy more feasible than when foreign investment takes the form of traditional FDI? Also, do the new forms offer any particular advantages over FDI from the social, as distinct from private, point of view?

In so far as the new forms of investment do in fact imply at least some increase in the control exercised by host countries, the ownership versus control issue also raises important questions from an international perspective. Put simply, do the gains in control by the host country imply equivalent losses by the foreign investor, with the system as a whole remaining unaffected? It is quite likely that the trade-offs involved are not always a zero-sum game, where the gains of one party are exactly offset by the losses of the other. Under some circumstances, the situation could be a positive-sum game, in which increased host-country ownership enhances effective host-country control of local accumulation without significantly reducing foreign investors' control over those variables with which they are most concerned. Indeed, the "strategic-initiative" hypothesis discussed in Chapter 4 suggests that in some cases foreign investors' control may even be strengthened, along with that of their host-country partners, implying that the new forms of investment may serve to reduce the supposed contradiction between the "national logic" of accumulation pursued by host-country élites and the "global logic" of accumulation pursued by multinational firms. A third possibility, however, is that the situation corresponds to a negative-sum game, in the sense that new forms of investment effectively reduce or restrict foreign investors' control without local élites or host governments being able to take profitable advantage – in private and/or social terms – of the control which they have wrested from foreign investors.

The purpose of this chapter is to explore such questions as these.

## I. THE ROLE OF SMALL- AND MEDIUM-SIZE FIRMS

Numerous studies have shown that traditional FDI in developing countries is almost completely dominated by large multinational firms. One hypothesis of considerable interest to developing and industrialised countries alike holds that small- and medium-size firms (SMF) have generally been unable to internationalise their activities through FDI because of their limited resource base – especially their financial and/or managerial resources – while the new forms greatly enhance their possibilities for international investment. The growing use, acceptance and familiarity with new forms of investment worldwide may, according to this hypothesis, gradually create an international institutional framework in which SMF can convert their unique talents and firm-specific advantages – for example, small-scale production technology – into capital which can be invested internationally without having to supply all the other assets incorporated in the traditional FDI "package". While it was argued in Chapter 4 that one *cause* of the growing use of new forms appears to be the growing number of "newcomers", including SMF, to multinational investment, it may thus also be hypothesised that an important *result* of the proliferation of new forms is, or will be, an increasing multinationalisation of SMF.

Should this hypothesis prove correct, a number of potentially important advantages for host countries can be identified. One might be significantly increased competition among potential foreign investors and suppliers of technology, etc., which would enhance the bargaining strength of host countries. This increased negotiating power could in turn facilitate host-country demands for increased local control and a larger share of rents generated by foreign investment resources. Also, a greater participation by SMF could represent a move both towards greater diversification of sources of such resources and less likelihood of transfer pricing[3]. This could lead to a reduction of the cost to host countries of foreign investment resources, including technology and the like.

Secondly, the participation via new forms of investment of SMF from industrialised countries might conceivably increase competition not only internationally, but also within the host economies. A significant increase in price competition on local markets could have far-reaching structural and developmental implications for these countries[4], a point we shall develop towards the end of this chapter.

Thirdly, a substantial increase in the participation of SMF might offer important advantages to host countries in the realm of technology transfer and the development of local technological capacity[5]. For example, SMF may tend to transfer newly developed technologies and knowledge more readily than do larger multinationals, either because the weaker world-market positions of smaller firms encourage them to penetrate new markets ahead of their larger competitors, and/or because they are less concerned with the longer-term risks of strengthening potential competitors since they lack the means for pursuing global strategies in marketing their technological advantages[6]. SMF may therefore also be less likely to pursue restrictive practices, such as tie-in clauses, export prohibitions, etc., and may tend to be more flexible in the transfer of process and production knowhow than established multinationals, which have a reputation for tending to limit transfers to designs and product technology.

It is also conceivable that technologies transferred by SMF would tend to be more appropriate to the needs of developing countries, either because they are more labour-intensive or, even if they are relatively sophisticated or capital-intensive (as is often the case of capital-goods producers), because they are better adapted to the smaller-scale production needs of many host countries. Furthermore, whereas multi-nationals have been subject to criticism for concentrating FDI in relatively high-income consumer-durables markets based on sophisticated and advertising-intensive marketing techniques – even "biasing" local consumption patterns – smaller firms may operate in sectors more closely matched to the development needs of many host countries. These sectors might include such traditional lower-income mass-consumer industries as food, textiles, clothing, and the like, which could be of particular interest both to less developed countries in relatively early stages of industrialisation, and to more industrialised developing countries with smaller markets seeking to diversify their industrial structure. They might also include capital goods, mechanical engineering, etc., which could well correspond both to needs of larger, more industrialised developing countries seeking to expand local production in their heavy industrial sector, and to those of less developed countries pursuing development of their physical infrastructure[7].

Lastly, the multinationalisation of SMF is of considerable potential interest to the home countries of these firms as well[8]. Despite trends towards increasing industrial concentration worldwide, SMF continue to account for a large proportion of total employment in most industrialised countries – as much as 70 per cent in some. During the past decade, the economic slowdown and increased competition from larger foreign and domestic firms in their home markets have threatened the very survival of many OECD-based SMF. Thus, although the multinationalisation of SMF via new forms of investment might increase the bargaining power of developing countries, the industrialised countries could benefit from it not only because North-South investment tensions would be lowered, but more directly, because revitalised SMF would inject new life and employment prospects into their home economies. This undoubtedly helps explain many industrialised countries' growing interest in promoting joint ventures, licensing, technical assistance and the like between their SMF and developing countries[9].

Hard evidence does not, however, lend much support to the hypothesis that the spread of new forms of investment is being accompanied by a multinationalisation of significant numbers of SMF. In fact, what limited empirical evidence we have suggests that, on the contrary, the new forms of investment, like traditional FDI, tend to be dominated by relatively large firms, both established multinationals and some relatively large "newcomers" such as major engineering firms, state enterprises, and relatively large firms from a few developing countries.

There are of course a few important exceptions. Perhaps the most notable has been the redeployment of certain traditional Japanese industries in a number of Asian countries in the early to mid-1970s, whereby a large number of Japanese SMF entered into minority-owned joint ventures. This phenomenon was referred to by Kojima in his well-known hypothesis: while investment by Western and especially U.S. firms occurs largely under oligopolistic conditions and is "anti-trade" oriented, much Japanese manufacturing investment is "trade creating" and is undertaken by SMF in relatively competitive industries in which host countries have a comparative advantage[10]. One could easily infer from Kojima's argument that such use of new forms of investment by smaller Japanese firms also serves to accentuate price competition within the host economies; but there is considerable reason to question the validity of this inference, both because of the predominantly export-oriented nature of these investments, and especially because of the centralising or "umbrella" role played by the major trading companies in setting-up, financing and controlling the imports and exports associated with these investments.

Another important example of SMF's use of new forms of investment in developing countries is that of capital-goods producers, particularly European firms, entering into licensing and turnkey-cum-technical assistance arrangements with local firms in some of the most rapidly industrialising developing countries. Probably the most widespread new form of investment involving SMF from the industrialised countries, however, is international subcontracting. In some cases – like French firms in Tunisia – SMF operate at home as independent principals and contract with local firms in developing countries, especially as a way to redeploy labour-intensive activities to lower-cost locations. But in many cases – such as Japanese firms in Asia or German firms in Latin America – SMF are linked to larger clients in their home countries as suppliers of specialised products or services and are induced to redeploy and/or to follow their multinational clients abroad.

Even so, the available evidence does not suggest a systematic or widespread multinationalisation of SMF in conjunction with the growing use of new forms of investment. One reason may be that despite the opportunities offered by new forms of investment for SMF to exploit their specialised assets in developing countries, these firms simply lack the managerial resources and information necessary to take advantage of such opportunities. For firms with little or no experience in unfamiliar markets, the costs, risks and uncertainties involved in identifying and evaluating opportunities, locating local partners, adapting to unfamiliar legal, administrative, linguistic and socio-political environments, and formalising their often highly personalised knowhow so as to be able to transmit it to local partners, may prove to be too high. Furthermore, for firms that lack the advantages of global marketing and financial networks, the need to maintain control over and limit the diffusion of their firm-specific knowhow or technological advantages may imply a greater need, other things equal, to insist on 100 per cent or majority ownership than do multinational firms[11].

And finally, the fact that in some developing countries, like Brazil or the Philippines for example, technology agreements appear to be subject to more severe requirements and proceedings than FDI projects, may further discourage SMF from participating more actively through new forms of investment. Although host governments generally favor joint ventures over majority/wholly foreign-owned FDI, government incentives and pressures often focus on strategic or high-profile sectors rather than on industries in which SMF may be more inclined to operate.

Contrary to the hypothesis that the new forms of investment will lead to the multinationalisation of significant numbers of SMF, then, a more realistic hypothesis might be that investment in developing countries through the new forms will generally be dominated by large firms, just as in the case of traditional FDI. While there may be an increase in the *number* of firms investing in developing countries via new forms as well as FDI, due in part to the increasing participation of "newcomer" European and Japanese firms, the larger firms will continue to occupy the commanding heights of North-South investment – if for no other reason than because there continues to exist a strong correlation between firms' size and firms' possession of monopolistic advantages, the *sine qua non* of all forms of foreign investment.

A more refined version of this hypothesis would hold that the new forms of investment reflect important changes in the nature of inter-firm competition – as expressed in the globalisation of oligopolistic inter-firm rivalry, mentioned in Chapter 4 – rather than a secular trend towards declining industrial concentration worldwide. The new forms may, in other words, be more closely correlated with changes in the international division of risks and responsibilities in which a relatively limited, if increasing, number of large firms and banks increasingly dominate international investment. But such a trend towards increasing oligopolisation of the global economy would hardly exclude the possibility of a proliferation of SMF operating internationally via new forms of investment. On the contrary, it would suggest a certain hierarchy of relations between smaller and larger firms – similar to those in international subcontracting or between smaller Japanese manufacturers and the large trading companies, for example – in which SMF could occupy numerous "niches"[12].

Whether such "niches" will be occupied primarily by SMF from industrialised countries is another question. A number of *developing-country-based* firms, which in some cases have had to fend off competition from large multinationals in their home markets, are finding that their competitive tactics – sometimes based on relatively small-scale and/or labour-intensive production processes, in contrast to developed-country multinationals' emphasis on more sophisticated technological and marketing advantages – lend themselves to successful investment in other developing countries. Thus, the last decade has witnessed an impressive growth of outward investment and technology exports from some of the more industrialised developing countries, notably Argentina, Brazil, Hong Kong, India, Korea, Singapore and Taiwan[13]. Although some of these "Third World multinationals" are relatively small by international standards, they tend to be among the larger firms in their home economies, and some are quite large even by international standards.

On the whole, firms based in developing countries reveal a rather high propensity to use new forms of investment to expand to other developing countries. One recent study, for example, found that of 602 manufacturing subsidiaries with equity from parents based in other developing countries, only 57 were wholly owned ventures, which makes a joint-venture rate of over 90 per cent[14]. Other studies show that suppliers of turnkey plants and technology from developing countries have become very active in recent years[15] – as brought to public attention, for example, when South Korean firms won out over competition from U.S. firms for some lucrative construction contracts in the Middle East[16]. If developing-country-based firms' international expansion via new forms of investment is sustained over the coming years, this may present a major challenge to potential investors from industrialised countries, both large and small[17].

In any case, it seems reasonable to conclude that the greater importance of new forms of investment in developing countries reflects a growing integration of, and co-ordination among, major industrial and financial investors internationally. In the context of a changing international division of risks and responsibilities, this may be made both possible and necessary by the "consolidation" of the State and local élites in developing countries, on the one hand, and by the tendency towards a globalisation of oligopolistic inter-firm (and bank) rivalry on the other. In this context, the North-South distinction in terms of investors' (firms and banks') nationality *per se,* though not irrelevant, would appear to be of decreasing significance.

## II. THE CHANGING DIVISION OF RISKS AND RESPONSIBILITIES BETWEEN FOREIGN INVESTORS AND HOST COUNTRIES

In Chapter 4 it was pointed out that one interesting implication of the "strategic-initiative" hypothesis and its focus on the role of structural changes in developing countries is that the new forms of investment may serve to open up new branches of economic activity to foreign investment. The idea is that, by combining the particular strengths of local élites and the international business and financial communities, new forms of investment may allow foreign firms to invest in industries or capitalise on business opportunities in developing countries to which traditional FDI is poorly adapted. An example is the hotel industry. International hotel chains have flourished in developing countries in recent years primarily via franchising and management contracts, presumably because they combine the advantages of host countries, not only rapid growth and the ability to attract tourists and business travellers, but also the ability to mobilise financial capital either locally or on international capital markets – with those offered by the hotel chains – international reservation systems and trade name.

In some cases, of course, new forms of investment may be used by foreign firms to penetrate industries in developing countries which local investors could have developed without them. Conversely, as pointed out by the "defensive reaction" hypothesis, new forms may be used in industries where, without host-government insistence on the participation of local firms, the investment would have been undertaken by foreign firms through traditional FDI. In such cases, the form of investment may play an important role in determining the shares of rent appropriated by local versus foreign investors, but they could be described as essentially zero-sum games as regards the total volume of investment and rents to be appropriated.

However, in other cases, new forms of investment could open the door to a capitalisation of sectors which have traditionally resisted modernisation, whether by local or foreign capital. An important, if extreme, example would be the production of food for local consumption, a sector which continues to be dominated by peasant and/or other "pre-capitalist" forms of productive organisation and which constitutes a major development bottleneck in many developing countries.

A few cases seem to illustrate this possibility. In Mexico, for example, government restrictions on land ownership by foreigners have induced some multinational investors to develop a system of contract farming. This system, which offers an interesting illustration of the possibility of separating ownership and control, has helped to convert some areas traditionally dominated by peasant agriculture into areas dominated by capitalist farming. A case in point is Del Monte's fruit and vegetable canning operations in Mexico's Bajio valley:

> "The Bajio's land tenure system was...incompatible with Del Monte's needs. Due to the valley's population density and the breakup of the large landed estates under Mexico's agrarian reform laws, the average landholding was small, ranging from ten to twenty acres... But Del Monte found the perfect tool for changing the valley's agriculture – contract farming. Under the contract system, the farmer or grower agrees to plant a set number of acres of a particular crop, and the company in return provides financial assistance which usually includes seeds and special machinery, as well as cash outlays for purchasing fertilizers and hiring farm labour. [...]
>
> "In Mexico, where agricultural credit is limited or non-existent, contract farming was an attractive offer. As such, it was influential in changing the structure of agriculture in the Bajio. [...] By skillfully using its financial leverage, Del Monte affected the valley in several ways: it introduced crops that had never been grown

there, favored the development of the larger growers at the expense of the smaller, more marginal producers, and gained operating control over large tracts of land[18]."

The social costs of this transformation from peasant agriculture to capitalist farming, borne to a considerable extent by the large number of increasingly marginalised smaller producers, many of whom become wage labourers, are significant. Nevertheless, the importance of the long-run structural implications should not be underestimated, and from the point of view of productivity, the results are impressive. According to Del Monte reports, gross income per acre has risen by as much as 50 per cent over a ten-year period[19].

Two large agricultural development projects currently being organised by the Brazilian government in the "backlands" of Rondonia and Matto Grosso/Minas Gerias might also be cited. The purpose of these highly original projects is to produce food for consumption in Brazil. They will involve considerable amounts of financial capital from the World Bank and the Inter-American Development Bank, technical assistance and equipment from foreign firms, and at least initially State ownership of the land, to be parcelled out among independent farmers but with the State retaining some centralised co-ordinating authority. Another example might be the development of large scale farming in Sudan, involving substantial amounts of financial capital from oil-exporting countries in the Gulf region and equipment and technical assistance from a number of firms based in industrialised countries.

It is, of course, far too early to predict either the success of these large agricultural investment projects or their eventual long-run impact on economic development in these countries. Nevertheless, the mere fact that new forms of investment, involving a three-way division of risks and responsibilities, are being used in a sector which has traditionally resisted modernisation in many developing countries, and whose capitalisation may be seen as vital to the overall development process in these countries, is of great potential significance. It remains to be seen whether new forms of investment will be increasingly used to combine the forces of local and international capital as a means of expanding the sphere of investment and accumulation in developing countries.

Thus, to carry this logic to its ultimate conclusion, it is conceivable that the new forms will do for growth and investment on a global scale over the coming decades, what the advent of the joint stock corporation did for growth and investment in the national context about a century ago. That is, just as the invention of the limited-liability corporation created the legal/institutional framework in which individual capitalists – entrepreneurs, owners of physical assets and financiers – could join forces, divide risks and responsibilities and separate ownership from control, thereby giving major impetus to the process of capital formation in today's industrialised countries, the new forms of investment – with their obvious similarities at the international level in terms of division of risks and responsibilities and the possibility of separating ownership from control – may hold analogous implications for growth and capital accumulation internationally. Given the vast development needs and growth potential of the developing countries at a time when growth in the industrialised countries as a group seems to have slowed considerably, it could even be argued that by opening important new avenues to profitable international investment and capital formation in the developing world, the new forms of investment may constitute a necessary, if not sufficient, condition for sustained or renewed growth and accumulation on a global scale.

Seen in this light, it would also make sense to argue, as did a former U.S. Assistant Secretary of the Treasury for International Affairs and his co-authors, that "The national interest of the United States...calls for a formula other than equity investment. American companies have experimented with one method of spreading risk: "unbundling" corporate services.... American policy should take unbundling one step further.

It should abandon entirely the idea of direct ownership...and encourage the provision of production and marketing skills through service or management contracts.... Such contracts, because they offer a highly leveraged return on corporate assets, can be extraordinarily lucrative."[20]. Such reasoning corresponds, in sum, to a macro version of the positive-sum-game interpretation of the new forms of investment mentioned at the outset of this chapter.

One must, however, be careful not to indulge in what might be called wishful thinking, or at least not to ignore possible macro risks which appear to be associated with the new forms of investment. Whereas under traditional FDI long-term investment decisions are usually made by the same economic agent (multinational firm) which assumes the risks of financing the operation and of marketing the output, under new forms of investment these decisions and risks may be divided among various groups and/or shifted, along with ownership, to the host-country's government or private firm, whose planning horizon is likely to be less international in scope. As long as the investment project can be financed with local savings and depends largely on host-country market demand, there is no inherent problem. But what happens when financing depends on major borrowing from international capital markets, or when long-run viability of the project depends on the project's export competitiveness?

One example might be investment in such basic industries as petrochemicals or steel, which many individual host countries see as vital to their development plans. Another might be major mining projects, which are often a vital source of foreign exchange. Under FDI a multinational firm could be expected to take into careful consideration levels of installed capacity and probable long-term worldwide demand trends before immobilising large sums of capital in such long-term productive investments. But under the new forms, investment decisions often fall on the host country and/or multinational banks. One result could be a long-run disequilibrium in global supply and demand, with a tendency towards over-production and/or over-capacity worldwide[21]. This undoubtedly explains, and may well be exacerbated by, the increasing interest shown by multinational firms in approaching the new forms of investment in these industries as *sales* operations – via turnkey and management contracts – rather than as investment operations[22].

It is of course conceivable that the long-term global investment planning perspective which multinational firms are relinquishing may be assumed by multinational banks and international financial organisations, at least to the extent that host countries require foreign loans to undertake their investment projects[23]. Such an hypothesis would be consistent with a number of studies of recent trends in offshore financial markets and multinational banking which see banks making more credit-allocation decisions on a global level, and focussing on international outcomes by firm and industry[24]. However, the enormous potential power of the banks to rationalise productive investment on a global scale tends to be undermined by pressures on banks to create new, relatively short-term assets, and by the relative instability of international financial markets – not to mention the international financial community's tendency to devote large sums of capital to short-term speculative-type activities. Nor do industrialised countries' national credit agencies, whose export credits and guarantees are often used in conjunction with certain new forms of investment, appear likely to resolve the problem of investment planning, since their decisions are heavily influenced by pressures to promote the competitive positions of firms from their own countries.

One obvious danger is that while some of the new forms of investment create lucrative new possibilities for firms to sell plant and equipment, consulting and management services, and so forth, to the developing countries, many of the latter run up enormous international debt to finance these projects. And, with foreign firms' profits increasingly "delinked" from the long-term viability of these investments, and/or as the pressures of global excess capacity mount as the projects come into production and depress world output prices, the borrowing countries may find it increasingly difficult to service their debt. These difficulties may in turn further exacerbate longer-term problems of stability for the system as a whole, both at the financial and at the "real" or industrial level.

In short, whether the economic slowdown which has plagued the world economy since the early 1970s is of a business-cycle nature or a more profound structural nature, certain new forms of investment may, by opening up new avenues to lucrative investment and *sales* opportunities for foreign firms in developing countries, offer responses to short-run problems felt by host countries and foreign firms alike, but risk exacerbating longer-run global financial and industrial disequilibria. In so far as the growing importance of new forms not only reflects but also reinforces the tendency of firms to shorten their investment-planning horizons (as discussed in Chapter 4), these disequilibria may be further accentuated. Such disequilibria would pose serious problems for the industrialised as well as the developing countries, and would almost surely aggravate North-South trade and investment relations as well. This would appear to call not only for public intervention to deal with financial disequilibria[25], but especially for increased inter-governmental co-ordination of industrial policy – among industrialised countries, among developing countries, and between the two groups.

## III.  IMPLICATIONS FOR HOST COUNTRIES

### A.  Ownership and Control

The "strategic-initiative" hypothesis, as seen from the foreign firm's point of view, suggests that effective control does not necessarily require ownership. A logical corollary to this hypothesis, when assessing the implications of new forms of investment from the host-country's viewpoint, is that ownership does not necessarily imply effective control.

According to one interpretation, the new forms of investment represent a necessary, though not sufficient, condition for host countries to establish the control required to pursue many of the development objectives cited in the introduction to this chapter. A striking example of host countries increasing both the size and degree of local control over rents in the extractive industries, for example, are the benefits achieved by the OPEC countries in conjunction with the shift from traditional FDI cum concessional agreements to new forms of investment in petroleum. And, as regards the extractive sector more generally, a recent document by the U.N.'s Centre on Transnational Corporations assessing new forms of investment in the petroleum and mining industries points out that, "the conclusion that host countries generally receive greatly improved conditions, terms, and benefits under the contemporary agreements than they did under the traditional concession is unavoidable"[26].

There is also evidence that a number of petroleum-exporting and a few importing developing countries have succeeded in increasing, via new forms of investment, their participation in downstream activities and, presumably, in the value added to be derived therefrom. Huge investments in which joint ventures and turnkey contracts play a dominant role have and are being undertaken in basic petrochemicals, for example, in the Gulf countries, Brazil and Korea, with major implications for the industry worldwide.

A similar trend towards more downstream processing, for example in smelting, is evident in a number of mineral exporting countries, as illustrated by the case of copper in

Peru[27]. It is unclear how far one can attribute such North-South redeployment of minerals processing – to the limited extent it has occurred – to host-country initiatives, or whether pressures in a number of industrialised countries, notably Japan, to redeploy such pollution-prone industries is of primary importance. For our purposes, what is noteworthy is that new forms of investment appear to be an important vehicle for such redeployment.

As for the broader question of local control, however, the evidence is less clearcut. The same U.N. study on the mining industry argues that, despite the sometimes spectacular host-country gains in volume or share of export revenues, "the actual reins of control generally remain in the hands of the transnational corporation as manager and operator." The document cites both the rapid innovation in minerals production and processing technology, which has surpassed the rate of effective technology transfer to host countries, and the recent period of high-cost capital, which has surpassed the financing capabilities of developing countries, as principal reasons for the host countries' relative lack of progress in increasing their role in operations management. It also makes the interesting observations that:

  i)   state ownership of mineral deposits managed (or serviced) by multinational firms operating under service contracts, and projects developed by joint ventures, do not necessarily yield greater fiscal returns for the country than would a comprehensive tax regime[28];

  ii)  the general trend towards increased profits accruing to host countries has also seen a number of increased risks and burdens being borne by the host countries[29].

This latter observation serves to highlight two important points, already mentioned in Chapter 2, which are just as relevant if not more to manufacturing projects than to those in the extractive sector. First, many developing countries may find that the balance-of-payments advantages to be gained from unbundling the traditional FDI package and using new forms of investment in order to restrict multinational firms' use of transfer pricing and to otherwise reduce the foreign-exchange cost of acquiring investment resources from abroad, are considerably less than expected. For one thing, licensing agreements are sometimes used by multinational firms as an alternative means to achieve similar ends, although host-country regulations of licensing in recent years appear to have had some effect in limiting this problem. More importantly, by further running up their foreign debt in order to finance certain new forms of investment at least as a partial substitute for foreign equity investment, some borrowing countries may have exacerbated what have turned out to be onerous debt-servicing obligations. These obligations, which have been severely accentuated by high real interest rates in recent years, are likely to outweigh whatever foreign-exchange savings may have been derived from reduced physical-capital costs due to unbundling[30].

Secondly, in trying to lessen their vulnerability to the oligopolistic rent-extracting powers of multinational firms, many developing countries may have achieved only limited success – due to their continued dependence on multinational firms for access to competitive technology and/or world markets – while at the same time considerably increasing their dependence on the IMF and the international banking community. Of considerable interest in this regard are the experiences of Algeria and Brazil which suggest that export credits from industrialised countries' national (often public) credit and financial agencies may not only offer somewhat more favourable terms, but most important, provide the host country with greater negotiating and decision-making power. Host-country control may remain limited under new forms of investment for a number of other reasons as well. Take, for example, a joint venture between the host government (majority partner) and a multinational firm (minority partner). In some cases, lack of effective control by the majority partner is due to such relatively trite reasons as: explicit host-government acknowledgement of the separation of ownership and control by reserving the right to appoint only a minority of the members of the board of directors[31]; the majority position of the government may be neutralised by devices for "minority protection" which confer veto power on the multinational firm in such critical areas of management and control as borrowing or spending funds to expand, issuing new shares, selling assets, terminating operations, etc.[32]; not uncommonly, a distinction between the nominal authority of the board of directors and effective control by management allows the government to dominate the board without effectively managing the enterprise[33].

Probably the single most important factor which may limit a host country's ability to assume more effective control of new forms of investment is a relative lack of technical expertise by local participants, be they members of the board of directors, managers, or workers. Among the countries covered by our study, this problem is perhaps most clearly illustrated by the Algerian experience, which stands in considerable contrast to that of such countries as Brazil or Korea. (A useful distinction may also be drawn here between the advantages obtained by Eastern European countries from new forms of investment in the East-West context, and those obtained by developing countries in the North-South context.) Some observers have thus gone so far as to argue that control through ownership without technical expertise is a mere illusion.

Control by multinational firms is also frequently maintained or reinforced by the phenomenon of interaffiliate transactions. As we have seen, many host countries have found themselves obliged to rely on the organisational structure of the corporations for access to specialised consulting and technical services, equipment and parts, and marketing. In addition to increasing the leverage and/or maximising the returns accruing to the foreign investor under the new forms, this device of interaffiliate transactions also may serve to perpetuate the effective control of the foreign firm despite its non- or minority-equity position. According to one author, "The common experience of most host countries is that the corporate structure of transnational corporations invariably denies the subsidiaries that measure of autonomy that would permit them to be fully integrated into the economic strategies of the host country[34]." Others have argued that in Mexico, for example, local ownership requirements achieved almost no benefits for the host country except as a bargaining chip to trade for better performance on other objectives[35].

Many ex-parent companies in fact openly recognise their intention to maintain effective control, contending that the surrender of control over individual components of their worldwide organisation is incompatible with the nature of their operations. Thus, although legally the foreign investor may be transformed into a junior partner in a local enterprise, in practice the acquisition by a host government (or state or private enterprise) of a majority equity interest in the local subsidiary of a multinational firm often amounts to virtually the same thing as acquiring minority participation in a global enterprise.

Along similar lines, many U.S.-based firms have been developing strategies based on inter-firm transnational alliances in marketing and finance. These strategies, particularly visible in extractive industries vulnerable to nationalisation, but analogous to those of manufacturers who produce specialised components in diverse offshore plants, have been described as follows:

"The strategy is to leave host governments no place to sell nationalised output. More than that, it attempts to cut the government off from sources of international finance...In the late 1960s, American companies in the copper, petroleum, natural gas, and nickel industries initiated a process of unbundling corporate services, separating the provision of [financial] capital from the provision of management skills, the provision of production technology, and the provision of marketing experience. They spread the risk of capital commitment by securing loans (in the subsidiary's name) from customers or by selling collection rights on contracts outstanding to financial intermediaries. As a consequence, fewer of their own assets were exposed to nationalisation, and a broad array of creditors stood ready to bring pressure against a nationalistic government. In addition, they wrote long-term contracts with major users for the output of vulnerable subsidiaries, so that a nationalisation threat would disrupt the markets of Europe, Japan, and the United States, simultaneously[36]."

Another interesting illustration of how foreign firms may enhance their control vis-à-vis host countries is Japan's use of long-term contracts and the "dominant buyer relationship" in her dealings with foreign, mostly developing-country, suppliers of mineral resources. Table II shows how, by carefully diversifying her sources, even with some possible sacrifice of economies of scale, Japan has succeeded in acquiring a favourable bargaining position with most of her minerals suppliers. Her trade is structured so that almost without exception a given country's exports to Japan represent a higher proportion of its total exports than they do of Japan's total imports of that commodity. This arrangement gives Japan, and notably her trading companies, considerable strength and flexibility in contract and investment negotiations with each supplying country individually. One author has thus concluded:

"despite the trend of greater national ownership which has taken shape in developing countries since World War II, and despite the new forms of interface this trend has fostered, the overall dominance of the mineral industry by transnational corporations, except for notable instances, has not universally and decisively declined. National ownership of production facilities, whether by the state or the private sector, by itself does not alter radically the ultimate flow of gains if transnational firms maintain their control over processing, marketing and distribution. This control...has, if anything, increased with modern advancements in sophisticated technology, and in accounting and communications techniques[37]."

Although difficult to test empirically, these assertions appear to be borne out, for example, by some of the difficulties Peru experienced in marketing her minerals production through her state-owned marketing corporations during the 1970s[38].

Seen in this light, then, it is not surprising that many multinational firms have overcome initial reservations about investing in minority or non-equity positions with host governments in developing countries. Such ventures may effectively defuse nationalist objections to foreign control of domestic resources without substantially threatening foreign investors' financial returns or access to raw materials. The host government's equity interest, often coupled with the presence of powerful members of the local élite on the board, may enhance access to local capital and facilities such as import licenses and other permits from government agencies, and strengthen relations between host governments and multinational firms more generally[39].

Finally, such ventures may also permit foreign investors to shift important risks associated with investment projects due, for example, to fluctuations in world-market prices, in international currency-exchange and interest rates, etc., on to the host country. That is, by sharing often only a limited degree of control with the host country, firms may be more than compensated by the degree to which risks inevitably associated with the investment project are "shared" by the host country.

An area in which multinational firms using FDI have sometimes come in for particularly severe criticism[40], is that of technology transfer and the development of local technological capacity. Sweeping generalisations about the advantages offered in this area to host countries by new forms of investment, relative to traditional FDI, must be treated with great caution.

There is some evidence to suggest that at least under certain conditions the new forms may offer important advantages to host countries. The classic example of course is Japan's experience, as a host country, in actively pursuing licensing while restricting inward foreign investment up to the mid-1960s. Among today's developing countries, one particularly interesting example is Brazil's pharmaceutical industry, where data show a fairly strong correlation between local equity participation in joint ventures with multinational firms and the latter's willingness to set up R&D facilities in the host country. These and other data from the Brazilian experience have led one author to draw a number of conclusions:

a) faced with rising, primarily political, pressures from local élites to set up R&D in the host country, managers of multinational firms may find themselves substituting one kind of risk – that of ensuring control over R&D at a distance – for another – political factors – also difficult to control at a distance;

b) given Brazil's highly attractive market, a surprisingly large amount of local political pressure was required to produce relatively modest changes in foreign firms' behaviour;

c) from the viewpoint of local élites, however, even these modest successes may be of critical importance in that they provide a base for incremental future changes;

d) given the importance of incrementalism in multinational firms' management decision-making, the relative success of local pressures in bringing about change in this area will vary not only from one industry to another, but from one firm to another. In any case they will tend to be more successful to the extent that local pressures parallel the forces of inter-firm rivalry, that is, that the pressures of international oligopolistic competition can be brought into play[41].

Korea's rapid technological advance during the 1960s and 1970s might also be cited in support of the hypothesis that new forms of investment offer important advantages in the realm of technology transfer and the development of local technological capacity. In important respects the Korean experience is reminiscent of postwar Japan: FDI has been of relatively limited importance as a proportion of gross domestic capital formation, and local firms have actively used licensing to acquire foreign technology. Turnkey plants, though of little significance in recent years, were also of some importance as a basis for technology transfer in the early years of Korean industrialisation. A recent World Bank study entitled "Korean Industrial Competence: Where It Came From" thus reports:

"In postwar Korea... electronics and certain chemicals perhaps are unique in their almost exclusive reliance on FDI for acquiring the very latest technology as well as market access. On the basis of licensing, Korea was able to acquire the most modern shipbuilding technology in the world, just as it was able to incorporate the most recent technological advances in its integrated steel mill. Other examples... further attest that Korean industry has been able to initiate, and in most cases successfully to operate, a variety of "high-technology" industrial activities by means of licensing and turnkey arrangements. [...] Electronics... appears to be an exception that proves a rule, for electronics is precisely the industry in which Korea has extensively relied on FDI to enter production, particularly for export, and has so far failed to gain local mastery of fundamental aspects of production know-how"[42].

Another source of technology transfer may have been international subcontracting, since "one of the most important sources of product design and quality control for Korean exporters has been the information that export buyers provide in specifying their orders and making plant inspections"[43].

"Korea's export-led industrialisation has overwhelmingly and in fundamental respects been directed and controlled by nationals [who have] relied heavily on indigenous effort through various forms of learning by doing and emphasized transactions at arm's length in the use of foreign resources.... For most of the industries that have been intensively developed to date, the technology for processes and for product design is not proprietary. With respect to acquiring technology or marketing overseas, there consequently are few advantages to be gained from either licensing or FDI, except in peculiar circumstances."[44]

The study also points out that Korea's technological mastery has progressed much further in plant operation, involving non-proprietory knowledge, than in either plant or product design.

What both the Brazilian and Korean experiences clearly imply is that while the new forms of investment may offer important advantages in the realm of technology transfer and development of local technological capacity, the new forms can in no way be regarded as a panacea. This is supported by the contrasting experiences of such countries as Tunisia and Algeria. The Tunisian government's development strategy relied heavily for about a decade on international subcontracting, with only limited and partial success in promoting technology transfer[45]. Algeria's experience stands in even sharper contrast, despite the major emphasis given to training of local personnel and technology transfer in the "product-in-hand" contracts which were the key element of Algeria's development strategy during the 1970s[46].

What the experiences of these and the other countries covered in our study seem to suggest, then, is that whether the potential advantages offered to developing countries by the new forms of investment are assessed in terms of local rent appropriation, technology transfer, or other relatively specific host-country objectives, which may in turn be situated within a broader ownership-control framework of analysis, the decisive factor seems to be foreign firms' willingness and interest in sharing rents, transferring technology, and otherwise sharing effective control with their host-country counterparts. In turn, their willingness and interest seems to depend above all on such factors as the size and perceived growth potential of the local market, on the one hand, and the nature of global inter-firm oligopolistic rivalry in specific industries, on the other. Host governments and local élites in the private sector may take profitable advantage of these factors in applying pressure on foreign firms to share ownership, rents, technology, etc. – as illustrated quite well by the experiences of Brazil[47] and Korea[48] – but rarely can they succeed without, or against, these factors.

Another conclusion which can be reasonably drawn is that a host country's ability to capitalise on the potential advantages offered by new forms of investment, relative to FDI, depends to a considerable extent on what some authors refer to as local skills of entrepreneurship and of learning by doing. Whether the development of such skills in a given country in turn depends on socio-cultural factors which lie beyond the scope of economic analysis, as some authors seem to hold, or whether it reflects the very nature of capital formation and structural change in a given country, the implication would seem to be that global economic conditions – both within the host country and internationally – are of greater relative importance than specific host-government foreign-investment policies in determining the advantages to be gained from new forms of investment. Increased local ownership and greater reliance on new forms of investment are certainly not *per se* a sufficient condition for the success of the "logic of national accumulation".

What is not so clear is whether the new forms of investment in developing countries correspond more to the logic of "national" or global accumulation. Perhaps the most realistic conclusion is that the growing importance of new forms of investment is in itself evidence that the two "logics" really are, or are increasingly, one and the same, where conflicts of interest among groups within a given national economy are as important as those which may exist or arise internationally.

Nevertheless, the potential advantages offered by new forms of investment to developing countries should not be underestimated. Korea's experience during her recent economic slowdown with wholly foreign-owned firms and joint ventures operating in the same industry provides some evidence, for example, that the latter may be more amenable to host-government industrial-policy measures (designed in this case to deal with the economic slowdown) than are wholly foreign-owned firms. This experience is of interest first of all because it suggests that, at least under certain circumstances, there are advantages to be gained from new forms of investment – difficult or impossible though it may be to measure those advantages – because of their greater responsiveness to host-government industrial policy measures. And secondly, it emphasizes the importance of a country's *having* a viable industrial policy in order to take advantage of the possibilities offered by new forms of investment.

## B. Group Interests

Till now, we have generally referred to "host-country élites" as if they were a largely homogeneous group within a given country and as if they represent the interests of the country as a whole. To conclude our discussion of the implications of the new forms of investment, however, it seems appropriate to at least consider the possibility that the new forms may have different implications for different groups within a given host economy.

To begin with, it is useful to recall the hypothesis that by taking advantage of the process of structural change in developing countries and combining the forces of local and foreign interests, the new forms of international investment may contribute to further structural change and to enlarging the sphere of capital formation in those countries. To illustrate this possibility we cited the example of the transformation of peasant agriculture to modern capitalist farming and noted in passing both the significant productivity gains, on the one hand, and social costs borne mostly by marginalised peasants on the other. By contributing to the capitalisation of certain "traditional" or "pre-capitalist" sectors of developing countries' economies, the new forms of international investment could, theoretically, have a major impact not only on productivity levels but also on accelerating the process of structural transformation – "modernisation" – with far-reaching implications for the global development process.

But it is equally possible, as shown by the marginalisation of small agriculturalists, that the new forms of investment may contribute to certain "development objectives" such as increased productivity, local control and rent appropriation, development of management skills and, where relevant, access to world markets, without making an appreciable contribution in such crucial areas as income distribution, employment of un- or low-skilled labor, etc. Or, to phrase the idea in another way, it is at least conceivable that the new forms of investment may do a lot to satisfy certain demands of host-country élites, including some of those demands contained in the United Nations' call for a New International Economic Order, while at the same time doing little to help improve living standards, satisfy basic needs, reduce marginalisation, or promote global development for the bulk of the host country's population.

To illustrate this idea, it is useful to recall our discussion of multinational firms' possible use of inter-affiliate transactions to retain control over joint ventures in which host-country partners hold majority ownership. We pointed out that although legally the foreign investor may be transformed into a junior partner, in practice the acquisition by a public or private enterprise in the host country of majority equity in the local subsidiary of a multinational firm often amounts to virtually the same thing as acquiring minority participation in a global enterprise. To this comment might be added another observation, made by the authors of *American Multinationals and American Interests:*

"In a world where multinational corporations are global oligopolies exercising substantial discretion in the conduct of international activities, bargaining by an individual state to get these corporations to serve its goals may not involve any economic losses to the state; the result may simply be collusion, active or tacit, between host governments and firms, their disagreements limited to how to divide up the spoils"[49].

This "collusion", as the authors call it, may find its clearest expression in the new forms of international investment. Their comments are suggestive of our earlier observation that by permitting local and foreign groups to combine forces within a new division of risks and responsibilities, the new forms may, in the extreme, do for capital accumulation at the international level what the limited-liability joint stock corporation did at the national level.

But what these authors fail to clarify is where the "spoils" – the division of which they see as the principal source of disagreement between host governments and foreign firms – come from. That is, if host governments and multinational firms are "colluding", against whom are they colluding?

Given the authors' focus on "American interests", as distinct from those of American multinationals, one possibility they may have in mind is suggested by our earlier discussion of the petroleum industry, where extractive rents and downstream profits rose phenomenally during the 1970s – in conjunction with the shift to new forms of investment, be it noted in passing – largely at the expense of final consumers in the industrialised as well as developing petroleum-importing countries. Another possibility they may have in mind is the potentially negative impact on employment levels in multinational firms' home countries, including the U.S., resulting from developing countries' growing use of incentive and performance requirements to induce industrial redeployment.

In looking at the "collusion" phenomenon from the host country's side, another possibility seems to be that local élites, whose interests are often represented by the action of host governments, may benefit substantially from the new or greater opportunities offered by new forms of investment for increased rent appropriation in the local economy at least partially at the expense of other groups in the local economy. Thus, when looked at from a broader social point of view, the new forms of investment may not differ significantly from traditional FDI. The fact that new forms of investment in the manufacturing sector (Cf. Chapter 3) appear to be used more frequently in industries serving the local market than those which are export-oriented, and in those which tend to involve more mature – hence, often, more labour-intensive – technologies, may be evidence that the "spoils" come from local consumers and/or labour.

Quite revealing are the experiences of a number of host governments which have sought to regulate international licensing agreements, often for balance-of-payments reasons, so as to limit royalty payments (or transfer pricing) and promote greater competition in the local product market. Not infrequently an important source of resistance to these measures has been wholly or majority locally owned firms, whose principal interest often coincides closely with that of their foreign licensors in maintaining their joint monopolistic position in the local market. Only subsequently does the local firm worry about negotiating with the foreign licensor over the division of the rents ("spoils") to be derived.

In a more general sense, then, a very important issue, which we only briefly alluded to in our section on SMF, is that of the implications of new forms of investment for market structure and industrial concentration in the host economy. The role of concentration and market structure in economic development can in fact be considerably greater than is commonly recognised[50]:

> "Economic development... depends crucially on inter-activity linkages and external economies. Consequently, we must be concerned with the extent to which competitive pressures lead to the actual transmission of pecuniary externalities in production and investment from one activity to another. Further... industrial market power also has important effects on dynamic efficiency, income distribution, the internal terms of trade, and macroeconomic conditions in the developing countries[51]."

This author makes a number of important additional observations. First, he explains that levels of concentration tend to be rather high in today's developing countries – even higher than is visible from the statistics that show relatively high levels in specific industries – because of the inter-sectoral ties within, i.e., the centralising role of, the "Groups" which are a special feature of industrial organisation in many developing countries[52]. He contrasts these high levels of concentration with the comparatively lower levels characteristic of many of today's developed economies during their 19th-century industrial development process[53]. He also points out a number of consequences of these high concentration levels, which lie at the very heart of today's development problems: unfavourable internal terms of trade for local agriculture and for less concentrated manufacturing activities; oligopolistic rivalry and uncertainty, which aggravate tendencies toward relatively high capital-labour ratios and severe under-utilisation of installed capacity in supposedly capital-scarce economies; monopolistic pricing and output policies, which accentuate unemployment and inflation; emphasis on the introduction of new and relatively "sophisticated" consumer products, often aimed only at markets for upper-income strata, and on high advertising and marketing expenditures, rather than on cost-cutting in existing product lines; and relatively low rates of technical innovation.

Secondly, and of particular relevance for our immediate purpose, he observes that entry by the "Groups" into new product markets "has often been facilitated by *joint ventures* with foreign firms or by international *licensing agreements*"[54].

Lastly, he notes that whereas in more highly industrialised countries today a certain degree of monopoly power may sometimes be considered justified as a necessary condition for R&D, no such rationale exists for oligopolists in most developing countries since they are generally not at the frontiers of technical knowledge. Consequently, in developing countries, "oligopolists gain little social legitimacy on dynamic considerations of technical progress. Indeed, the proclivity of local capitalists to enter new activities by importing technology through licensing agreements or joint ventures with foreign companies has contributed further to nationalist hostility against them"[55].

The "hostility" to which this author refers may occasionally come from groups of organised or unorganised workers or peasants. But far more frequently it comes from members of the local business community who are unable to internationalise their assets via new forms of investment, and whose competitive position in the local economy is increasingly threatened and sometimes marginalised[56] by their competitors' – that is, the Groups' – associations with foreign firms in joint ventures, licensing agreements, etc.

To summarise and simplify a bit, there is considerable evidence to suggest that the new forms of investment in developing countries both reflect and contribute to increasing concentration through what might be described as a simultaneous process of horizontal international integration and vertical "hierarchisation" or "disintegration" within developing countries. Horizontal international integration takes place in the sense that local élites or "Groups" may be finding that the new forms of investment offer important advantages, relative to traditional FDI, for internationalising their assets,

112

strengthening their ties and/or improving the terms of their relations with their counterparts in the international business and financial communities – all of which serve to increase their economic and sometimes political power at home as well. That such international integration is taking place – with local élites not always playing the role of junior partners[57] – is manifested most clearly by the growing importance of the new forms of investment in developing countries. But it is also increasingly apparent in the use of new forms of investment by firms and "Groups" from developing countries, including the so-called Third World multinationals, exporters of technology[58], etc., especially in expanding into other developing countries. To a lesser degree, it is apparent in recent North-South bilateral intergovernmental investment treaties calling for reciprocal protection, that is, for protection of investment by developing countries in industrialised countries as well as vice-versa[59].

The other dimension of the process – internal "hierarchisation" or "disintegration" – lies in the fact that the new forms of investment may reinforce or accelerate industrial concentration within individual developing countries. This reflects both the increasing dominance of a limited number of large private "Groups" and/or state firms which are the principal participants in new forms of investment in the host economy, and the weakening of the relative position of large numbers of local firms – especially small- to medium-size firms – which are unable to internationalise their assets via direct participation in new forms of investment.

An alternative hypothesis might of course be that whereas traditional FDI tends to concentrate in highly oligopolistic markets, often accentuating the degree of concentration in the host economy[60], the new forms of investment are more likely to have a positive impact on competition within the economy both because they open the door to more potential foreign competitors for local investment opportunities, notably SMF, and because investment under the new forms tends to go into more "mature", price-competitive industries. As pointed out in Section I of this chapter, however, there is little evidence to suggest either a widespread multinationalisation of SMF via new forms of investment in developing countries, or that new forms of investment in "mature" manufacturing industries make any discernable contribution to price competition within the host economy.

The Singaporean experience with new forms of investment is revealing. Compared to the other host countries in our study, Singapore's "local élites" have for some time been highly integrated into the international economy and are therefore less inclined to turn either to local government or to new forms of investment in their country in order to internationalise their assets or consolidate their bargaining position vis-à-vis either the international business and financial communities or other groups in Singapore. Nor are there any extractive industries in the country which might induce local élites to pursue new forms of investment more actively. Moreover, labour and other "non-élites" appear to have shown little interest in promoting new forms of investment in Singapore. In other words, the relative *lack* of interest in new forms of investment in Singapore suggests that this country is the exception which confirms the rule: seen from the point of view of the individual host country, the new forms of investment serve above all as a vehicle for local élites seeking to internationalise their economic bases, to strengthen their negotiating position vis-à-vis the international business and financial communities and to consolidate their position vis-à-vis other groups within the host economy. When viewed from a broader social perspective, however, there is little evidence that the new forms of investment are intrinsically either more or less advantageous to host countries than traditional FDI.

Thus, to summarise and conclude, within a global investment context characterised by changing international investment strategies and an evolving division of risks and responsibilities among the principal participants, the new forms of investment appear to offer both new potential advantages and risks to host developing countries. In general, perhaps the most important risks are those resulting from the possible "delinking" of major investment decisions from effective control over technology and markets internationally, and the financial and "real" disequilibria which may result. Among the potential advantages to host countries, perhaps the most important is the possibility for increased host-government control over the processes of investment and capital formation in the local economy. At least from the larger social/developmental perspective, the benefits to be derived by an individual host country from new forms of investment, relative to traditional FDI, thus appear to depend to a large extent on the effectiveness of the country's overall industrial policy. Much depends of course on the relative bargaining strength of the host government and/or local élites in attempting to assert their control over the investment process. Their bargaining strength in turn depends on such factors as the size and dynamism of the local market, on the strength of local technological, managerial and entrepreneurial capacity, and on the dynamics of oligopolistic inter-firm rivalry on a global scale. But, given the central importance of the host country government both in international negotiations and in setting the host country's industrial policy, much also depends on the strength of various groups within the country in attempting to assert their control over the State.

# NOTES AND REFERENCES

1. Cf. Evans, op. cit.; see also R.E. Caves, "The Multinational Enterprise and the theory of industrial organization," in J. Dunning (ed.), *Economic Analysis and the Multinational Enterprise* (London, Allen and Unwin, 1974).

2. See footnote 47 below.

3. A study of small U.K. firms found that such firms are not set up to take advantage of transfer pricing (G. Newbould, P. Buckley and J. Thurwell, *Going International – The Experience of Smaller Companies Overseas,* Associated Business Press, London, 1978.)

4. Cf. N. Leff, "Monopoly Capitalism and Public Policy in Developing Countries", in *Kyklos,* Vol. 32, 1979.

5. For a more detailed discussion of these points, see E. White, "The role of small and medium-sized enterprise in the international transfer of technology: Issues for research," paper prepared for UNCTAD, November, 1980 (TD/B/C.6/64), especially pp. 27-34.

6. "There is one important distinctive feature in the way that smaller firms try to capitalize on their innovative advantages through transfer of technology transactions. Such firms, although highly innovative in several sectors, normally lack sufficient resources and organization to protect their advantages through the international patent system or to exploit the innovation directly... It follows that they may be willing to transfer their technology at an earlier stage, moving ahead of the competition of larger competitors." (*Ibid.,* p. 21)

7. See, e.g., the experience of several French agriculture machine SMF in Latin America, and other SMF with infrastructure projects in Africa, reported in various issues of *Moniteur du Commerce International,* February and April, 1978 (cited in *Ibid.,* pp. 28 and 34).

8. See for example, A.D. Little Inc., "Technology transfer to Latin America from small and medium sized U.S. firms: broadening the channels" (prepared for U.S. State Department, 1978); and A. Weil, "Les transferts de technolgie aux pays en voie de développement par les petites et moyennes entreprises" (prepared for the French Industry Ministry, 1979).

9. Government measures taken along these lines over the last decade by industrialized countries include: the creation of public Development Finance Corporations, notably by members of the EEC; subsidisation of export credits and longer-term loans for financing equity investments in joint ventures; establishment of investment guarantee systems and, most recently, active pursuit of bilateral inter-governmental investment protection treaties. In some cases these public measures explicitly provide for special treatment for SMF; even where they do not, these measures may be seen as generally responding to the particular risk perceptions and sensitivities of SMF more than of established multinationals. Cf. OECD DAC Secretariat, *Investing in Developing Countries* (Fifth revised edition); E. White, op. cit.; and on the subject of inter-governmental agreements, A. Gourdain-Mitsotaki, "Les Accords Intergouvernementaux Relatifs aux Investissements", *op. cit.*

10. K. Kojima, Direct Foreign Investment, op. cit. For a critique of Kojima's position, see for example R.H. Mason, "A Comment on Professor Kojima's 'Japanese Type versus American Type of Technology Transfer'", in *Hitotsubashi Journal of Economics,* Vol. 20, No. 2, February 1980.

11. "The available empirical evidence seems to indicate that so far there is not [any] inclination on the part of small and medium enterprises for joint ventures with large local ownership. On the contrary, the information on small parent companies in the United States, United Kingdom and the Federal Republic of Germany reveals that they have clearly tended to favour wholly owned subsidiaries or majority control systems. Also medium-size French firms operating in Brazil are predominantly organized as 100 per cent subsidiaries." (White, *op. cit.,* pp. 35-36).

12. Thus, for example, L. Wells, in his article on "The Internationalization of Firms from the Developing Countries", in Agmon and Kindelberger (eds.), *Multinationals from Small Countries,* observes that many such "niches" are left by major multinationals in their operations in developing countries.

13. Cf. L. Wells, *Ibid.;* K. Kumar and M. McLeod, *op. cit.*

14. Wells. *Ibid.*. Chapter VII.

15. World Bank study of technology exports by developing countries (directed by C. Dahlman).

16. Whereas from June of 1975 through April of 1978, U.S. firms accounted for some 10.3 per cent of the Middle Eastern construction market, from May 1978 through June 1979 this share fell to only about 1.6 per cent, while during this same period Korean firms' share rose to over ten times that of U.S. firms (Korean firms won over $3.3 billion contracts in Saudi Arabia alone, compared to U.S. firms' $0.35 billion for the Middle Eastern region in that year). Reported in *Engineering News Record,* Mac-Graw-Hill, and cited in the *International Herald Tribune* December 11, 1979.

17. In addition to the phenomenon of South-South investment, other studies have focussed on "multinational marriages", i.e., international joint ventures involving firms from industrialised countries but in which the dominant partner(s) are from developing countries. Heenen and Keegan go so far as to argue that, "chief executive officers from wealthy countries should be mindful of "reverse takeovers" – that is, instances where a developing country investor gains a controlling interest in an enterprise based in a developed nation. [...] Inevitably ... one nation's competitive dominance passes to another. Today the Japanese, tomorrow the Brazilians, the Mexicans, the Koreans, and others." D.A. Heenen and W.J. Keegan, "The Rise of Third World Multinationals," *Harvard Business Review,* January-February 1979, pp. 108-109.

18. R. Burbach and P. Flynn, *Agribusiness in the Americas,* (New York, Monthly Review, 1980), pp. 184-185.

19. *Ibid.*

20. C. Fred Bergsten, T. Horst and T.H. Moran, *American Multinationals and American Interests,* Brookings Institution, Washington D.C., 1978, pp. 159-160.

21. See Mikesell's comment cited in footnote 28 of Chapter 3.

22. See our discussion of investment trends in the mining industry, in Section I of Chapter 3.

23. See Suratgar's comment cited in the very last sentence of Chapter 3.

24. See e.g. R.B. Cohen, "Structural Change in International Banking and its Implications for the U.S. Economy," prepared for the Joint Economic Committee, U.S. Congress, Washington D.C., December 1980.

25. The dangers of international financial instability have been brought to public attention by Mexico's, and quite recently if less spectacularly, by Brazil's debt-servicing problems. These disequilibria may in turn call for substantial public intervention by multilateral agencies and/or OECD governments to prevent major bank failures – leading at least one author to argue that, ultimately, it is the tax-payer who will shoulder the burden of these disequilibria. (cf. "La Dette du Tiers-Monde et la Crise Financière Internationale", *Le Monde Diplomatique,* November 1982).

26. UNCTC doc. ST/CTC/29, *op. cit.,* p. 234.

27. See Chapter 3, Section I, Part B.

28. Peru's experience with production-sharing contracts in the petroleum sector for several years illustrates this point well.

29. UNCTC doc. ST/CTC/29, *op. cit.,* pp. 236-238.

30. It is interesting to note that during a brief period (1980-1981) Brazil attempted to pressure foreign investors to convert their debt into equity capital. When these attempts met with little success, they were dropped.

31. Such was the case, for example, under the joint-venture agreement between the Jamaican Government and Kaiser Aluminum & Chemical Corp.

32. Such was the case under agreements between: Panama's State Mining Corporation and Texasgulf Inc. (1976); Zambia and the Roan Selection Trust Ltd. (1970); Ghana and Lonrho Ltd. of London (1973); and Ghana and Consolidated African Trust (1973). (Reported in S.K.B. Asante, "Restructuring Transnational Mineral Agreements" *The American Journal of International Law,* Vol. 73, 1979).

33. A very interesting illustration of this point is provided by the Anaconda v. OPIC litigation, cited in footnote 22 of Chapter 3.

34. Asante, *op. cit.,* p. 341.

35. D. Bennett and K. Sharpe, in their "Controlling the Multinationals: The Ill Logic of Mexicanisation" (Feb. 1977).

36. Bergsten, et al., *op. cit.,* pp. 393-94.

37. B. Widyono, "Transnational Corporations in Mineral Resources Development: A Conceptual Framework for Research," paper presented at the International Conference on International Mineral

Resources Development, Emerging Legal and Institutional Arrangements, organized by the German Foundation for International Development (DSE) in co-operation with the United Nations, West Berlin, 11-15 August, 1980.

38. Cf. F. Sanchez Albaverra, *Mineria, Capital Transnacional y Poder en el Peru* (DESCO, Lima, 1981).

39. Along these lines, it is interesting to note that in Mexico, for example, several major U.S. multinationals (including Chrysler, Del Monte, Continental Can, DuPont, Ford, Gillette, Monsato and others) initiated efforts to form joint ventures shortly after the 1975 enactment of a new foreign investment law in order to obtain the tax and other incentives reserved by mexicanized operations. In fact, foreign investment in Mexico declined in 1971-72 and then rose after the passage of the new law. (Taken from Bergsten, et al., pp. 348-349).

40. As Dunning has pointed out, because of their domination of high-technology sectors, multinational firms are sometimes regarded as "the main inhibitor of indiginous technology-creating activities and of the advancement of the dynamic comparative advantage of developing countries." [J. Dunning, "Alternative Channels and Modes of International Resource Transmission," in T. Sagafi-nejad, et al (eds.) *Controlling International Technology Transfer* (Pergamon, New York, 1981), p. 15].

41. Evans, *op. cit.*, pp. 176-193.

42. L.E. Westphal, Y.W. Rhee and G. Pursell, World Bank Staff Working Paper No. 469, July 1981, pp. 65-68.

43. *Ibid.*, p. 3.

44. *Ibid.*, p. 65.

45. Cf. A. Ghorbel, *op. cit.*

46. Cf. K. Abdallah-Khodja, *op. cit.*

47. Referring to the Brazilian experience, Evans thus argues, "To put the argument in its most simplistic form, the best cards on the side of locals are political. The multinationals' best cards are technological. [But there] is an additional factor that makes the bargaining difficult from a nationalist point of view... When the multinationals are not confident about future profits then they will be likely to respond to demands for local control by refraining from increased investment, thereby threatening overall expansion. Changes in the proportions of Brazilian joint ventures over time make the connection between the economic context and multinational willingness to share control blatantly clear. During the rapid growth of the fifties... the majority of multinationals starting manufacturing operations in Brazil were willing to share control. As soon as the lean times of the early sixties began, the proportion of new joint ventures dropped and the tendency to turn old joint ventures into wholly owned subsidiaries was accelerated [...]. The proportion of subsidiaries formed by acquisition of local companies rose at the same time... "denationalization" was exacerbated. Brazil in the early sixties illustrates perfectly the extent to which an attractive "investment climate" is the sine qua non of bargaining over control. Without the promise of profits, political pressure will undermine expansion without increasing local control." (Evans, *op. cit.*, pp. 203-206.) It is worth adding that, with Brazil's economic "miracle" of the late 1960s and early 1970s, the situation was once again much more favorable to the "nationalists'" bargaining position, undoubtedly reinforced since the mid-1970s by the proliferation of "newcomer" multinationals seeking to establish themselves in Brazil.

48. The above-cited World Bank study thus concludes, "Indeed, Korea's remarkable industrialisation would not have occurred without the design and implementation of effective government policies that have fostered industrial dynamism." As regards the willingness of foreign firms to "co-operate" with the government's policies, the study makes the following observations when discussing the current attempt to shift the economy towards more technologically sophisticated industries: "What seems apparent from recent experience is that the shift... implies greater reliance on licensing as the mode of acquiring technology. [...] What is not so apparent is whether firms overseas will license technology without restricting its use. They may impose several restrictions on the sales of licensed products. They may prefer to give access to technology only through FDI. Or they may even deny access."

49. Bergsten, et al., *op. cit.*, p. 332.

50. This lack of recognition is perhaps due to a common belief that for developing countries emphasis should be placed on the contribution of foreign investment resources to growth of output rather than on structural "distortions" which inhibit inefficiency in a neo-classical sense, and/or to a belief that when faced with the monopolistic powers of foreign investors, and despite the "efficiency costs" involved, developing countries derive important advantages from high levels of local concentration (in both private and state enterprises) in negotiating with foreign capital.

51. N. Leff, *op. cit.*, p. 7/9.

52. "The Group is a multi-company firm somewhat similar to the *zaibatsu* of pre-World War II Japan, and to conglomerates in contemporary more-developed countries. Drawing their capital from sources which transcend a single family and often possessing their own bank as well, the Groups have displayed considerable entrepreneurial capacity in investing and producing in many of the new activities which comprise the "modern" sector in developing countries... often involving substantial vertical integration rather than simply growth within a single product line." *Ibid.*, pp. 722-723.

53. *Ibid.*, p. 727. Although he does not pursue this historical comparison, it is arguable that in a market-economy context, the key to global structural transformation and development, as distinct from growth of industrial output *per se*, lies in the inter-sectoral linkages and pecuniary externalities – viz. the qualitative transformation of domestic agriculture introduced by the Industrial Revolution – which result from the type of relatively unconcentrated market structures and active price competition characteristic of most of today's developed market economies in the 19th century.

54. *Ibid.*, p. 723 (our emphasis).

55. *Ibid.*, p. 728. This lack of "social legitimacy" is suggestive of a larger set of problems relating to the legitimacy or democratisation of economic and political power in many developing countries.

56. Referring to Hirschman's well known article on "The Political Economy of Import-Substituting Industrialization in Latin america" (Quarterly Journal of Economies, February 1968) the author goes on to point out that, "In these conditions private capitalism is often viewed unfavorably in the less-developed countries. Moreover the disillusion is especially great because industrialization was expected to reduce the concentration of economic power. Earlier, a small number of large land-owning families held dominant economic power; the only change which appears to have resulted from industrial development is that economic power is now concentrated in the hands of a relatively small number of Groups." Furthermore, "under current oligopolistic conditions, industrial development in many developing countries leads to an increase in political tensions and instability. The net outcome in many cases has been military rule." (*Ibid.*, pp. 728, 730).

57. Evans (*op. cit.*, pp. 157-158) cites the interesting example of Atunes in Brazil, who has used pyramiding to control a Brazilian mining firm in which he is only a minority partner with such foreign firms as Mitsui and Bethlehem Steel.

58. See forthcoming World Bank study of technology exports from developing countries.

59. Cf. A. Gourdain – Mitsotaki, *op. cit.*

60. For a good summary of alternative arguments on this point, see R. Newfarmer, "International Industrial Organization and Development: A Survey", in R. Newfarmer (ed.), *International Oligopoly and Development,* forthcoming.

Table 1.   STRUCTURE OF JAPAN'S MINERAL-ORE IMPORTS
FROM DEVELOPING COUNTRIES IN 1973

| Mineral | Supplier | Japanese Share of Suppliers Total Exports   % | Suppliers Share of Total Japanese Imports   % |
|---|---|---|---|
| Iron-ore | India | 98.7 | 15.0 |
| | Brazil | 27.3 | 9.0 |
| | Chile | 96.6 | 6.7 |
| Copper-ore | Philippines | 86.9 | 22.9 |
| | Chile | 71.5 | 6.9 |
| Nickel-ore | New Caledonia | 64.5 | 43.0 |
| Bauxite | Indonesia | 93.3 | 18.0 |
| | Malaysia | 95.5 | 16.7 |
| Lead-ore | Peru | 37.3 | 16.4 |
| Zinc-ore | Peru | 50.7 | 28.6 |
| Manganese-ore | India | 92.9 | 16.4 |
| Chromium-ore | India | 100.0 | 21.3 |
| Tungsten-ore | Korea | 41.0 | 32.2 |
| | Thailand | 21.5 | 16.9 |

*Source:*  K. Kojima, *Direct Foreign Investment, A Japanese Model of Multinational Business Operations* (Praeger, New York, 1978) pp. 207-208.

*Appendix*

# SOME AGGREGATE MEASURES OF NEW FORMS OF INVESTMENT

by

Graham Vickery

The "new" forms of capital and organisational links between OECD countries and developing countries are examined here by dissecting the aggregate statistics of OECD countries.

Aspects such as trade in capital goods or independent licence and technical assistance transactions can be measured. However, it is not easy to detect the general growth and evolution of new forms of investment in aggregate trade or balance of payments statistics. Many of the links between enterprises (i.e. minority direct investment, joint ventures, technical and management services, and capital and equipment flows) cannot easily be seen in the balance of payments time-series that are routinely collected.

Section I presents some general trends. Transactions involving industrial property rights and technical services are then examined in detail. This is followed by a brief examination of trade in capital goods in Section III, and of financial flows in Section IV. Finally a summary of trends in the new forms of investment relative to traditional majority direct investment is presented.

The approach is necessarily general and mostly deals with broad trends rather than with details by country or industry. "Traditional" foreign direct investment is always compared with the "new" links between OECD countries and developing countries, with the test being whether the new forms are growing more or less rapidly than traditional investment, or in different ways.

## I. GENERAL TRENDS

### A. Direct investment

Total additions to direct investment grew in current terms in the period 1970-1981. In real terms the annual flows grew at an average rate of over 4 per cent per annum between 1970 and 1979 and then dropped sharply in 1980 before returning to the trend growth rate in 1981. (See Table 1 for aggregate figures). The downturn in 1980 was largely due to equity and intercompany inflows into the U.S., and lower reinvestment of earnings by U.S. petroleum companies in 1980[1].

### B. Receipts for technology: industrial property rights and technical services

Receipts for technology showed a consistent and steady increase of 15 per cent per annum in current terms (about 6 per cent per annum in real terms) during the period. Values are shown in Table 1.

119

| | Values (billion current US $) | | | | | | Rate of growth 1970-1981) (%) | |
|---|---|---|---|---|---|---|---|---|
| | 1970 | 1977 | 1978 | 1979 | 1980 | 1981 | Current values % | Constant values % |
| Direct investment: net[1] | 3.7 | 9.5 | 10.9 | 12.7 | 9.8 | 14.6 | 13.3 | 4 |
| Receipts for technology[2] | 0.6 | 1.5 | 1.8 | 2.0 | 2.6 | 2.9e | 15.1 | 6 |
| Capital goods[3] | 16.7 | 78.3 | 94.8 | 102.8 | 122.6 | 135.0e | 20.9 | 12 |
| Private export credits: | | | | | | | | |
| gross[1] | 5.2 | 18.1 | 21.8 | 22.9 | 27.8 | 29.4 | 17.0 | 7 |
| net[1] | 2.1 | 8.5 | 9.4 | 10.4 | 11.5 | 10.6 | 15.7 | 6 |
| Bank sector and bond lending: | | | | | | | | |
| gross[4] | | 21.6 | 37.7 | 47.9 | 36.7 | 50.0 | | |
| net[1, 5] | 3.3 | 18.7 | 25.5 | 20.8 | 21.7 | 27.4e | 21.2 | 11 |

1. Includes developing OECD: DAC definitions. OECD, *Development Cooperation, 1982 Review.* Constant values derived with DAC GNP deflator.
2. Royalties and fees, technical services. Author's calculations based on data for France, Germany, Italy, Japan, Netherlands, U.K., U.S. Estimates for 1970, 1971, 1981 for some countries. Definitions vary between countries. Not including developing OECD.
3. Author's calculations based on OECD, *Trade by Commodities.* Not including developing OECD. Constant values derived with UN machinery unit value indices.
4. OECD, *Financial Statistics Monthly,* external bonds plus international medium and long-term bank loans. Not including developing OECD.
5. From all sources. *Development Cooperation, op. cit..* Bank sector plus bond lending.

This group of receipts covers: *(i)* receipts of royalties and fees for the rights to use intangible industrial property (patents, licences, trademarks) and technical know-how, and for the supply of management and consultancy services; and *(ii)* receipts for engineering services and technical assistance that are linked to industrial and civil engineering, construction, and the supply of equipment. When examining aggregate data for different countries, it is important to remember that receipts for the right to exploit intangible industrial property are different in nature and timing from receipts for the provision of engineering services. There are considerable differences between OECD countries in the coverage of service and technical assistance activities. These differences imply that national data for different countries should be compared very cautiously. Furthermore, transactions are not necessarily between independent firms. Data for transactions between affiliated firms are included in aggregates shown in Table 1 and affiliated transactions grew strongly in the period 1970-1981.

## C. Exports of capital goods

Exports of capital goods to developing countries grew rapidly during the period. They showed robust increases in both current (21 per cent) and real (12 per cent) terms. Some of these exports were linked to direct investment and are examined below. However the strength and steadiness of growth compared with foreign direct investment suggests that there was an increasingly independent and flexible strand to industrial-isation, construction and capital formation in developing countries.

Export credits, both gross and net, have also grown strongly to finance export of capital equipment on concessional terms.

## D. Other financial flows

Bank sector and bond lending rose dramatically in the period 1970-1981. Some of these loans and financial flows went to service ever-increasing debt and balance of payments deficits, particularly as the world economy slowed after the second oil price rise. However a significant proportion went into productive investment in industry and in physical infrastructure, until high interest rates exacerbated financial difficulties.

The general picture during the period 1970-1981 can be summarised as follows: direct investment grew more slowly than transactions in industrial property rights and technical services, but both of these were outstripped by capital goods trade and capital goods financing, and by financial flows.

Do these trends suggest that traditional direct investment is being replaced by new forms of financial and economic links between OECD and developing countries? Or do the trends give a misleading picture which must be modified after closer examination?

## II.  INDUSTRIAL PROPERTY RIGHTS AND TECHNICAL SERVICES

### A.  General features

Receipts for technology cover two different kinds of activity:

   *i)*  licensing and similar transactions, that transfer rights to use intangible industrial property and know-how usually in return for continuing royalty payments, and long-term management and technical services that have a similar aspect of continuity; and

   *ii)*  engineering and technical assistance services which are linked to construction and engineering projects and which are limited in time to the building and start-up of a project or industrial complex. The extent to which this second group of transactions is included in data of a particular OECD country has an important influence on trends.

General trends are given in Table 2 for six major OECD countries. It is clear from this table that, despite differences in definition between countries, a slowly decreasing proportion of total receipts went to the U.S., as other OECD countries (France, Japan) increased their share of total technological inputs going to developing countries.

If foreign technical services and the exploitation of intangible industrial property rights are an increasingly important part of industrial and economic development in developing countries, then payments for them would be expected to grow in real terms

Table 2.  VALUES OF RECEIPTS FOR INDUSTRIAL PROPERTY RIGHTS, TECHNICAL AND RELATED SERVICES FROM DEVELOPING COUNTRIES

(million $)

| | | 1970 | 1971 | 1972 | 1973 | 1974 | 1975 | 1976 | 1977 | 1978 | 1979 | 1980 |
|---|---|---|---|---|---|---|---|---|---|---|---|---|
| France | (A) | 21.6 | 21.6 | 48.3 | 68.1 | 74.2 | 128.1 | 124.6 | 158.9 | 146.1 | 160.1 | 251.1 |
| | (B) | 42.5 | 40.0 | 77.3 | 89.3 | 94.4 | 128.1 | 126.4 | 152.2 | 117.3 | 110.0 | 153.4 |
| Germany | (A) | 26.6 | 34.9 | 41.5 | 40.9 | 59.4 | 65.3 | 38.5 | 44.5 | 64.4 | 74.0 | 69.2 |
| | (B) | 54.2 | 63.1 | 65.0 | 50.7 | 66.7 | 65.3 | 38.1 | 39.2 | 47.3 | 47.8 | 42.3 |
| Italy | (A) | | | 9.1 | 6.2 | 14.5 | 15.6 | 18.3 | 43.5 | 25.0 | 38.9 | 49.0 |
| | (B) | | | 12.6 | 7.7 | 17.0 | 15.6 | 19.8 | 41.8 | 20.3 | 26.8 | 28.9 |
| Japan | (A) | | | 59.2 | 84.8 | 93.3 | 114.1 | 145.2 | 173.9 | 300.4 | 315.1 | 411.5 |
| | (B) | | | 87.7 | 101.9 | 98.8 | 114.1 | 134.4 | 133.7 | 173.4 | 202.3 | 242.3 |
| U.K. | (A) | 31.8 | 30.3 | 30.6 | 38.7 | 51.0 | 51.6 | 95.8 | 103.7 | 118.1 | 100.4 | 128.7 |
| | (B) | 54.5 | 46.6 | 42.5 | 51.2 | 61.5 | 51.6 | 102.7 | 100.9 | 94.3 | 63.0 | 61.9 |
| U.S. | (A) | 445 | 475 | 483 | 552 | 674 | 781 | 761 | 754 | 983 | 1 144 | 1 410 |
| | (B) | 611 | 622 | 607 | 656 | 737 | 781 | 723 | 677 | 826 | 882 | 999 |

(A)  current $
(B)  constant 1975 $
*Sources:*  Author's calculations based on national sources. Artistic and film receipts excluded. Definitions vary between countries. Constant $ values calculated by deflating with national GDP price indices in purchasers' values (1975 = 100) and converting into 1975 $: OECD, *National Accounts, Main Aggregates* 1951-1980; IMF, *International Financial Statistics.*

(Table 2), and developing countries would be the source of a growing share of the worldwide receipts of OECD countries. This trend could be accentuated if technical inputs were closely linked to the high rates of industrial and economic growth experienced by many developing countries. However, the share of technological receipts from developing countries did not increase dramatically between 1970 and 1980. Graphic 1 shows receipts from developing countries as a percentage of total world-wide technological receipts for six OECD countries.

Japan clearly receives a higher proportion of total receipts from developing countries than do the other OECD countries. Developing countries were the source of about one-half of total Japanese receipts for technology exports, whereas the share for the other five major countries did not reach one-third of the total. France and Italy include technical assistance and engineering services in their data and both of these countries showed a generally rising trend in the share coming from developing countries with peaks in the mid-1970's. The U.K. captures a small proportion of total technical assistance and engineering services in royalty data and also showed a peak in the share from developing countries in 1976-1978.

Japan only includes "technical guidance" in the published data which showed a declining share from developing countries through to 1977 with a subsequent recovery. The U.S. collects contract operations of engineering and technical service firms separately (see below), and royalty and fee receipts showed a declining trend through to 1977 with a subsequent recovery. Germany also collects data on construction services separately and showed a declining share of receipts for technology (patents, inventions, processes) throughout the period.

Intangible property rights transactions are much more important for countries that have a reasonable technical and industrial infrastructure than for those with a less developed infrastructure. The former can make use of licensing arrangements, while the latter rely on foreign technical assistance and engineering services to build industry and establish the technical infrastructure. Payments for licences come mainly from industrial countries, whereas payments for engineering services come from developing countries. France and Italy separately identify technical assistance in their technology balance of payments, and they both had rapid increases in receipts for engineering and similar services from OPEC countries in the mid-East during the 1970's[2].

In summary, total technnological receipts showed some upward trend due to growth of receipts for engineering and technical services. They also reflected some movement towards independent arrangements by developing countries during the period 1970-1980, but this movement was not dramatic.

## B. Affiliated versus unaffiliated transactions

### i) U.K. and U.S.

Only the U.K. and the U.S. publish detailed figures that distinguish between affiliated and independent transactions. If there is a general shift by developing countries towards independent licensing or non-equity and minority equity arrangements, then independent receipts should increase as a proportion of total receipts from affiliated and independent sources[3].

Whereas the U.S. showed no significant increase in the share of independent transactions across all industry, for the U.K. there was a dramatic increase in 1976-78, with a subsequent decline. Graphic 2 shows independent receipts as a percentage of total independent and affiliated receipts. Detailed examination of U.K. data suggests that this rise was partly due to increases in receipts from supplying independent engineering and technical services to Asia, including the mid-East. It was also partly due to large increases that were not allocated by country.

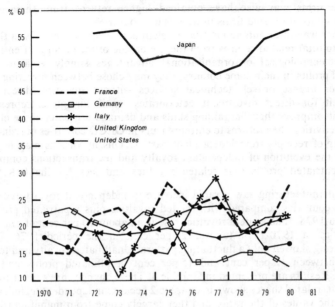

Graphic 1   **TECHNOLOGY RECEIPTS FROM DEVELOPING COUNTRIES AS % OF TECHNOLOGY RECEIPTS FROM ALL SOURCES**

Legend:
- France
- Germany
- Italy
- United Kingdom
- United States

Japan

**Source :** Author's calculations from national sources.

Graphic 2   **TECHNOLOGY RECEIPTS FROM UNRELATED ENTERPRISES AS % TOTAL TECHNOLOGY RECEIPTS FROM DEVELOPING COUNTRIES**

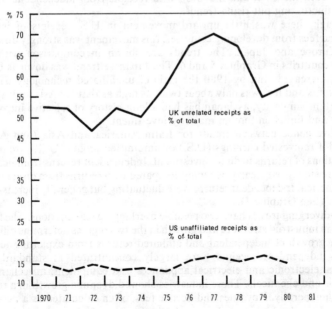

UK unrelated receipts as % of total

US unaffiliated receipts as % of total

**Source :** Author's calculations from national sources.

123

Thus it appears that U.K. firms increased their supply of technical assistance to unrelated enterprises, or turned to unrelated sales of intangible industrial property, or both. U.K. firms may also have obtained higher returns from their technology transactions with unrelated firms in developing countries.

Another way of disentangling this problem is to examine changes in the ratio of unrelated to total related returns from the use or sale of technology. If entrepreneurs that have technological or organisational advantages simply wish to maximise repatriated profits in their home country, they may chose between investing in foreign countries or license or sell technical services without investing directly. If the environment for direct investment deteriorates, or if foreign entrepreneurs and governments improve their bargaining skills and demand a greater share of equity in domestic activities, then returns to entrepreneurs in OECD countries may increasingly be made up of receipts from independent parties. This hypothesis may be tested by examining the evolution of independent royalty and fee transactions compared with related repatriated profits plus related royalties and fees for the U.K.[4] and the U.S.[5].

U.K. manufacturing saw a rapid increase in independent royalty receipts from developing countries compared with related royalties plus repatriated profits in the period 1976-1978. Independent royalties rose from about 10 per cent of related profits and royalties in 1970-1974 to over 20 per cent in the period 1976-1978. U.S. manufacturing showed only a fluctuating pattern. Unaffiliated royalty and fee receipts remained between 12 per cent and 15 per cent of affiliated profits and royalties combined[6]. Results are presented in Graphic 3. These changes are similar to those for independent/related shares shown in Graphic 2 because independent technical receipts determine the values of the ratios and they largely come from manufacturing[7].

By region, the clear divergence in trends between Latin America, Asia and Africa is shown in Graphic 4. For both the U.K. and the U.S., there was a general downward trend in independent royalties and fees compared with related royalties and profits from Latin America. For Asia and Africa combined (predominantly Asia), the trend was the reverse for both the U.K. and the U.S., with receipts from independent transactions showing a fluctuating but rising trend[8].

Although there was little upward movement in U.S. receipts of independent royalties and fees from developing countries, this movement was strongly downward for Canada, Europe and Japan. The trends are shown in comparison with those of developing countries in Graphics 5 and 6. The Japanese trend was down as U.S. direct investment increased, and by 1980 the ratio of unaffiliated technology payments to affiliated profits and fees was only about twice as high as that for Asia and Africa. This is an important similarity, as Japan has had a long history of selective introduction of technology and limits on foreign majority investment.

The divergence between trends for Latin America and Asia (and Africa) are maintained if reinvested earnings (U.S.) or unremitted profits (U.K.) are included in the calculations of returns to direct investment. Independent returns from licensing and services were slowly but clearly declining compared with returns from direct investment in Latin America. Independent returns were fluctuating but generally increasing in Asia and Africa. (See Graphic 7).

These diverging trends have two possible overlapping explanations. The first is that differences in industrial structure and growth in the two regions determine differences in the relative growth of independent and affiliated returns from exploiting technology.

Asian independent receipts were largely concentrated in standard elecronic components, electronic and electrical appliances and equipment, miscellaneous consumer goods and chemicals. These industries showed dynamic growth in a region with high growth generally. Royalties and licence fees, often calculated as a percentage of sales, showed similar high growth rates. Latin American independent receipts largely

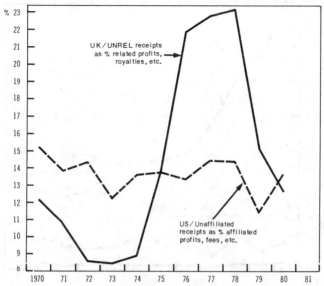

*Source :* Estimates based on data from *Business Monitor MA4,* and *Survey of Current Business.*

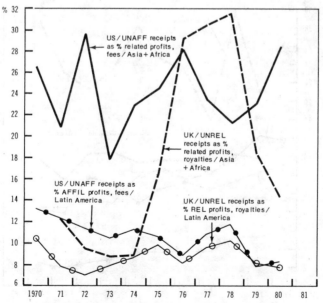

*Source :* Estimates based on data from *Business Monitor MA4,* and *Survey of Current Business.*

125

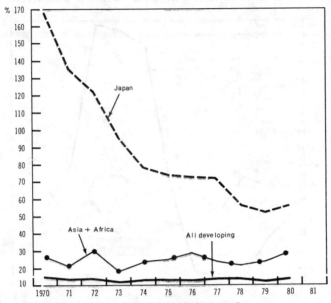

Graphic 5   UNAFF TECHNOLOGY RECEIPTS/PROFITS, FEES ETC.: MANUFACTURING

Source : Estimates based on data from Survey of Current Business, op. cit.

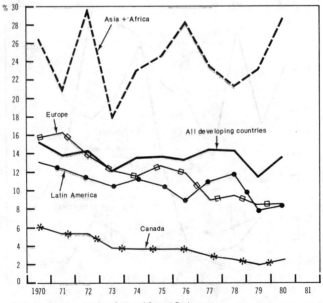

Graphic 6   UNAFF TECHNOLOGY RECEIPTS/PROFITS, FEES ETC.: MANUFACTURING

Source : Estimates based on data from Survey of Current Business.

126

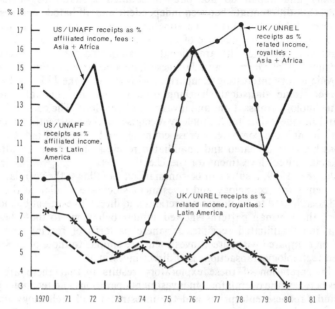

Graphic 7 "INDEPENDENT" TECHNOLOGY RECEIPTS AS % OF
"RELATED" INCOME, FEES ETC.: DEVELOPING REGIONS, MANUFACTURING

Source : Estimates based on data from Business Monitor MA4, and Survey of Current Business.

came from the heavy machinery, chemical and traditional industries. These industries have shown relatively lower growth (with the exception of chemicals) in a lower growth region.

The second explanation involves the regulations and controls on technology transactions and foreign investment introduced in Latin America during the early part of the 1970s. These controls were in part designed to increase local participation in industry and to limit payments for technology.

However, in the 1970's Latin America experienced a relative reduction in independent payments of royalties to the U.K and U.S., strong growth in direct investment (particularly from Germany and Japan) and continued growth in affiliated profit and royalty payments to parent companies (in the U.S.). This may have been due to closer scrutiny of royalty payments by regulatory bodies and attempts to ensure a higher real transfer of technology per unit of payment (which results in lower licence payments). Furthermore, large international companies with valuable technology have greater resources to devote to mastering new regulations and maintaining their presence in expanding markets than do independent companies, and international companies can maintain higher royalty and profit flows and high rates of reinvestment. Finally, in some industries or product groups, there may be few ways of acquiring technology other than through 100 per cent or majority equity investment by foreign firms.

Overall, there were few signs that the general investment climate deteriorated sharply during the period, although there were some notable exceptions. The probable explanation of the increase in receipts from independent enterprises in some developing countries is that governments and entrepreneurs gained and retained greater equity in high-growth domestic activities.

127

## ii) Germany and Japan

Germany and Japan do not publish detailed breakdowns of technological transactions that differentiate between independent and affiliated concerns[9]. This is a pity as it seems likely that part of the impetus for new forms of investment probably comes from the increasing presence of new investors from Germany and Japan that complement and compete with traditional investors and forms of investment. The detailed structures of German and Japanese independent and affiliated transactions would provide a very interesting comparison with those of the U.K. and U.S.

However, some statistical sleuthing does provide insights into German and Japanese technology transactions and investment behaviour. The correlations between German and Japanese data for technology receipts and their respective stock of foreign direct investment were compared across countries and across all industries with the correlations between affiliated and unaffiliated receipts of fees and royalties and the stock of foreign direct investment for the U.S.[10].

For the year 1979, results can be summarised as follows: the correlation between German receipts for technology and investment stock are similar to the correlation between U.S. affiliated technology transactions and direct investment by industry only. By country, the German patterns showed similar behaviour to those between U.S. investment and unaffiliated receipts. Japanese patterns of receipts for technology exports when compared with direct investment are similar to those of U.S. patterns of unaffiliated technology transactions and direct investment.

One interpretation of these exploratory results is that there are significant differences between the overall foreign investment operations and technology exports of German and Japanese enterprises and the investment and technology links of U.S. affiliated enterprises.

Furthermore, for Japan, a large proportion of technology receipts probably came from unaffiliated enterprises, but the choices by Japanese enterprises between unaffiliated and affiliated operations are similar to those of U.S. enterprises when they are operating in the same industries and countries.

Japanese technology exports may substitute for direct investment by allowing Japanese enterprises to reap returns where direct investment is limited. German receipts show a more complex pattern. For Germany, technology exports may complement direct investment or substitute for it.

These results may partly be due to the relative newness of German and Japanese investment and the dynamics that determine flows of affiliated receipts to parents. But they also reflect differences between Germany and Japan and other countries in the industries and countries that they are investing and setting up new organisational arrangements in, and the influence of unrelated contractual arrangements on patterns of technology receipts when compared with patterns of direct investment.

## C. Majority-owned affiliates and unaffiliated royalties and fees

The foregoing discussion does not distinguish between majority-owned affiliates and minority-owned affiliates. For example, U.S. affiliates may have as little as 10 per cent equity ownership by the U.S. "parent" company. However, in most countries most affiliates are also majority-owned: more than 50 per cent of their equity is controlled by their foreign parent. In these countries most royalties and fees also come from affiliates. On the other hand, governments that have been concerned in the past with limiting direct investment and promoting independent licensing have also sought to limit majority-owned investment. This general relation is illustrated in Graphic 8. The percentage of total U.S. investment assets controlled by majority-owned subsidiaries is plotted against technology receipts from affiliates expressed as a percentage of total receipts from affiliated and unaffiliated enterprises.

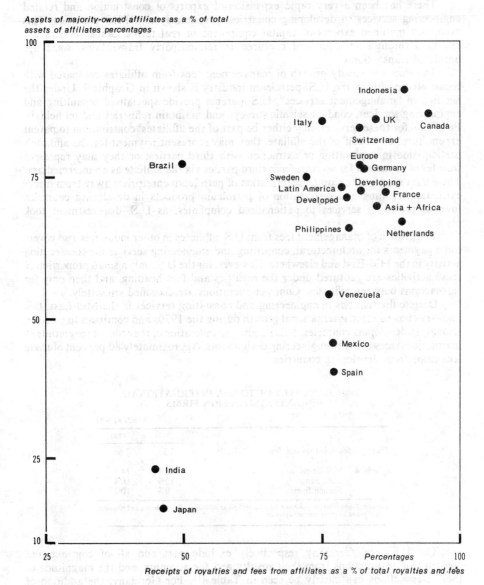

Assets of majority-owned affiliates as a % of total
assets of affiliates percentages

Receipts of royalties and fees from affiliates as a % of total royalties and fees

**Source :** Estimates based on data from *Survey of Current Business.*

As expected, majority-owned affiliates and affiliated royalties are highly concentrated in the same countries. Canada and Indonesia are high on both majority-owned
affiliates and related party payments for technology, while India and Japan are low on
both counts.

## D. Management fees and technical and engineering services

There has been a very rapid expansion of exports of construction and related engineering services to developing countries, particularly to OPEC countries. This expansion matched exports of capital equipment in real terms. Some services are extended through affiliates and captured in related-party transactions, some are unrelated transactions.

The slow but steady growth of management fees from affiliates compared with repatriated profits in the U.S. petroleum industry is shown in Graphic 9. Under the heading of "management services", U.S. parents provide specialised consulting and engineering services, conduct seismic surveys and maintain refineries and oil fields[11]. Payments for these services may either be part of the affiliates' contribution to parent expenditures on behalf of the affiliate; they may represent payment for the affiliate's participation in exploration or extraction with third parties; or they may represent transfer of payments for services from third parties via the affiliate as an intermediary. These data suggest the slow transformation of petroleum enterprises away from direct extraction, refining and distribution of petroleum products in developing countries towards providing services to nationalised companies, as U.S. disinvestment took place.

The growth of management fees from U.S. affiliates in other industries also covers some payments for architectural, consulting and engineering services for construction activity in the Mid-East and elsewhere. However, for the U.S. only a small proportion of these activities are captured under the royalties and fees heading, and then only for transactions between affiliates. Contract operations are classified separately.

Despite fluctuations in engineering and consulting services in the Mid-East, this industry showed rapid international growth during the 1970s and continues to perform strongly in developing countries. Table 3 gives an indication of the order of magnitude of international fees going to engineering design firms. Approximately 80 per cent of these fees came from developing countries.

Table 3.  SURVEY OF TOP 150 INTERNATIONAL
ENGINEERING DESIGN FIRMS

|  |  | (billion US $) | |
| --- | --- | --- | --- |
|  |  | 1979 | 1980 |
| Total professional service fees | | 2.1 | 2.6 |
| of which: | U.S. firms | 38% | 34% |
|  | U.K. firms | 15% | 16% |
|  | French firms | 9% | 10% |

Source:   Engineering News-Record. Services include architecture, all engineering and planning, and construction management.

The U.S. and Germany respectively exclude part and all of contract and construction transactions from their royalty and fee accounts, and the magnitude of these transactions can clearly be seen in Table 4[12]. For Germany, the addition of receipts for construction services to receipts for patents, inventions and processes in Table 2 gives a better picture of exports of technical services and know-how by German firms.

The U.S. data also round out the U.S. royalty and fee data by showing the importance of the operations of international contractors. These receipts are the unaffiliated counterparts of affiliated payments of management fees to parents for technical or construction services illustrated in Graphic 9 for the petroleum industry.

Table 4.   EXPORTS OF CONSTRUCTION AND CONTRACTING SERVICES

(million $)

| | 1970 | 1977 | 1978 | 1979 | 1980 |
|---|---|---|---|---|---|
| **Germany:**  construction services, assembly and repairs: balance: | | | | | |
| to OPEC | | 1 041 | 1 107 | 1 268 | 1 658 |
| Other developing | | 41 | 153 | 127 | 234 |
| Total developing + OPEC | −4 | 1 082 | 1 260 | 1 395 | 1 892 |
| **USA:**  contract operations of U.S. construction, engineering and technical service firms: net receipts: | | | | | |
| OPEC | 64 | | 767 | 405 | 650 |
| Other developing | 103 | | 295 | 347 | 539 |
| Total developing + OPEC | 167 | | 1 062 | 752 | 1 189 |

*Sources:*  Statistical supplement to the *Monthly Report of the Deutsche Bundesbank,* Reihe 3, July, 1981; *Survey of Current Business,* November 1981, pp. 39-40.

Graphic 9   MANAGEMENT FEES AS % PROFITS : US PETROLEUM

**Source :** Estimates based on data from *Business Monitor* MA4, and *Survey of Current Business.*

What can be summarised from the information presented above?

There is some evidence from balance of payments data of an increase in independent technology agreements involving licences and technical assistance in the period 1970-1980. This was more marked in Asian countries than in Latin America. However, Latin American data are masked by investment and technology transfer regulations and controls and require country-by-country or case study work to clarify the picture.

German and Japanese data suggest that the international operations of their enterprises differ in some way from those of the U.S. But this also requires a case study approach to obtain further information rather than over-reliance on detailed statistical studies.

Independent international contracting and technical services grew rapidly during the period 1970-1980, particularly to OPEC countries. They involved transport, power and related physical infrastructure, as well as petroleum and mineral extraction and processing. They also provided an industrial base and contributed to further industrial development in non-OPEC countries.

## III.  CAPITAL GOODS

Capital goods exports from OECD countries to developing countries grew rapidly in the period 1970-1980 (see Table 1 for overall values in current terms and growth rates). A high share of total capital goods exports went to developing countries; this share remained stable over time despite the efforts and interest of developing countries in building up their domestic production of machinery, equipment and transport capital goods industries. The developing country share of OECD exports of capital goods is shown in Table 5.

A significant proportion of total capital equipment exports goes to affiliates of foreign companies. Detailed data which give an indication of the share of capital goods flows that are destined for affiliates are available for the U.S. from the 1977 Investment Benchmark Survey. Some of these data are summarised in Table 6.

Machinery exports from parents and non-U.S. affiliates to affiliates in developing countries were almost one-fifth of the value of U.S. machinery exports to developing countries. Total machinery exports to affiliates from all sources, including unaffiliated and non-U.S. sources, were equivalent to one-quarter of total U.S. machinery exports to developing countries.

These figures clearly show the importance of exports of capital equipment to affiliates in developing countries from U.S. parents and affiliates. Affiliates use

Table 5.  DESTINATION OF OECD EXPORTS OF CAPITAL GOODS

(per cent of total exports of capital goods)

| | 1968 | 1970 | 1971 | 1972 | 1973 | 1974 | 1975 | 1976 | 1977 | 1978 | 1979 | 1980 |
|---|---|---|---|---|---|---|---|---|---|---|---|---|
| Developing countries | 31 | 30 | 30 | 30 | 31 | 34 | 40 | 39 | 40 | 36 | 35 | 36 |
| of which:  OPEC | 5 | 5 | 6 | 6 | 6 | 8 | 14 | 16 | 17 | 16 | 12 | 13 |

Source:  Author's calculations from OECD, Trade by Commodities. Includes transport equipment and agricultural and telecommunications capital goods.

Table 6.  EXPORTS OF MACHINERY AND CAPITAL GOODS TO DEVELOPING COUNTRIES AND TO AFFILIATES IN DEVELOPING COUNTRIES:  1977

| | |
|---|---|
| Total U.S. exports of machinery to developing countries | $13.7 billion |
| From parents and affiliates to affiliates: | (per cent) |
| From parents in U.S. | 14.5 |
| From non-U.S. affiliates of U.S. parents | 4.0 |
| Sub-total | 18.5 |
| To affiliates from all sources: | |
| From U.S. | 18.0 |
| From other countries | 6.1 |
| Sub-total | 24.1 |

Source:  U.S. Department of Commerce, U.S. Direct Investment Abroad 1977 and OECD, Trade by Commodities. Machinery = SITC 71 + 72, and includes some consumer goods and intermediates.

company equipment wherever and whenever possible; on average over three-quarters of their machinery imports come from within the same firm. In 1977, imports of machinery were equivalent to about 40 per cent of total capital expenditures by U.S. affiliates. These calculations assume that transfer pricing does not give a significant upward bias to the value of machinery sales to affiliates.

Japanese exports of goods to developing Asian countries are also moderately well correlated with both direct investment and technological exports to these countries[13]. This suggests that export trade is closely linked with direct investment and technological affiliation.

Thus, a significant share of capital goods and machinery exports to developing countries is between parents and affiliates; that is, it takes place within the framework of traditional direct investment and should not be seen as evidence of rapid growth of new forms. Whether this is a declining share, which is being displaced by trade involving new investment forms, is not clear owing to the paucity of information regarding related party trade in capital goods and machinery.

## IV. CAPITAL FLOWS

International capital flows to developing countries have shown very large increases and rather volatile behaviour, particularly in the periods following the major oil price increases in 1973 and 1979. These flows are in part independent, in the sense that they go to national enterprises and government institutions, but in part they also go to finance foreign affiliates of OECD-based firms.

Following the 1973 oil price rise, multinational enterprises covered their financing needs particularly with external funds. This was well-documented by the U.S. Department of Commerce for U.S. majority-owned foreign affiliates[14]. In most cases, external funds came from foreign financial institutions as short-term borrowings, and from other foreign creditors, primarily unpaid suppliers. This pattern was probably repeated, with some differences, following the 1979 oil price rise.

Fluctuations in the international economy are clearly widening the "gap" between the financing requirements of multi-nationals and their internal sources of funds. One measure of this gap is shown in Graphics 10-13 for U.S. affiliates in developing countries; the gap is always present in manufacturing industry and it widens in periods of economic turmoil.

"Capital outflows" from the U.S. in Graphics 10-13 consist of equity and inter-company account outflows plus reinvested earnings. Reinvested earnings come from undistributed profits, depreciation and similar charges. Debt and equity financing by foreign affiliates of the U.S. parent are not included in the data represented in the Graphics. "Capital expenditures" in Graphics 10-13 are estimates of all physical asset investment without changes in inventories[15]. Inventories also tend to rise during periods of abrupt change in economic activity. For example, inventories increased in manufacturing in 1977 by $0.72 billion and probably showed greater increases in 1979-80. The financing of inventory build-up probably requires extra funds external to the firm.

To close the financing gap shown in the graphics, U.S. affiliates in developing countries have recourse mainly to: debt financing from foreign affiliates of the parent; debt financing from unrelated foreign financial institutions or creditors; debt financing from unrelated financial institutions at home; or sale of equity to foreign or home residents.

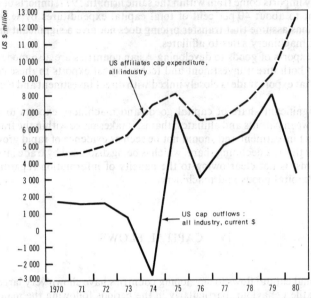

Graphic 10  US CAP OUTFLOWS, CAP EXPENDITURES : TOTAL

US affiliates cap expenditure, all industry

US cap outflows : all industry, current $

**Source :** Estimates based on *Survey of Current Business*, various issues. Capital outflows = reinvested earnings of incorporated affiliates plus equity and intercompany account outflows ;- values are inflows. Valuation adjustments excluded. Capital expenditures estimated for all affiliates from majority-owned affiliate data.

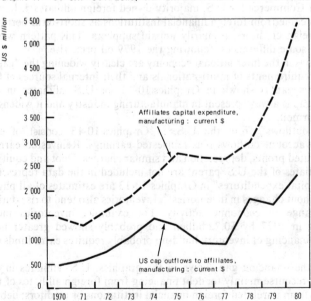

Graphic 11  US CAP OUTFLOWS, CAP EXPENDITURES : MANUFACTURING

Affiliates capital expenditure, manufacturing : current $

US cap outflows to affiliates, manufacturing : current $

**Source :** Estimates based on *Survey of Current Business*, various issues. Capital outflows = reinvested earnings of incorporated affiliates plus equity and intercompany account outflows ;- values are inflows. Valuation adjustments excluded. Capital expenditures estimated for all affiliates from majority-owned affiliate data.

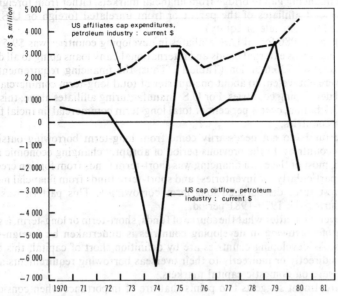

*Graphic 12* **US CAP OUTFLOW, CAP EXPENDITURE : PETROLEUM**

US affiliates cap expenditures, petroleum industry : current $

US cap outflow, petroleum industry : current $

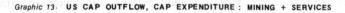

**Source :** Estimates based on *Survey of Current Business,* various issues. Capital outflows = reinvested earnings of incorporated affiliates plus equity and intercompany account outflows ;- values are inflows. Valuation adjustments excluded. Capital expenditures estimated for all affiliates from majority-owned affiliate data.

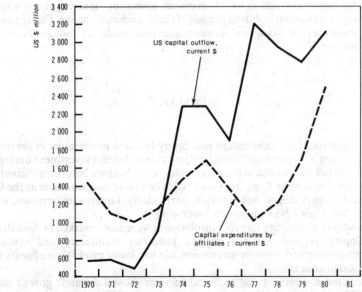

*Graphic 13.* **US CAP OUTFLOW, CAP EXPENDITURE : MINING + SERVICES**

US capital outflow, current $

Capital expenditures by affiliates : current $

**Source :** Estimates based on *Survey of Current Business,* various issues. Capital outflows = reinvested earnings of incorporated affiliates plus equity and intercompany account outflows ;- values are inflows. Valuation adjustments excluded. Capital expenditures estimated for all affiliates from majority-owned affiliate data.

Graphics 10 and 11 show clearly that U.S. affiliates in developing countries have a significant financing gap to bridge from financial markets, either from foreign financial or non-financial affiliates of the parent or from unrelated foreign or U.S. financial institutions (or from sale of equity).

This gap in 1980 for all U.S. affiliates in developing countries was $9.5 billion. In the same year, gross external bonds and international bank loans going to all developing countries totalled $36.6 billion (Table 1). Thus, the financing requirements of U.S. affiliates were equivalent to about one-quarter of total long-term commercial financial flows to all developing countries. For U.S. manufacturing affiliates alone, this financing gap was $3.1 billion, over 8 per cent of total long-term commercial financial flows to all developing countries.

These funds do not necessarily come from long-term borrowing outside of the developing countries. In the previous period of abruptly changing economic activity in 1974-1976, most of the extra financing was short-term funds from foreign creditors and suppliers (particularly for inventories) and short-term funds from financial institutions. High interest rates discouraged long-term borrowing[16]. This pattern was probably repeated during the 1979-1981 period.

However, no matter what the source of funds, short-term or long-term, a significant proportion of borrowing in developing countries is undertaken by foreign-controlled enterprises. As developing countries are by definition short of capital, this borrowing contributes directly or indirectly to their overseas borrowing requirements and places added pressure on domestic capital markets.

This treatment suggests two points that are of importance when considering the changing nature of direct investment in developing countries. These are:

– part of aggregate of borrowings from international capital markets (short-term or long-term, or both) goes to cover the financing requirements of multinational companies;
– the sum of inter-company account outflows and reinvested earnings is a misleading proxy for the state of traditional investment by multinationals. It under-represents additions to overseas assets by ignoring borrowing by affiliates, particularly during periods of rapid economic change. Foreign capital expenditures or sales are a more accurate guide to foreign investment behaviour.


## V. SUMMARY


There is evidence that independent non-equity forms of involvement in developing countries increased relative to traditional majority-owned direct investment during the period 1970-1981. This was due in part to changes in the balance between affiliated and independent involvement by firms from such traditional investing countries as the U.K. and U.S., and in part due to new arrivals, particularly Japanese enterprises, which appear to exploit their advantages with lower equity.

Low-equity or non-equity forms of involvement were more marked in Asia than in other developing regions. Latin American countries maintained and continued independent licensing and minority investment, but to a lesser extent than appears to be the case in Asian countries.

International contracting and technical services showed dynamic growth during the period 1970-1981. Much of this activity took place in OPEC countries, particularly for the building of infrastructure.

Nevertheless, the durability of traditional investment forms should not be underestimated. One-quarter of the value of U.S. capital goods and machinery flows to developing countries go to affiliates of U.S. multinational firms. Borrowing from international capital markets by developing countries is partly attributable to financing requirements of foreign multinationals, particularly during periods of instability in the international economy.

We have not concentrated on the economic or technological contribution of changes and continuities in external participation in industrial and commercial development. Some aggregate data have been investigated. These data suggest that developing countries have maintained, and in some cases increased, independent development of domestic industry and commerce. Whether this is due to government policy, increased domestic bargaining power, changing domestic economic structures, or changes in the strategies of overseas participants, or a mixture of all of these, cannot be decided from the evidence presented here.

The economic and technological significance of these changes requires detailed study of individual countries and industries. Whether the trends described will continue into the future is unclear, particularly because major developing countries have recently changed their policies towards foreign investment and are more flexible in permitting majority foreign investment. At the same time, large-scale international borrowing is being re-assessed and is more restricted than in the recent past.

# NOTES AND REFERENCES

1. These figures also exclude valuation adjustments and transactions with the Netherlands Antilles for the U.S. See U.S. Department of Commerce, *Survey of Current Business,* June and August, 1981.

2. Since 1979 Italy has collected data on "non-connected technical assistance", that is independent of other transactions; France includes "technical assistance" in its annual returns.

3. Throughout the discussion of affiliated and unaffiliated transactions it is assumed that $1 (or £1) of returns from affiliates retained a stable relation with $1 (or £1) of returns from independent firms, i.e. that unit returns from affiliates for a particular technology have not been consistently increasing relative to those from independent sources, or vice-versa. It is also assumed that there have not been dramatic changes in the industry composition of affiliated returns vis-a-vis independent returns. These are bold assumptions which require further detailed research work.

4. U.K. unrelated royalties and similar transactions expressed as a percentage of: interest and dividends from subsidiaries and associates and net profits of overseas branches plus royalties from related concerns. Royalties estimated from total royalty receipts from manufacturing. Reinvested earnings for manufacturing estimated from total reinvested earnings. From 1979 the classification of overseas fellow subsidiaries has changed. These are now treated as related concerns. The result of this change is that related party transactions are tighter, unrelated are lower.

5. U.S. royalties and fees from unaffiliated foreign residents expressed as a percentage of: repatriated interest, dividends and earnings of unincorporated affiliates plus royalties and fees from affiliated foreign residents. Excluding films and TV tape rentals. Unaffiliated values for manufacturing estimated from totals for period 1970-1977.

6. Manufacturing industry does not present the problems of wide fluctuations in profits and inter-company flows experienced by the petroleum industry due to disinvestment, or by banking due to rapid changes in international capital markets. Values in Graphics 3 and 4 should not be over-interpreted; all values are partly estimated. However, general directions of movements are probably reasonably accurate. The U.S. reports very few unaffiliated fees and royalties outside of manufacturing.

7. The estimation procedure may have allowed some non-manufacturing engineering and construction royalties to remain in independent royalty receipts for the U.K. and some engineering and petroleum industry royalties and fees to remain in U.S. data. However this bias would be consistently present throughout the period and is unlikely to have affected trends.

8. Disaggregated data for the U.K. must be treated with caution because of the large proportion of receipts that are not allocated by country or region.

9. Germany does distinguish enterprises in which there is a major foreign interest from those in which there is not. However there is no separate category for German enterprises with foreign interests of their own.

10. Correlation results: Germany, Japan, U.S. Data from national sources were reorganised to give matching sets. Data availability determined countries and industries chosen. For comparisons across the year 1979, for Germany 14 countries and 9 industries were readily available, for Japan 12 countries and 8 industries. These data refer to developed and developing countries and to total receipts by industry.

### CORRELATION COEFFICIENTS:

*Stocks of direct investment, receipts for technology exports: 1979*

Germany Japan U.S.: Affiliated Unaffiliated Total

|  | Germany | Japan | U.S. Affiliated | Unaffiliated Total |
|---|---|---|---|---|
| 9 industries | 0.556 | 0.627 | −0.204 | 0.532 |
| 14 countries | 0.234 | 0.801 | 0.216 | 0.694 |
| 8 industries | −0.178 | 0.829 | −0.0096 | 0.777 |
| 12 countries | 0.807 | 0.881 | 0.841 | 0.886 |

138

11. *Survey of Current Business*, January 1980, p. 34.

12. "Construction services, assembly and repairs" for Germany is a larger, more heterogeneous grouping than that of the U.S. for "contractor's services". However, the orders of magnitude are comparable

13. See G. Vickery, "International Technology Transactions: Data and Interpretation" DSTI/SPR/81.34/Secretariat, Workshop on the Technological Balance of Payments, 14th-15th December, 1981.

14. See Ida May Mantell, "Sources and Uses of Funds of Majority-Owned Foreign Affiliates of U.S. Companies, 1973-76", U.S. Department of Commerce, May 1979.

15. Other uses of funds such as changes in current receivables, cash and other short-term assets, are ignored in this treatment.

16. Ida May Mantell, *op. cit.*

# OECD SALES AGENTS
## DÉPOSITAIRES DES PUBLICATIONS DE L'OCDE

**ARGENTINA – ARGENTINE**
Carlos Hirsch S.R.L., Florida 165, 4° Piso (Galería Guemes)
1333 BUENOS AIRES, Tel. 33.1787.2391 y 30.7122

**AUSTRALIA – AUSTRALIE**
Australia and New Zealand Book Company Pty. Ltd.,
10 Aquatic Drive, Frenchs Forest, N.S.W. 2086
P.O. Box 459, BROOKVALE, N.S.W. 2100. Tel. (02) 452.44.11

**AUSTRIA – AUTRICHE**
OECD Publications and Information Center
4 Simrockstrasse 5300 Bonn (Germany). Tel. (0228) 21.60.45
Local Agent/Agent local :
Gerold and Co., Graben 31, WIEN 1. Tel. 52.22.35

**BELGIUM – BELGIQUE**
Jean De Lannoy, Service Publications OCDE
avenue du Roi 202, B-1060 BRUXELLES. Tel. 02/538.51.69

**BRAZIL – BRÉSIL**
Mestre Jou S.A., Rua Guaipa 518,
Caixa Postal 24090, 05089 SAO PAULO 10. Tel. 261.1920
Rua Senador Dantas 19 s/205-6, RIO DE JANEIRO GB.
Tel. 232.07.32

**CANADA**
Renouf Publishing Company Limited,
2182 ouest, rue Ste-Catherine,
MONTRÉAL, Qué. H3H 1M7. Tel. (514)937.3519
OTTAWA, Ont. K1P 5A6, 61 Sparks Street

**DENMARK – DANEMARK**
Munksgaard Export and Subscription Service
35, Nørre Søgade
DK 1370 KØBENHAVN K. Tel. +45.1.12.85.70

**FINLAND – FINLANDE**
Akateeminen Kirjakauppa
Keskuskatu 1, 00100 HELSINKI 10. Tel. 65.11.22

**FRANCE**
Bureau des Publications de l'OCDE,
2 rue André-Pascal, 75775 PARIS CEDEX 16. Tel. (1) 524.81.67
Principal correspondant :
13602 AIX-EN-PROVENCE : Librairie de l'Université.
Tel. 26.18.08

**GERMANY – ALLEMAGNE**
OECD Publications and Information Center
4 Simrockstrasse 5300 BONN Tel. (0228) 21.60.45

**GREECE – GRÈCE**
Librairie Kauffmann, 28 rue du Stade,
ATHÈNES 132. Tel. 322.21.60

**HONG-KONG**
Government Information Services,
Publications/Sales Section, Baskerville House,
2nd Floor, 22 Ice House Street

**ICELAND – ISLANDE**
Snaebjörn Jönsson and Co., h.f.,
Hafnarstraeti 4 and 9, P.O.B. 1131, REYKJAVIK.
Tel. 13133/14281/11936

**INDIA – INDE**
Oxford Book and Stationery Co. :
NEW DELHI-1, Scindia House. Tel. 45896
CALCUTTA 700016, 17 Park Street. Tel. 240832

**INDONESIA – INDONÉSIE**
PDIN-LIPI, P.O. Box 3065/JKT., JAKARTA, Tel. 583467

**IRELAND – IRLANDE**
TDC Publishers – Library Suppliers
12 North Frederick Street, DUBLIN 1 Tel. 744835-749677

**ITALY – ITALIE**
Libreria Commissionaria Sansoni :
Via Lamarmora 45, 50121 FIRENZE. Tel. 579751/584468
Via Bartolini 29, 20155 MILANO. Tel. 365083
Sub-depositari :
Ugo Tassi
Via A. Farnese 28, 00192 ROMA. Tel. 310590
Editrice e Libreria Herder,
Piazza Montecitorio 120, 00186 ROMA. Tel. 6794628
Costantino Ercolano, Via Generale Orsini 46, 80132 NAPOLI. Tel. 405210
Libreria Hoepli, Via Hoepli 5, 20121 MILANO. Tel. 865446
Libreria Scientifica, Dott. Lucio de Biasio "Aeiou"
Via Meravigli 16, 20123 MILANO. Tel. 807679
Libreria Zanichelli
Piazza Galvani 1/A, 40124 Bologna Tel. 237389
Libreria Lattes, Via Garibaldi 3, 10122 TORINO. Tel. 519274
La diffusione delle edizioni OCSE è inoltre assicurata dalle migliori librerie nelle
città più importanti.

**JAPAN – JAPON**
OECD Publications and Information Center,
Landic Akasaka Bldg., 2-3-4 Akasaka,
Minato-ku, TOKYO 107 Tel. 586.2016

**KOREA – CORÉE**
Pan Korea Book Corporation,
P.O. Box n° 101 Kwangwhamun, SÉOUL. Tel. 72.7369

**LEBANON – LIBAN**
Documenta Scientifica/Redico,
Edison Building, Bliss Street, P.O. Box 5641, BEIRUT.
Tel. 354429 – 344425

**MALAYSIA – MALAISIE**
University of Malaya Co-operative Bookshop Ltd.
P.O. Box 1127, Jalan Pantai Baru
KUALA LUMPUR. Tel. 51425, 54058, 54361

**THE NETHERLANDS – PAYS-BAS**
Staatsuitgeverij, Verzendboekhandel,
Chr. Plantijnstraat 1 Postbus 20014
2500 EA S-GRAVENHAGE. Tel. nr. 070.789911
Voor bestellingen: Tel. 070.789208

**NEW ZEALAND – NOUVELLE-ZÉLANDE**
Publications Section,
Government Printing Office Bookshops:
AUCKLAND: Retail Bookshop: 25 Rutland Street,
Mail Orders: 85 Beach Road, Private Bag C.P.O.
HAMILTON: Retail: Ward Street,
Mail Orders, P.O. Box 857
WELLINGTON: Retail: Mulgrave Street (Head Office),
Cubacade World Trade Centre
Mail Orders: Private Bag
CHRISTCHURCH: Retail: 159 Hereford Street,
Mail Orders: Private Bag
DUNEDIN: Retail: Princes Street
Mail Order: P.O. Box 1104

**NORWAY – NORVÈGE**
J.G. TANUM A/S
P.O. Box 1177 Sentrum OSLO 1. Tel. (02) 80.12.60

**PAKISTAN**
Mirza Book Agency, 65 Shahrah Quaid-E-Azam, LAHORE 3.
Tel. 66839

**PHILIPPINES**
National Book Store, Inc.
Library Services Division, P.O. Box 1934, MANILA.
Tel. Nos. 49.43.06 to 09, 40.53.45, 49.45.12

**PORTUGAL**
Livraria Portugal, Rua do Carmo 70-74,
1117 LISBOA CODEX. Tel. 360582/3

**SINGAPORE – SINGAPOUR**
Information Publications Pte Ltd,
Pei-Fu Industrial Building,
24 New Industrial Road N° 02-06
SINGAPORE 1953, Tel. 2831786, 2831798

**SPAIN – ESPAGNE**
Mundi-Prensa Libros, S.A.
Castelló 37, Apartado 1223, MADRID-1. Tel. 275.46.55
Libreria Bosch, Ronda Universidad 11, BARCELONA 7.
Tel. 317.53.08, 317.53.58

**SWEDEN – SUÈDE**
AB CE Fritzes Kungl Hovbokhandel,
Box 16 356, S 103 27 STH, Regeringsgatan 12,
DS STOCKHOLM. Tel. 08/23.89.00
Subscription Agency/Abonnements:
Wennergren-Williams AB,
Box 13004, S104 25 STOCKHOLM.
Tel. 08/54.12.00

**SWITZERLAND – SUISSE**
OECD Publications and Information Center
4 Simrockstrasse 5300 BONN (Germany). Tel. (0228) 21.60.45
Local Agents/Agents locaux
Librairie Payot, 6 rue Grenus, 1211 GENÈVE 11. Tel. 022.31.89.50

**TAIWAN – FORMOSE**
Good Faith Worldwide Int'l Co., Ltd.
9th floor, No. 118, Sec. 2,
Chung Hsiao E. Road
TAIPEI. Tel. 391.7396/391.7397

**THAILAND – THAILANDE**
Suksit Siam Co., Ltd., 1715 Rama IV Rd,
Samyan, BANGKOK 5. Tel. 2511630

**TURKEY – TURQUIE**
Kültur Yayinlari Is-Türk Ltd. Sti.
Atatürk Bulvari No : 191/Kat. 21
Kavaklidere/ANKARA. Tel. 17 02 66
Dolmabahce Cad. No : 29
BESIKTAS/ISTANBUL. Tel. 60 71 88

**UNITED KINGDOM – ROYAUME-UNI**
H.M. Stationery Office,
P.O.B. 276, LONDON SW8 5DT.
(postal orders only)
Telephone orders: (01) 622.3316, or
49 High Holborn, LONDON WC1V 6 HB (personal callers)
Branches at: EDINBURGH, BIRMINGHAM, BRISTOL,
MANCHESTER, BELFAST.

**UNITED STATES OF AMERICA – ÉTATS-UNIS**
OECD Publications and Information Center, Suite 1207,
1750 Pennsylvania Ave., N.W. WASHINGTON, D.C.20006 – 4582
Tel. (202) 724.1857

**VENEZUELA**
Libreria del Este, Avda. F. Miranda 52, Edificio Galipan,
CARACAS 106. Tel. 32.23.01/33.26.04/31.58.38

**YUGOSLAVIA – YOUGOSLAVIE**
Jugoslovenska Knjiga, Knez Mihajlova 2, P.O.B. 36, BEOGRAD.
Tel. 621.992

Les commandes provenant de pays où l'OCDE n'a pas encore désigné de dépositaire peuvent être adressées à :
OCDE, Bureau des Publications, 2, rue André-Pascal, 75775 PARIS CEDEX 16.

Orders and inquiries from countries where sales agents have not yet been appointed may be sent to:
OECD, Publications Office, 2, rue André-Pascal, 75775 PARIS CEDEX 16.

67738-06-1984

OECD PUBLICATIONS, 2, rue André-Pascal, 75775 PARIS CEDEX 16 - No. 42819 1984
PRINTED IN FRANCE
(41 84 02 1) ISBN 92-64-12590-6